MW00780164

Codename Revolution

Codename Revolution

The Nintendo Wii Platform

Steven E. Jones and George K. Thiruvathukal

The MIT Press   Cambridge, Massachusetts   London, England

MIT Press books may be purchased at special quantity discounts for business or sales promotional
use. For information, please email special_sales@mitpress.mit.edu or write to Special Sales Department, The MIT Press, 55 Hayward Street, Cambridge, MA 02142.

This book was set in Filosofia and Helvetica Neue by the MIT Press. Printed and bound in the
United States of America.

Library of Congress Cataloging-in-Publication Data

Jones, Steven E., 1959–
Codename revolution : the Nintendo Wii platform / Steven E. Jones and George K. Thiruvathukal.
    p. cm. — (Platform studies)
Includes bibliographical references and index.
ISBN 978-0-262-01680-3 (hardcover : alk. paper)
1. Video games—Social aspects. 2. Nintendo Wii video games. I. Thiruvathukal, George K. (George
Kuriakose) II. Title.
GV1469.17.S63J66 2012
794.8—dc23
2011026378

10 9 8 7 6 5 4 3 2 1

Contents

Series Foreword

How can someone create a breakthrough game for a mobile phone or a compelling work of art for an immersive 3D environment without understanding that the mobile phone and the 3D environment are different sorts of computing platforms? The best artists, writers, programmers, and designers are well aware that certain platforms facilitate certain types of computational expression and innovation. Likewise, computer science and engineering has long considered how underlying computing systems can be analyzed and improved. As important as scientific and engineering approaches are, and as significant as work by creative artists has been, there is also much to be learned from the sustained, intensive, humanistic study of digital media. We believe it is time for those of us in the humanities to seriously consider the lowest level of computing systems, and understand how these systems relate to culture and creativity.

The Platform Studies book series has been established to promote the investigation of underlying computing systems, and how they enable, constrain, shape, and support the creative work that is done on them. The series investigates the foundations of digital media: the computing systems, both hardware and software, that developers and users depend on for artistic, literary, gaming, and other creative development. Books in the series certainly vary in their approaches, but they all also share certain features:

- A focus on a single platform or a closely related family of platforms
- Technical rigor and an in-depth investigation of how computing technologies work

- An awareness and discussion of how computing platforms exist in a context of culture and society, being developed based on cultural concepts and then contributing to culture in a variety of ways—for instance, by affecting how people perceive computing

This particular title, *Codename Revolution*—a collaboration between a scholar in textual studies and a computer scientist—offers a close look at how platforms and their design can foster social engagement with computing and gaming. The book also provides a comprehensive study of a current-generation, state-of-the-art platform that was released in 2006, has been extremely influential, and is still significant in the market.

Acknowledgments

For general inspiration and feedback while this book was in progress, we wish to thank our students, including in particular the members of Jones's graduate seminar in digital humanities in fall 2009. Also, Jones would like to thank Sari Gilbert and Charles Shami for inviting him to speak at the Savannah College of Art and Design's Game Developers' Exchange in April 2010, where a portion of the large audience that had just been wowed by industry speakers demonstrating impressive explosions, ballistics, and gameplay previews, politely stayed around for his presentation on the Wii. Since then, similarly responsive audiences eleswhere have repeatedly made the question-and-answer periods as long as the talks, and twice as educational. For the past two years, both Jones and Thiruvathukal have benefited from opportunities to present material from the project at various conferences, from the Society for Textual Scholarship and the Digital Humanities conference to the Modern Language Association, where peer audiences of scholars across several disciplines played an important role in helping us formulate and refine the arguments.

At Loyola University Chicago, we'd like to thank Peter Shillingsburg for his moral and practical support as well as leadership, especially during the start-up phase of our jointly administered Center for Textual Studies and Digital Humanities. Conversations and formal exchanges with many students and colleagues, here and abroad, were extremely useful along the way, though not all the participants were aware that they were helping us work on the book at the time. To name just a few: Pedro Prieto Alarcón, Jasper Cragwall, Neil Fraistat, Allen Frantzen (a joint collaborator who introduced the two of us), Ron Greenberg, Chris Grubbs, Doug Guerra, William Honig, Paul Jay, (the other) Steve Jones, Matthew Kirschenbaum, Jason Kolkey, Konstantin Läufer, Adrienne Massanari, Federico Meschini, Peter Nabicht, James Newman, Chandra Sekharan, Joyce Wexler, Zach Whalen, and Talmadge Wright. At the MIT Press, we're grateful to Doug Sery for his editorial guidance; Katie Helke for her timely responses and deft coordination; Deborah Cantor-Adams, Cindy Milstein, and others who facilitated the production of the book; and Ian Bogost and Nick Montfort, the founding editors of the Platform Studies series and whose *Racing the Beam* paved the way. Anonymous readers helped us sharpen the final version of the book, and we're grateful to them. In a published review of Jones's previous book, Nina Huntemann remarked that one of its chapters would make a worthwhile contribution to the Platform Studies series, thus confirming a plot already hatched. The original illustrations are by Henry Jones.

We'd like to thank Evander Preston, the mad genius of Pass-a-Grille Beach, for inspiration during a final collaborative revision session. Thanks to Rohan and Maya, for knowing at such a young age that it's acceptable to be simultaneously both in and out of the game. Thanks to Emi and Hannah for a special emergency equipment donation (more Wii Remotes and a Zapper), and finally, to Heidi and Nina for playing along.

Introduction: Starting with Revolution: $\begin{bmatrix} 1 \end{bmatrix}$
The Wii as a Platform

Over ten years ago, Robert D. Putnam published an influential work of
sociology, *Bowling Alone*, about the loss of social community in the United
States—a loss symbolized by the title's sad image.[1] Americans were increasingly likely to go bowling by themselves rather than in groups or a league,
Putnam found, and this was just one example of a more general loss of
involvement in civic life. Though the book maintains proper skepticism
about causation and correlation, it represents technology and the media
as at least contributing to the problem, and repeats a number of clichés
about "computer and video games" as being "solitary" and alienating. For
example, Putnam cites statistics to show that in the 1990s American boys
were more likely than girls to use computers to play games; girls, in contrast, were more likely to use computers for email. Putnam interprets this
as evidence that girls are "more socially adept," based on the unsupported
premise that games are less social than email.[2]

More than a decade after *Bowling Alone* appeared, civic life in the
United States may still be in decline (such broad trends are notoriously
difficult to both define and measure), but bowling—and still sometimes
with others—seems to have remained at least moderately popular. Now,
however, for many people, the idea of bowling as a social activity is probably more likely to call to mind *Wii Sports* than actual bowling. Google
"bowling" in an image search, and the results are almost certain to turn up
one or two images of Wii Bowling among the group shots in matching
T-shirts as well as images of crowded alleys. When we tried it for this
chapter (June 2010), among the top-twenty images was one of a Wii Bowling
league T-shirt for sale, with a pin replacing each *i*, and a blurry action shot

of a senior citizen throwing their whole body into Wii Bowling at a local public library. In fact, googling "Wii Bowling seniors" resulted in 1,940,000 results, many including links to how-to articles or stories about retirement homes setting up leagues. The Wii has not replaced what Putnam saw as lost in US culture—civic involvement and broad social commitments; that's not the point. But the topic of bowling as a social activity has been redefined since 2006 to feature Nintendo's bowling simulation game.

This is just one anecdotal example of the widespread cultural influence of the Wii, the video game console that from its introduction in 2006 until 2010 (when competitors introduced similar systems) was synonymous with the mimetic motion-control interface (you stand up and swing your arm to bowl, like the person in our search-results image), and with the kind of public and playful social interactions once associated with card games and bowling leagues. "Entertainment" is literally Nintendo's middle name. The company was established in the nineteenth century as a playing-card manufacturer and, interestingly enough in this context, once turned disused bowling alleys into multimedia shooting ranges, or places where new kinds of social games replaced the once-central bowling leagues in Japan. That history is important for this book, which takes a detailed look at this most influential video game platform of the past decade at a moment when its successor, Wii U, is on the horizon, marking a kind of completion of the primary lifecycle of the original Wii.[3]

By the time it went on sale in North America, in November 2006, the Wii had already generated a good deal of interest in the press, and on discussion boards and blogs. Codenamed "Revolution" during development, the fifth home console released by the Kyoto-based entertainment company was marketed in advance as a categorical exception—a system for the untapped majority of the market that doesn't play video games or only plays them casually. The Wii helped to usher in the larger trend that Jesper Juul calls the "casual revolution" and "a breakthrough moment in the history of video games." So-called social games on the Internet such as *FarmVille* that use Facebook and other social networks as their host platforms have emerged roughly in parallel with the Wii. Unlike these online social games, the Wii home console is what Juul describes as "mimetic-interface" gaming: the system mirrors the player's movements. But social and mimetic-interface games like *Wii Sports* are different manifestations of the same casual revolution, Juul argues.[4] In both cases, the emphasis is on the social contexts that give the games meaning and the social interactions that are encouraged by the games, even if those interactions are not at the center of actual gameplay—which may involve asynchronous online interactions such as in *FarmVille*, using the controller as a token or pointer device for group activities taking place in the living room, or local multi-player or co-op modes with players who are in the same physical space together, as in the case of *Wii Party*.[5]

In addition to the shared stress on social contexts, both online social and Wii games are part of a "breakthrough moment" in gaming that is oddly, paradoxically backward looking:

> This is the moment in which the simplicity of early video games is being rediscovered, while new flexible designs are letting video games fit into the lives of players. Video games are being reinvented, and so is our image of those who play the games. This is the moment when we realize that everybody can be a video game player.[6]

Whether by design or default (and probably some combination of both), Nintendo helped to bring about this moment of retro-reinvention with the Wii. Even before any actual design began, the company seems to have conceived of the new console as simple, accessible, and "for everyone"—a revolution that meant a return to the ideal of family fun that had been associated with its brand since the 1980s. The attention of the press was quickly focused on the wireless motion-sensitive controller for the system, the Wii Remote (nicknamed the "Wiimote"), in part because people looked funny in photogenic ways when they played with it. People stood up more often than they sat on the couch, and used their whole bodies, waving their arms around as if they were wielding swords, rolling a bowling ball, or swinging a tennis racquet instead of concentrating on small-motor-control actions with their thumbs, as the traditional joypad would have required them to do.

Compared to learning complicated button combinations while controlling analog sticks on a typical game-control pad, using the Wii is remarkably easy. The plain-white rectangular wand shaped like a television remote works by mapping the player's gestures to what's happening in the game world and how the game world is represented on the television screen. In this way, the mimetic interface shifts attention from the game world or what's on the screen to the player's body in physical space, out in the living room. As Juul says, "Casual game design is about . . . using space in a different way than one experiences in recent three-dimensional video games."[7] It's about shifting attention to player space, and as we argue more than once throughout this book, player space is social space, where actual or potential interactions with other people are assumed.

Four years after the release of the Wii, Microsoft's Kinect extension for the Xbox 360 and Sony's Move for the PS3 were created to compete for the mimetic-interface market that Nintendo had opened up. (We'll have more to say about the initial phase of that competition in the book's final chapter.) But in a more profound way than the precursors to these platforms and the Wii's immediate competition in 2006—the Xbox 360 and the PS3 with traditional controls—the Wii depends on what happens in that "empty" space *between* its interconnected components, that space between the player and the screen—a space mediated by a network of peripheral devices and imagined as a possibility space where social interactions are the ideal context for gameplay.

This book considers the Wii as a social platform. Of course, in one sense, all platforms are social systems, and game platforms especially so. But the Wii is "about using space in a different way" than in most recent mainstream games with 3D game worlds, as Juul contends.[8] It's designed around the notion that gameplay ideally happens in a shared space where social interactions, at least potential ones, are at the heart of the experience. Rather than being designed to maximize the immersive graphics of the virtual battlefield, kingdom, dungeon, or city in which the game takes place, the Wii's somatic and mimetic network of controller objects were expressly made with the physical living room in mind.

There's certainly nothing inherently more social in the Wii's hardware and software components than in those of any other game platform. The Xbox and PlayStation, along with other legacy historical systems, are frequently and even perhaps typically used in social settings, whether local area network (LAN) parties with multiple players sitting in the same space but connected via headsets and sharing a virtual game space, or more loosely defined groups in which two players wield controls, for example, while several others watch and comment. And that's not to mention online social interactions, whether through services such as Xbox Live or massively multiplayer online role-playing games played on the personal computer (PC). In fact, we believe that most gameplay is fundamentally social in one or more of these ways, contrary to mainstream stereotypes. Again, there's nothing inherently more social about using a Wii Remote instead of a traditional two-handed joypad. It's the overall design of the system that makes the difference, and this design is shaped by preconceptions about what the system is for and how it's to be used. It's a difference of degree rather than of kind, a difference in relative emphasis, but the Wii was the first home video game platform consciously designed as a whole— from initial concept to prototype to shipped product—to first and foremost promote social gameplay out in physical space. That's what we mean when we call the Wii a social platform. Engineering the social space of gameplay is its whole point, its explicit reason for being.

As the series foreword makes clear, platform studies is an approach that looks at the relation of hardware and software as a system, from the electronics inside the console box to the peripheral controllers, and at how the affordances and constraints of a particular system invite as well as shape the development of creative works—such as video games and gamelike entertainments. Affordances is a term taken from human-computer interaction (HCI) studies for what a system allows a user to do, or increasingly, what a system suggests to a user that they *might* do.[9] It's a way of talking about games and game systems as producing possibility spaces. In this view, the user is key to the realization of a platform's affordances, but also its constraints (restrictions on what can be done or imagined). That's the basis of our underlying premise that any platform is always ultimately a social phenomenon. A platform depends on the user's engaged imagination, multiple users' imaginations as developers in turn imagine them, and the larger social contexts that shape and are shaped by those imaginations. In the case of a video game system, users are important to every phase of its life cycle, whether as system designers, programmers, software developers, or consumers and players—the so-called end users. It's impossible, finally, to separate particular hardware and software configurations from the social and cultural contexts that influenced them. So we pay a good deal of attention to how the Wii has been marketed, citing press releases, keynote presentations, and ad campaigns, all of which make up the persuasive rhetoric that contributes to Nintendo's "blue-ocean" and "nimble-dinosaur" strategies (to use the metaphors developed by marketing itself). Marketing is framing. It projects certain economic, demographic, and social realities that affect a platform's reception and ultimate meaning.

The Nintendo Wii vividly illustrates how this framing influences the design as well as reception of a system. The result in this case was a product with an aura about it, a popular image that captured the collective imagination. This was in part because the system appeared in the charged atmosphere of Nintendo fandom and its backlash, but also because it claimed to provide a new experience in gaming while appealing to the users' familiarity with the company along with leveraged tested and available technologies. The motion-sensitive interface was not an entirely new idea in 2006. Yet it had never before been deployed as the main controller for a game platform. That much was new. Nintendo's decision to make it the chief characteristic of a new system resulted in a platform with significant cultural influence—beginning with a refocusing of discussions surrounding video game and console system designs away from ever-more realistic, immersive game spaces, and toward the player's physical and psychological experience of gameplay. The Wii's cultural influence didn't stem from the motion-sensitive controllers alone. It also depended on the foundation of Nintendo's reputation and software catalog, which includes some of the most beloved franchises in history and carries a good deal of cultural capital among so-called core gamers. Smaller, less expensive, innovative, accessible, casual, family-friendly, classic, revolutionary, and fun—all of these descriptors have been successfully associated with the Wii by Nintendo marketing, and echoes of that marketing in the press and wider culture. To study the Wii as a platform requires us to pay attention to the links between system design, framing, and cultural response.

Our Approach

In general, we've approached the writing of this book from the perspectives of our different academic disciplines: textual studies and computer science. One of us is an English professor who studies the material texts of literary works—for example, how manuscripts, print technologies, and publishing all work together as a system to afford and constrain the meaning of poetic texts. The study of material texts and game studies have begun to combine in volatile and interesting ways in the past two decades, thanks to the catalyst of digital media. So as a textual studies scholar, Jones found himself teaching and studying electronic texts and new media, and presenting papers at digital humanities conferences, where he heard compelling presentations by theorists of video games and new media. In that context, Jones came to write a book in 2008 on the relation of textual studies to video games, and extending that work led him to the present book.[10]

The other one of us, Thiruvathukal, is a computer science professor whose interests are in high-performance computing, but also more recently, distributed systems and pervasive computing—a space dominated by low-powered devices. He sees systems as the anatomy and physiology of platforms, and is intrigued by applications of computing to culture—including computing history, digital humanities, gaming, and environmental science. That's how Thiruvathukal came to coauthor the present book.

Together we codirect a university Center for Textual Studies and Digital Humanities that supports interdisciplinary research and education at the intersection of computing, the humanities, and social sciences— English, history, art, communication, new media, sociology, and library and information science. The center supports a variety of computing applications and humanities projects, including ways to create new digital environments for the collaborative editing and publishing of texts and images, from modernist novels to nineteenth-century political cartoons. The whole point of digital humanities work, as the term implies, is to bring computer science and information technology together with the objects of humanities research—books, manuscripts, artworks, photographs, prints, artifacts, records, and electronic data; in other words, to connect computing with culture. That's essentially the same method and perspective we bring to this book. In this case, the research object is the Wii as a platform—which includes the console, Wii Remote, Nunchuk, Balance Board, firmware and operating system (OS) system software, and disc or downloaded game software as well as the culture of the commercial video game business, for example, along with the larger phenomena of casual gaming and popular understandings of what video game systems are and might become.

Both of us have been around long enough so that we played video games in the heyday of the arcades as well as the early home console and PC eras. We've owned many game systems over the years and currently between us, own consoles by all three major current competitors. But in truth, until we began researching them in recent years, we both found ourselves playing games less and less, since like many in our demographic group we've discovered that having children and academic jobs has made it increasingly less likely that we have time and energy for extended bouts of gaming. So in our own lives, we're part of the larger cultural shift associated with the Wii—the rise of casual gaming. For pleasure and research, we now play games on our mobile devices, phones, and tablets as much as or more than we do on home consoles. The truth is that we're both mostly casual gamers. But we still take seriously the study of video games, which we agree are one of today's most pervasive and significant forms of expressive culture.

We take games seriously as objects of attention even when the games themselves are intentionally self-mocking. When we were writing chapter 5, on channels of access, distribution, and transmission on the Wii, we found that the then-new *WarioWare D.I.Y.* game for the DS had taken the series' self-referential humor about making and selling games to new levels (in more than one sense). It's a game about making games, or in this case the five-second microgames for which the series is famous. So we used the tutorials, played around with the built-in editor, and made some microgames of our own, starting with one called Make Room!!!, in which you have to tap or click to move a coffee table out of the way to provide what the *Wii Operations Manual* calls "adequate space" for gameplay. The idea for this microgame emerged from our theoretical discussions about competing ways to configure game space and the idea promoted by the Wii that the physical living room is the space where what's most important to games really happens (as opposed to the imaginary, virtual game space).

Playing the Wii often involves moving furniture—constraints of an external and physical sort.[11] But *WarioWare D.I.Y.*, as deliberately playful as it is, offered us a number of unexpected serious insights along with its unexpected pleasures. Though there's no coding required, the editor and tutorials provide a fairly sophisticated introduction to the usual procedures for building games with existing object-oriented editors and game-engine interfaces. The game allows you to import existing assets and repurpose them in a new game—for instance, a crucial feature of real-world game development. This seemingly trivial game about making games reminds users of the importance of marketing and dissemination, reaching an audience of players, since you have to name your imaginary game-development studio (we chose "EvertInc.," a title whose significance will become clear in chapter 4), design logos, and manufacture cartridges—the physical medium through which your software reaches the market—and then distribute the results through various local or widely distributed channels—in this case, DS to DS, or using the Internet, asynchronously dropped and picked up later by an authorized end user (anyone who gives you their Nintendo Friend Code).

In terms of reminding the user of how a platform helps to determine a game's experience, *WarioWare D.I.Y.* highlights the differences between playing your microgame on the handheld DS versus the Wii hooked up to a television screen, including the basic fact that you use a stylus and touch screen for the handheld as opposed to the Wii Remote cursor and A button for the Wii. The more we spent time with it, the more we came to see that this playfully satirical game about games, in a franchise that has always parodied a greedy and opportunistic head (Wario) of a game development company (WarioWare Inc.), was surprisingly educational, as a microscale playable meditation on the game-development process.

Throughout the book, we zoom in on the relevant specifics of the technology involved, even at the level of the tiny microelectromechanical systems (MEMS) devices built into integrated circuits in the Wii's controllers. These devices are what allow the Wii Remote to capture the player's physical movements, and their existence has called for new software from the development community to take advantage of what they afford in the way of gameplay. So *Wii Sports Resort* games, for example, take a certain form and experiment with particular modes of gameplay, because of the decision to manufacture and market motion-sensitive controllers.

In most cases, however, the technology is far from a simple one-way determinant. A third-party action-adventure game like *Red Steel*, created for the launch of the Wii and to make use of the original Wii Remote, could fail in many respects (as it did)—in part because of the graphic and processing limitations of the system—but then be revived (or "rebooted") in a sequel, *Red Steel 2*, after Nintendo released an add-on to the controller, MotionPlus, that incorporated a MEMS "tuning fork" gyroscope, which greatly enhanced the Wii Remote's ability to measure and map player movements. The second game's relative success was a direct consequence of changes in the hardware. It was a matter of the developers' learning to work within the constraints of the platform *and* being given a new set of affordances that make for realistic-feeling (as opposed to realistic-looking) swordplay. The expressive and creative cultural artifact, *Red Steel 2*, is a direct result of new computing technology in the first place. At the same time, games like *Red Steel 2* (and what was learned from the first *Red Steel*) were the reason for the creation of new computing technology. Any full understanding of that game—including even its diegetic story line, as limited as it is—must take into account the web of economic and technological factors that made the game possible as well as shaped its possibilities. From our point of view, no material technology stands apart from culture. And no cultural event transcends material technologies. So our approach demands a kind of interweaving of the two.

If "platforms are layered—from hardware through operating system and into other software layers—and they relate to modular components, such as optional controllers and cards," then the platform itself is a kind of layer in the "stack" that represents the structure of digital media objects in their social contexts.[12] Ian Bogost and Nick Montfort, whose book on the Atari VCS, *Racing the Beam*, inaugurated the present series, provide a useful diagram that represents the five levels of possible attention to digital media or creative computing, with the platform as the foundation, and moving up through software and architectural layers (code, form/function, interface, and reception/operation) to include the creative work itself (such as a video game).[13] Culture can be understood as the highest-level layer or context surrounding the whole, or as something like the solution that inevitably pervades every layer in the media object, helping to shape it and be shaped by it in turn. We'd go even further to suggest that culture (or social context) pervades and shapes every sublayer of the platform layer, too, from the technology of transistors to the art of game design. This makes game consoles particularly interesting cases for platform studies to consider because they so obviously depend on the social and cultural layer if they are to have any meaning. Again, the Wii is an especially vivid example of this general dependency because it was designed to focus on what happens in the social space, shaped by culture, in which games are imagined and played.

As we've said, every platform is a social platform to some degree—and not only digital platforms. Take books. The printing press along with the institutions of print culture can be seen as a kind of platform for producing and disseminating texts in the material form of codex books. After Johannes Gutenberg developed printing from movable type (in Europe), machines were deployed to impress paper with texts using pieces of metal type that were locked into wooden *formes* and inked. This allowed for a high degree of uniformity across multiple copies of the same work and the wide dissemination of texts in book form—a form with a two-page-opening interface (the codex) that was brilliantly suited to the various reading practices that emerged along with it.

The higher-level connections between print technologies and something often called print culture, and between print culture and culture in general, are extremely complicated, and their precise nature has been the subject of serious debate among book historians.[14] But that there are *some* such connections—that print technologies have cultural effects—is accepted by most historians. There are positive effects—the invention of steam-driven printing presses in the early nineteenth century opened up mass-market publishing—and negative effects—the Romantic poet William Blake and, later, Victorian Pre-Raphaelite poets returned to handcrafted books in part as a reaction to new printing technologies.

Either way, printing platforms affect creative works, such as poems. Yet compared to a computing platform like a video game console, print looks more like a culturewide technological regime or medium. More precisely, the gift-book annual anthologies of the English Regency period, triple-decker (three-volume) novels of the Victorian era, do-it-yourself (DIY) cut-and-paste photocopying of zines in the 1980s and 1990s—all specific configurations of text technologies that shaped the creation and reception of various forms of writing—were specific *platforms* within the larger *medium* or *field* of print. In this sense, video game consoles are specific platforms within the larger field of computing.

In our own era, we're seeing the rise of the electronic book in various competing platforms for producing and delivering texts. These now include not only PCs but also handheld mobile e-book platforms, whether Amazon's Kindle, various applications for mobile phones, or Apple's iBooks for the iPad. Where are the boundaries defining the iPad, for example, as a platform for publishing e-books? To begin with, there are the specific hardware and software technical specifications, including everything from the multitouch interface and screen resolution to battery life and form factor—the shape and size of the tablet itself. In addition, there are layers of software, from the text files in the ePub format, to the code that allows for bookmarking, copying of selected text to the clipboard, searching, and dictionary lookup from within the selected text (but oddly, not annotation), to the interface design for the full-color display that animates page turning when touched and stacks cover images of the books in your collection in a graphic bookcase image. All these features are part of the iPad's iBooks platform for e-books.

But that's not the end of it. The online software channel by which the e-books are published, distributed, purchased, and downloaded, the iBooks section of the iTunes Store, is also a crucial layer in the platform—in some ways the most important layer of all, because publishing and distribution, not just reading, is the purpose of this platform. Even before the iPad was first released, iBooks at iTunes was controversial, provoking public debate about Apple's negotiated role as a bookselling "agent" mediating between publishers and readers. And that new model of electronic book publishing in turn had specific consequences for the price of e-books, not only by Apple on the iTunes Store, but also in response, by its competitor Amazon. The competition with Amazon's Kindle app for the iPad and other devices may be the primary motivating factor in the construction of Apple's own channels of distribution. One survey showed that as of fall 2010, while 75 percent of surveyed users read books on their iPads, about 7 percent of them preferred to read e-books on the iPad via the Kindle app instead of using Apple's own iBooks app.[15]

The point is that the iPad iBooks platform is the sum total of its layered components—from the microchips to the multitouch interface, to the available software, to the publishing channel for that software (the actual e-books), and its reception by users. A video game platform like Nintendo's Wii demands detailed attention to precisely this kind of multilayered structure. Games, too, are produced, distributed, received, and played via a multilayered system of components, from hardware to software to economic and social institutions. Platform studies has to remain aware of this complexity.

In that spirit, chapter 5 focuses on the software design and structure of the Wii's system function interface, or the so-called Wii Channels. More than just a set of menus, these represent a set of *channels of distribution* for software and services, pipelines of transmission extending the platform beyond the local console and its components. Just as the Bluetooth, infrared, and WiFi communications connect the Wii's devices, creating a kind of personal area network (PAN) as the local space in which the platform is experienced, so the WiFi- or Ethernet-enabled channels—in conjunction with the institutions and businesses to which they connect—establish the larger network at the platform's outer edge. These channels notably include access to the WiiWare service, which offers games for download, often made by independent third-party developers for the Wii and its special affordances, and the Virtual Console, by which emulated games from earlier platforms—those of Nintendo and others—can be downloaded and played on the Wii, alongside new games by Nintendo or other developers. So it's possible, for example, to turn on the Wii, access different channels (including the Disc Channel to the optical drive for running games on DVD-ROMs), and play multiple generations of Mario games, starting with the first iconic appearance in *Donkey Kong* and concluding with the newer games designed specifically for the Wii, such as *Mario Galaxy 2.*

Cross-Platform Mario

Mario is a useful example, serving as a controlled case study of the ways in which changes in a platform alter the detailed expressions of creative works. Nintendo's most iconic and beloved character, and the company mascot, Mario the plumber is now reportedly recognized by more children in the United States than recognize Disney Corporation's eighty-year-old mascot, Mickey Mouse. According to Wikipedia (which is a particularly useful source for such facts), the Mario franchise consists of over 115 game titles, not counting remakes, and has sold well over an estimated 200 million copies worldwide to become the top-selling video game series in history.[16] One widely reproduced image shows a life-size 3D Mario standing with his real-life creator, Shigeru Miyamoto—an image reminiscent of Walt Disney with Mickey Mouse, as seen in the famous statue at Disneyland, for example. (2010's *Disney Epic Mickey*, a Wii exclusive that we discuss in chapter 7, contains a visual parody of that same statue.)

Nothing better represents the art of classic video game design than Mario. When you place him in context, however, and follow Mario across the various platformer games and game platforms on which he has appeared, it quickly becomes clear how closely platform is tied to creative expression, from artistic character design, to the design of gameplay mechanics and genres, to the impact all this has on the wider culture.

Like other important origin stories, this one has been told many times, and most readers will be familiar with at least parts of it. But it bears repeating here in the context of platform and culture. Miyamoto began as an industrial designer who created toys. His work, though, was always about function as much as form. A famous early invention of his at Nintendo was a set of clothes hangers for children in the shape of cartoon animals. His first serious game design job at Nintendo was for an arcade game based on the cartoon *Popeye*, for which the company never received the intellectual property rights. So Popeye, Bluto, and Olive Oyl became new characters: Jumpman, a carpenter who jumps over barrels rolled at him by the ape as he runs on platforms in an abstract construction site; Donkey Kong, whose name the Japanese designers thought of as English slang for "stupid ape"; and Pauline, the carpenter's damsel-in-distress girlfriend, and among the first in a long line of imprisoned females in video games. The arcade game *Donkey Kong* was produced in 1981.

There were critical differences, in terms of technology and the gameplay experience, between these early arcade-cabinet games and the several home consoles for which later Mario games were created. Until recently, every new Nintendo system was launched along with the release of a new Mario game. *Super Mario Bros.* was released for the NES in 1985. It was closely associated with the innovations of that system and in turn lent its own aura to the NES as a platform, in a kind of symbiotic development loop. That game, which sold probably over twenty million copies worldwide, made Mario a cultural icon. The most complex video game to that point (so complex that a supplemental processor was included in the game cartridge), *Super Mario Bros.* was the first of its era to make reaching the story's conclusion the primary goal. Although you were scored on your gameplay, the fundamental motivation of the game was to save the princess and see what happened in the conclusion. Side scrolling took the gameplay from screen to screen, extending the playing field along the horizontal axis, allowing the gameplay to move through dozens of display screens in each level.[17] Continuing to extend the dimensions—literally and figuratively—of the game world became a hallmark of the Mario series as a whole.

The little carpenter was turned into a plumber in order to fit in with the urban setting and its navigable pipes. Interestingly, Miyamoto first thought of naming him "Mr. Video," because he was planned from the outset as a generic hero in many video games across multiple platforms, as someone who would appear over and over again in games, a kind of figure for the ability of any effective creative expression to thrive across platforms. Mario's basic characteristics were designed with these general plans in mind, and at the same time in direct response to the specific constraints and affordances of the platform for which he was first created in *Donkey Kong*. The basic controls of the arcade cabinet for that game—which already existed to play another game, *Radar Scope*—were givens. Miyamoto had no choice but to work with them. So he says that he invented the jumping move—for which Mario became famous and which spawned a whole style of side-scrolling platformer gameplay—as a response to the hardware, specifically to the fact that the cabinet already had a big button—used to fire the weapon in *Radar Scope*—that could be programmed to make the little character jump. Thus Jumpman was born. He was later renamed Mario, one story goes, after the developers' landlord, but probably also in an attempt to appeal to US culture as Nintendo imagined it.

This is a point worth reiterating: everything about the design of the original Mario, from using the arcade cabinet's button to make him jump to his basic appearance, was shaped by the circumstances of the hardware and software available at the time of *each* of his incarnations. The platform helped to determine the artistic design. As Nintendo president Iwata has said, "The entire design was a case of form being dictated by function"—where form means character and game design, and function basically means platform. This is true not only for Mario, of course. All "video game development at that time was essentially a matter of working out how things could be achieved within the limitations imposed by the hardware," Iwata observes.[18] As writer Tom Bissell puts it, the 1up mushrooms, fire flowers, and coins in blocks, all the icons of Mario games, may look like strangely hallucinatory symbolism, or what he dubs "ineffable Nipponese weirdity," but they're actually the direct result of working within the constraints of the medium, on a given platform, at a given moment.

> In film and literature, such surrealistic fantasy typically occurs at the outer edge of experimentalism, but early video games depended on symbols for the simple reason that the technological limitations of the time made realism impossible.[19]

The particular form of surrealistic fantasy imagined by Miyamoto was one possible response (in this case, a brilliant one) to the constraints of the medium and platform, and the same remains true for his video game designs today, though the constraints are different from what he faced circa 1980. In the case of making a Mario game for the Wii, Miyamoto was able to do amazing things again, this time with physics and world design, precisely because his symbolic vocabulary was already a powerful but non-realistic one, and the new platform, the Wii, had its own technological limitations.

The appearance of the first Mario, Miyamoto has explained, was a matter of using as few pixels as possible to reduce the demands on programming and animation. Early Mario was essentially a sixteen-by-sixteen-pixel spritelike figure, almost a game token or marker turned into a playable character, in many ways not all that far removed in time and the complexity of design from the abstract rocket ships of *Space Wars*, one of the first computer games from the 1970s. Miyamoto has said that "overseas" (meaning primarily US) games at the time used mostly inexpressive "matchstick figures" for characters because they were trying too hard to represent the realistic proportions of human bodies in the eight-bit environment—a judgment that echoes the rationale for the Wii's revolutionary turn away from realistic graphics as its primary goal. As a result, the facial features and gestures of these stick figures were more or less invisible, incapable of inspiring identification and empathy in the player.

Miyamoto turned instead to manga and anime art styles for inspiration. He cites Osamu Tezuka in particular, the great progenitor of modern manga, and the creator of *Kimba the White Lion* and *Astro Boy* (*Mighty Atom*), as an influence. So he exaggerated the features and distorted the proportions of his character, which had the advantage of economizing on the use of every pixel. Paradoxically, the abstraction of Mario may make him seem *more* alive and expressive than pseudorealistically proportioned stick figures would, in part because it makes him seem an integral part of the limited palette afforded by the game environment, and in part because it calls on the player's imagination to fill in the gaps.[20] Mario has a bright red cap to avoid the inevitable disappointing results of trying to depict (and animate) his hair. He has a mustache to avoid having to draw and animate a mouth. His overalls are a kind of clothing that differentiates limbs from torso in a way that makes possible the simple animations of running and jumping. And so on. This use of a cartoon aesthetic extends beyond the character himself. The famous ubiquitous pipes in later Mario games, into which he can move to be transported to dungeons and other locations, came from a manga visual convention, according to Miyamoto, in which pipes lying around everywhere often suggested urban settings.

Form being dictated by function, working out how to achieve designs within the constraints imposed by the platform, and making a creative virtue of necessity has become a design ethos at Nintendo. "Nintendoness," as Miyamoto has said, is not about seeking the "tech edge."[21] And this pragmatic ethos was at the heart of the Wii's development process. You can see it at work in the cartoon avatars and nonplayable characters (NPCs) created for the Wii, called Miis. Miyamoto is the creative force behind their design as well, and he has said that they were inspired by traditional carved *Kokeshi* dolls, but the same idea informs them: economize on representation in order to concentrate on other features (such as simulated motions). Mario is more than a company mascot and valuable intellectual property; he's an embodiment of this Nintendo design ethos. So it's not only a matter of branding or planting "Easter eggs" when we find images of Mario everywhere across the Wii platform, even mixed into crowds of Miis, as if to reinforce their ultimate genetic kinship. Each of these images of Mario is a kind of marker of the persistence of that design philosophy, an indicator of the Wii developers' aspirations to create expressive software with which players can identify, and that is engaging and fun, but within fairly severe constraints in terms of power, graphics capability, storage, and energy use.

The Wii Shop Channel uses a classic-looking Mario (or sometimes his brother Luigi) as its animated download meter. Accompanied by the familiar sound effects, he runs across the screen, jumping to hit blocks above his head and retrieve coins (an apt metaphor in this case, since your credit card or Wii Points card is in most cases being charged for a download when you see it). You can find images of Mario making cameo appearances everywhere in software for the Wii. As you skydive down to WuHu Island at the beginning of *Wii Sports Resort*, and are maneuvering your Mii avatar in the wind in order to catch the hands of other skydiving Miis and get your picture snapped, you may see the familiar little plumber in a skydiving outfit falling through the sky among the Miis. It's an odd effect. Later, down on the island and running a race, you may discover a graffiti mural painted on a stone wall depicting Mario's wide-eyed face. It's a kind of aesthetic haunting of the latest Nintendo game worlds by the most universal of its intellectual properties, and there's nothing accidental about its symbolism.

Games developed by Nintendo for the Wii console have included several that feature Mario (along with two games so far in the other cornerstone Nintendo franchise, *The Legend of Zelda*). Some are fairly perfunctory, while others are among the most critically acclaimed and popular games in recent years on any platform. *Mario Kart Wii* is one of a series of spin-offs that has remained popular in the Wii version. Mario is only one of the Nintendo characters that you can play as, or you can play as your own Mii, as you race others, including online players via the Nintendo WiFi Connection. Online play is quick to set up and easy, lending itself to casual bouts of one race at a time. You steer with the Wii Remote turned sideways in two hands or by fitting it into a plastic shell shaped like a steering wheel. An installment of the *Mario Party* series for the Wii is a board-based game for multiple players with numerous minigames, some of which make use of the Wii Remote's motion sensitivity.

New Super Mario Bros. Wii is a different kind of game and an interesting case study, which was both eagerly anticipated by serious fans and also somewhat disappointing to many of them. It allows for a multiplayer co-op mode, inviting the kind of social gameplay for which the Wii is known, but as one critic noted, it rewards the player for concentrated single-player efforts instead: "When you add multiple players in that game they often end up bumping and pushing one another into enemies and hazards. The effect there is to discourage people from playing together."[22] The game is ultimately too difficult for many of the casual players that the Wii was designed to attract. But more experienced, hard-core players may object to features such as the Super Guide, a kind of in-game help character (Luigi) that shows up when called, as too easy. The fit between game and platform in this case seems to many not quite right.

Super Paper Mario Wii (2007), on the other hand, seems at home on the Wii. It has been characterized as a kind of conceptual sequel to the RPG *Paper Mario* for the Nintendo 64 (2000–2001). The Nintendo 64 game was developed by Intelligent Systems for Nintendo (with the input of Miyamoto) and already had a retro style, deliberately 2D looking, as if characters were made from paper cutouts and then set against 3D backgrounds containing a series of obstacles, puzzles, quests, and battles. *Super Paper Mario* is a creative variation that blends elements from other Mario games as well (interestingly, including *Super Mario Bros.*) to make a platformer RPG for the Wii. Two-dimensional characters run, jump, and interact with blocks and the familiar turtle enemies (Koopas), and fight boss battles in order to rescue a princess, but with some surreal twists. At one point, the 1up mushroom turns Mario into a gigantic avatar, but this super Mario is a blown-up image of a highly pixelated old-school Mario from earlier eight-bit games. The result is a blocky abstraction of Mario-ness, the grain of the pixels boldly showing, a self-conscious representation of the character as an icon. *Super Paper Mario* was originally developed for the GameCube platform, but was shifted to the Wii at the end of its cycle. To play it, you mostly use the Wii Remote held sideways in two hands so that it resembles the old NES controller, but you can also use the Wii Remote (with "Pixl" characters as cursors of a sort) to point at the screen in order to reveal hidden doors or other secrets, and at key moments you can shake the controller to get extra points.

The real innovation of this Wii game, however, along with its sense of fit on the new platform has little directly to do with the Wii's technical affordances and constraints. Instead, the development of the new platform codenamed Revolution (which was almost certainly already under way as the game was still being designed for its precursor platform, the GameCube) seems to have created a kind of innovative atmosphere at Nintendo and promoted attention across various divisions of the company to the conceptual design problem of how "dimensions" differ in games.

In *Super Paper Mario*, you can push the A button to flip from two to three dimensions. When you do, a portal, a cutout door, appears in the flat backdrop, rotates with your character, and the setting flips to a 3D view. So rows of blocks that were impassible in side-scrolling platform mode are now revealed as only one-block deep, and you can find a way around them. What looked like a distant backdrop of mountains flips to reveal itself as a close-up narrow ramp that you can climb onto and use to cross behind a chasm. You can only stay in the third dimension for a limited time without losing your health, so you play mostly in 2D, always knowing that things are not as they appear. Your characters, though, remain 2D cutouts, sometimes twirling to reveal their flatness, like playing-card images (an appropriate visual metaphor in a game from Nintendo, the company that got its start manufacturing cards). *Super Paper Mario* reveals a general self-consciousness about game history at Nintendo that has also been built into the Wii: the sense of controlling a deep canon, and of what that in turn affords—always-available multiple "dimensions," or multiple perspectives on game design and gameplay.[23]

Nothing has attracted as much critical praise among software titles for the Wii as the two *Super Mario Galaxy* games (2007 and 2010), 3D platformers that take place mostly in space. Comically shaped cartoon planetary bodies, asteroids, and planets serve as the 3D "platforms" on which Mario runs and jumps. The games toy with radical shifts in perspective, using a planetary-level zoom, so that Mario appears to be running on spheres at one moment and, with a zoom in, across the larger plane of the planet's surface. Zooming out makes the scale shift, like an artificial garden created bonsai-style in a container, so that houses and trees loom out of proportion and can be seen from space, along with a tiny Mario (and his enemies) running around the surface of the sphere. In the game a planet can seem room or world sized, depending on a quick shift in perspective, making the earlier *Super Paper Mario*'s flipping from 2D to 3D look like a conceptual run-through for *Galaxy*. Mario's movements are liberated: from jumping over obstacles and gaps, he becomes free to run around in multiple directions and three dimensions. Though you move around using the Nunchuk analog thumbstick, both games, but especially the second, make use of the Wii Remote for pointing and clicking to control the camera, your motion, and various objects—coins, stars, rocket enemies with Mickey Mouse—style (or for that matter, Mario-style) arms with gloved hands.

Both *Super Mario Galaxy* games have been extremely successful, in terms of sales and their critical receptions. Most critics have listed them as the best games designed for the Wii, and many have judged them some of the best games of all time. We'd suggest that the success of these games is due in part to the fact that they demonstrate Nintendo's chief asset: its repeated ability to make something engaging, entertaining, and fun, within fairly severe constraints—from the eight-bit world of the NES to the relatively low-powered, standard-definition graphics of the platform codenamed Revolution. The meaning of a Nintendo platform is always bound up with the legacy of Nintendo's creative assets. In December 2010, Nintendo released a limited edition, red-colored *Super Mario All-Stars* Wii, complete with a soundtrack CD and a history booklet, to commemorate the twenty-fifth anniversary of *Super Mario Bros.*

In response to this legacy, we pay special attention in this book to Nintendo's own games and software for the Wii—even software that's arguably less than gamelike (*Wii Fit Plus*, for example) or not a game at all (as is true for many of the services provided by Wii Channels). Throughout, we select software for discussion that illustrates some particular aspect of the platform, some constraint or affordance, not based on formal or critical criteria, or on how good a game is. We've also chosen software that emphasizes what we see as the most important and unique features of the Wii as a console, so we favor, for instance, the casual over the hard-core side of the genre spectrum. Where it's possible to some degree to address both sides of the spectrum, we do so, as in the case of the Wii exclusive *Red Steel 2* (a first-person shooter [FPS]), which was designed to take advantage of the unique features of the Wii's motion-control system.

The Book's Plan

A video game console is a platform made up of separate but interrelated components, and this book is organized accordingly. Each chapter focuses on a major component of the Wii as a platform (see figure 1.1). Chapter 2 looks at the console itself, the housing of the motherboard and chipset, the computing heart of the system, as well as the symbolic object whose design sets the Wii apart in the marketplace. We summarize technical specifications, in this and other components, not for their own sake, but rather in order better to understand the specific affordances and constraints of the system, including especially its perceived and actual limitations when it comes to power and graphics capabilities. We briefly examine one aspect of the decision to make the Wii a relatively lower-powered console that's often overlooked: the fact that with lower power comes lower power consumption. The Wii consumes much less electricity than comparable devices in its generation. This too is part of the overarching strategy to sell the console to what Nintendo constructs as "moms"—obviously a domesticated gender-specific idea of how to gain entrée to the vast untapped market of those who do not own a console of any kind and do not think of themselves as gamers but might be induced to purchase this one. The stated goal of Nintendo designers is for the slim and efficient console to become an unobtrusive fixture in the idealized family living room.

1.1 The Nintendo Wii platform

Chapter 3 centers on the most recognizable iconic object associated with the Wii—the Wii Remote. Styled to resemble a traditional television remote control, the rectangular device is wireless and allows you to point and click to control in-game actions, but its most "revolutionary" feature is its use of a MEMS accelerometer and (once it was added) MEMS gyroscope to measure the player's motions in multiple dimensions. We place the Wii Remote in the historical context of other somatic interface devices as well as metaphorically in the context of the HCI concept of the "magic crayon" and in the tradition of the mouse as a controller device. We suggest how the addition of the MotionPlus attachment as an upgrade for the controller encouraged certain software features not possible or less viable using the original Wii Remote alone, as exemplified in the change from a third-party action-adventure game exclusively for the Wii, *Red Steel* (for the launch of the Wii in 2006), to the "reboot" sequel, *Red Steel 2* (in 2010), along with the proof-of-concept motion-sensitive gameplay of Nintendo's own *WarioWare: Smooth Moves*, *Wii Sports*, and *Wii Sports Resort*.

In chapter 4, we explore a different Nintendo software title meant to leverage the system's new technology, *Wii Fit Plus*, which came bundled with another peripheral controller, the Wii Balance Board. The Wii Balance Board, which you stand on, uses stress gauges to measure the body's weight and motion fairly precisely, so that you use your whole body to control the game. But this device also has a history, as we show, and was introduced as part of the larger strategy by Nintendo to take over the family living room, as can be seen in the strange new channel for the Wii, so far available only in Japan, Wii no Ma (roughly, "Wii living room"). The Wii Balance Board, literally a "platform" you stand on, exemplifies the system's shift from imaginary game space to physical player space. This emphasis has been the most notable effect of the Wii's advent, and has altered the landscape of game development and the popular view of gaming. This shift to player space is the direct result of the platform's specific material conditions: the fact that it was designed to wirelessly link easy-to-use motion-sensitive peripherals to the console, and use a preponderance of abstract or stylized graphics in the software (at least in first-party titles and during the first few years of the platform's presence in the market).

As we mentioned above, chapter 5 takes up the Wii Channels interface and all that it represents in the way of Nintendo's distribution system—which as we argue is also an important part of the whole platform. We look at the television metaphor governing the idea of channels and how that fits into the Wii's overall strategy, and tour a number of the particular channels as examples of the diverse range of services they offer—many of these services pointedly not games. Then we pay special attention to the Virtual Console, available via the Wii Shop Channel, which relies on emulation to give players access to the deep catalog of older Nintendo games as well as games written for other platforms. We close with a discussion of the WiiWare service, also available via the Wii Shop Channel, which offers smaller games from relatively more independent developers, making them available to the Wii's market of first-time or lapsed and casual gamers—and also delivering that market to third-party and independent developers. After a detailed exploration of *World of Goo*, considered by many to be one of the best WiiWare games by the independent developer 2D Boy, we turn to *WarioWare D.I.Y.*—which allows players to make their own microgames on the handheld DS and upload them to the Wii—and look at how the game itself is based on the structures of the game-development process. These examples help us to examine the commercial and creative issues at stake in the Wii's channels of distribution and access.

Chapter 6 studies in more general terms our claim that the Wii is a social platform, which we define more broadly than merely, for instance, whether its games afford multiplayer modes. For us, the social nature of a platform is best seen in what its design encourages users to do. So we begin with the problem of open or "generative" versus closed or "appliancized" platforms, and look at various mods and hacks that people have performed on the Wii, in order to show that even a decidedly closed game console can in fact be cracked open—and almost always is—to some degree by determined users. We then turn to how users are encouraged by the design and marketing of the Wii to play games on the system that are particularly inflected for social play, from party games to music and rhythm games, such as Nintendo's own *Wii Music* and *The Beatles: Rock Band*, but also *Donkey Konga* and the independent *Bit.Trip* series (available via WiiWare). All game platforms require users to realize their potentialities, and in that sense, every platform is social. But the Wii is explicitly designed to provoke user activities that demonstrate its identity as a social platform, both in terms of perception and practical reality, even if, in the end, it remains a closed and proprietary one with limited opportunities for what most people think of as social modes of gaming—especially online multiplayer modes. In the case of the Wii, social gaming is defined in terms of social contexts and physical space, but also in relation to the public image of the platform, how it's perceived, and the style of gameplay promoted by the system. The Wii is a social platform not because it's especially good for multiplayer games (it is not) but insofar as it is designed to treat player space as physical social space, designed to afford, or at least create the perceived possibility of, watching others play and playing for the pleasure of social interaction. In this sense, the Wii is a social platform by design, and at least until late 2010, this set it apart from its competitors.

The term revolutionary has become a cliché when applied to any new consumer technology, but we nonetheless take seriously the questions surrounding the idea of technological change and the new when it comes to computing platforms. The final chapter, chapter 7, connects the whole idea of revolution in a video game platform with some of the specific economic and technological conditions that encourage as well as delimit the possibilities of making something new in this arena of computing and culture. The context of the chapter is provided by the new competitive motion-control game systems by Sony and Microsoft, first revealed in detail at the E3 2010 conference in Los Angeles and released during 2010. These new versions of motion control may in the end overtake the Wii in precision (Sony's Move) or the technology of somatic mimesis (Microsoft's Kinect). But early on, they were both characterized by many in the press as "playing catch-up" to Nintendo, and their appearance in the rough-and-tumble console market seemed to validate Nintendo's claims to have initiated a new paradigm in console controls with the Wii. The very fact of these new platforms shows that Nintendo fundamentally changed the console market with the Wii's introduction in 2006.

In the end, we see some important differences between Microsoft's advertised interpretation of motion control in the Kinect—as an evolution of gaming with "no gadgets" and moving beyond the "object"—and Nintendo's more openly gadget-centered, object-focused, relational approach to fostering player-system interactions. Rather than erasing the intermediate space between player and system, as Kinect seems to want to do or claim it can do, the Wii highlights that intermediate space as the center of the action, the place where gaming is meaningfully experienced, where the player's body encounters the materiality of the platform. Either way, however, the newly competitive console environment of the Move, Kinect, and the Wii is obviously going to be extremely significant for future studies of video games and game platforms—which lends credence to the idea that as a platform, Nintendo's Wii console has indeed fostered a kind of revolution.

The Nintendo Wii, released in 2006, is the company's fifth home console, coming after the GameCube (2001), Nintendo 64 (1996–2002), the sixteen-bit Super Nintendo Entertainment System or SNES (1990–2000), and the eight-bit NES (1983–1994, or Famicom—"Family Computer"). These home video game systems were at first a departure for a traditional company that was founded, as mentioned earlier, in the nineteenth century to manufacture playing cards, and made its name and initial capital in the public space of the arcades, most famously with *Donkey Kong*.

By definition, a console like the Wii is usually hooked up to a television set and serves as the computing heart of a video game entertainment platform in the home. Even in this sense, as naming a home entertainment device, the term console has a long history. As early as the 1920s, it would have referred to a piece of furniture, a cabinet designed to hold a radio receiver or phonograph record player along with its wiring, speakers, fittings, and so on, and mounted with control knobs, illuminated dials, and other displays. Later, televisions came in "console models" in large wooden cabinets that amounted to substantial pieces of furniture. Console can also refer to any encased control panel—for instance, the levers, stops, and pulls of an organ, which are separate from the body of the musical instrument itself. Starting with the first historical example of a home video game console, the Magnavox Odyssey in 1972, during the 1970s the term came to mean the main box housing "a new variety of electronic game that can be hooked up to the family TV set."[1] Much as the concept "desktop computer" does, a console contains and unifies a variety of system components, and allows users a convenient, ergonomic, and attractive way to organize as well as consolidate a system's controls. In this sense, like the old radio consoles, a video game console is also a piece of furniture designed to fit into a domestic space—nowadays usually as part of a media or entertainment hub—and look natural there, even aesthetically pleasing, while at the same time serving its functional purpose.

The Kyoto-based multinational corporation Nintendo moved into the home market in 1975 when it became the Japanese distributor for the Magnavox Odyssey console. A decade later, when it named its own first home platform Family Computer (in Japan) and Nintendo Entertainment System (in North America and Europe), it was staking a claim in that new market territory—the domestic space. During the 1985 rollout of the NES in New York, the company's sales staff members were instructed to refer to the NES as an "entertainment system" rather than a "video game." The system not only included a light-gun controller, the Zapper, but also the Robotic Operating Buddy (R.O.B.), a small robot with optical-sensor eyes that stacked blocks or moved gyroscopic tops to interact with the game on the television screen.

The R.O.B. and the nomenclature of the NES have been treated by most historians as marketing moves by Nintendo—a way to gain retail exposure for its system (which looked as though a mechanical toy was its centerpiece) in the midst of the hostile economic climate following the video game market crash of 1983.[2] But they're also useful reminders of the domestic space into which consoles had to fit at the time (and since) as well as signs of the modular—sometimes almost cobbled together—nature of home-console systems. The console itself contains the central processors and so on, but the overall platform includes the crucial television set as a component, along with a whole cabinet full of possible controllers, peripherals, props, control pads, guns, steering wheels, lightsabers, robots, microphones, guitars, and drums, connected by a tangle of cables or, increasingly, wirelessly. Inside the industrial design of its casing, the console itself is a complicated bundle of parts and components, circuit boards and integrated circuits, transistors, solder, and cables.

Form Factor and Technical Architecture

The Wii console was designed in the face of this messy, complicated reality to seem simple and self-contained. Different-colored models have been demonstrated, and the first prototype shown publicly was black (the introduction in 2010 of a black Wii for the consumer market made headlines), but when it was released in 2006 the console came only in white, perhaps to invoke comparison with Apple's iconic first iPods. When the console is standing vertically (it's designed to work either this way or lying horizontally—yet only in these two positions, because the DVD-ROM drive requires gravity to keep the DVD in place), the slant of the base visually exaggerates the front height and perspective lines. This design gives the box a sense of dramatic sweep, despite its small size (figure 2.1). Its overall "emotional design," however, seems to be calculated to invoke an affective response associated with simple fun. As design theorist Donald Norman has argued, this response is not only appealing to users but also may cause them to forgive the limitations of the console, since research shows that "someone who is relaxed, happy, in a pleasant mood, is more creative, more able to overlook and cope with minor problems with a device—especially if it's fun to work with." He cites as an example a reviewer of the Mini Cooper who advised his readers to overlook the car's faults "because it was so much fun."[3] The Wii only *invokes* a *feeling* of simplicity, though. The Wii, like other computing devices, is actually a relatively complex system.

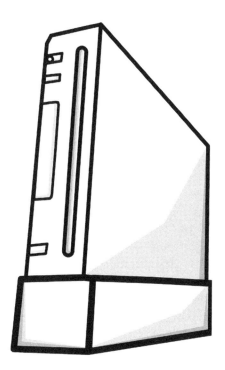

2.1 The Nintendo Wii console

Besides the Mini Cooper, the Wii console might remind some users of other aesthetically simple consumer objects, especially Apple's original iPod or, for that matter, Nintendo's own popular handheld portable DS system. Compact size is one thing that all these objects have in common. The prototype Wii, literally a black box with no controllers and still known as the Revolution, was first presented at the E3 conference in 2005, where Nintendo's president, Satoru Iwata, held it aloft in one hand to emphasize that it was "by far the smallest console" that Nintendo had ever built, at about the size of a stack of three DVD cases.[4] (He would later say that he actually picked up three plastic DVD cases and showed the stack to Nintendo engineers as a design challenge.) Taking the cue, one live blogger compared the new box to Apple's Mac Mini. A kind of parallel evolution has taken place with Apple and Nintendo systems in recent years. The GameCube was in development during 2000–2001, at the same time that Apple was developing its own distinctive Mac G4 Cube. Besides the shared shape, both systems aimed at similar low-profile designs, suggesting that they were taking part in larger trends in computing during this period. And then the next-generation console from Nintendo, the Wii, was nearing the end of its development in 2005, just as the Mac Mini appeared—another minimal form-factor, service-oriented, "right-sized" device. As many have noticed, the iPod can be seen as an even more apt parallel to the Wii in terms of marketing as well as computing design.

The Wii is smaller than competing consoles in the same generation—roughly 6 by 8.5 by 1.7 inches as opposed to roughly 10 by 12 by 3 inches for the Xbox and PS3—and lighter—2.7 pounds as opposed to 10 or 11 pounds for the other two. Even after both competitors came out with "slim" models in 2010, they remained significantly larger than the Wii. Nintendo's developers strategically sacrificed power, storage, and other features inside the box to keep it small and cool running, and achieve the semiotic effect of simplicity for the sake of marketing, not to mention to keep the price below $250. Originally, Nintendo hoped to set the price at about $100; by 2010, the price had been reduced to around $200 for an enhanced bundle. Aesthetic and technical simplicity, smallness, efficiency, and relatively lower cost were all entangled in the original design in ways that make them hard to separate for analysis. In fact, these features and limitations are all connected. So that it would not overheat, the small console had to draw less electricity, but this of course was a consumer advantage in terms of the cost of operation—and success at using less power and running cooler meant that the console could claim to be quiet as well as visually simple and unobtrusive.[5]

The console's design imperative—to signify simplicity—shows up even in the superficial details, such as, for example, the fact that the case's screws are covered with tiny white plastic flaps or rubber feet to create a smooth, uniform surface. But concealed behind the smooth, compact shell of the slim white box—literally hidden behind a series of trapdoors— are the inevitable complicated details, the technology that does the work necessary to any modern console, serving as a reminder of the importance of other components and peripherals (or potential components and peripherals) that complete the platform. It's important to get a sense of just how much is packed into the deceptively simple form factor, so we want to take a moment to tour the console's components.

With the console standing vertically, a long trapdoor on the top reveals four ports for GameCube controllers. Just behind that, a small door covers two slots for GameCube memory cards—signs of the Wii's most hardwired form of backward compatibility. The GameCube (2001) was a sixty-four-bit system and the first Nintendo console to use an optical drive for loading games (mini DVD-ROMs). Nintendo has repeatedly called attention to this backward compatibility, in concert with the availability of the back catalog by way of the Virtual Console. For the GameCube, Nintendo had partnered with IBM to produce a custom 486 MHz PowerPC chip, called "Gekko," as its central processing unit (CPU) and a 162 MHz ATI GPU (graphics processor unit), codenamed "Flipper". The Wii makes use of an updated version ("Broadway") of the same basic PowerPC architecture for its 729 MHz processor and 243 MHz ATI ("Hollywood") chip. In general, the internal architecture for the Wii's chipset is a kind of direct extension of the GameCube's "Dolphin" system. The GameCube can be seen as anticipating the Wii's simplicity of design since it was also a small box (a five-inch cube). Unlike the Wii, however, it came in a range of colors from the start.

To return to the Wii: a drive slot runs down the front of the console for optical discs (Wii and GameCube discs will work). It glows blue when the console is on, when a disc is inserted, and when it's receiving data over the Internet via the WiiConnect24 service. It turns orange when in standby mode, and red when turned off. A small door on the console's front to the left of the optical disc slot, below the reset button and above the eject button, opens to reveal a secure digital (SD) card slot for much-needed expanded storage (support for secure digital high capacity [SDHC] was added in 2009, allowing for up to 32 GB of additional storage), along with a small synchronization button above the slot. On the back of the box there are two USB ports, where dongles for wireless music-game controllers, for example, can be attached; their blinking lights dangling from the back of the console are reminders of a potential channel of wireless communication with, say, plastic guitar controllers, microphones, or drum-pad sets in *Rock Band* or *Guitar Hero*. On the back, there is also a connection for the cable to the slim LED sensor bar that sits on the top or in front of the television, and communicates with the infrared sensor camera in the Wii Remote controller, as well as AV out and DC power input connections. The lithium battery holder is under a cover on the bottom of the console, beside an air intake (there's also an air vent on the back).

Inside the box, the motherboard's various integrated circuits include a 512 MB NAND-embedded flash memory card and other memory, 88 MB of main memory, and 3 MB of short-term framebuffer memory, which is used to hold the color values of every pixel on the screen, up to 480i, 480p, or 576i (depending on the locale of the system), as well as the primary CPU and GPU chipset. Among additional components, the console case contains, for instance, the 802.11 B/G WiFi card with two antennae, a heat sink structure, and a fan for cooling the board as well as the actual optical disc drive and its logic board, divided from the main board by a metal plate. Some parts inside the Wii are labeled with a number starting with an RVL prefix, a reminder of the system's codename: Revolution.

Power (Constraints)

Being a computing powerhouse would have been impossible for the Wii, given its quiet and efficient technologies as well as small, slim design. Nintendo set out from the beginning to head off unfavorable comparisons over raw power by taking another tack altogether. Miyamoto publicly described the Wii in terms of natural selection, insisting that "power isn't everything for a console. Too many powerful consoles can't coexist. It's like having only ferocious dinosaurs. They might fight and hasten their own extinction."[6] The Wii has competed by being nimble and attractive, and for several years after its release it dominated a hitherto-uncrowded but extremely wide demographic niche in the console environment—a niche that the Wii has helped to create since its appearance in 2006—or the demographic segment of users that Juul has called the casual revolution.[7] These are first-time gamers, older adult or female gamers, and consumers who might not even choose to identify themselves as gamers. About a year before the Wii appeared, Donald Norman pointed out the disconnect between the idea of the core gamer and the actual market for video games, which by then included roughly as many women as men:

Despite the broader audience, the physical design of the game consoles has not been changed to meet the growing popularity. The design focus upon young, excitable males limits the potential audience, excluding not only many girls and women but also many men. This rich potential is completely untapped.[8]

The Wii was designed precisely to tap this potential market. Miyamoto has said that in conceiving of the system, the company asked itself, "What might convince moms to buy this for their kids?" and he admits that the developers deliberately aimed for a low-cost console because it would "make moms happy."

> Our goal was to come up with a machine that moms would want—easy to use, quick to start up, not a huge energy drain, and quiet while it was running. Rather than just picking new technology, we thought seriously about what a game console should be.[9]

Clearly "moms" is a gendered, even sexist marketing construct—one that assumes a traditional association between women and domestic space, for example, and represents a calculated attempt to leverage a stereotypical home economics in order to sell a home console. The idea of consumer moms is partway between traditional market segmentation and the newer design and marketing technique of creating "personas" to represent end users, or what some theorists have called "imaginary friends"—user *types* constructed by a company to guide the design and marketing processes.[10]

Nintendo has clearly marketed the Wii to women in general, especially in the case of *Wii Fit*, though with surprisingly little of the kind of "girl-games" stereotypes or "pink-PlayStation essentialism" (and restriction to Barbie games) that was everywhere in the 1990s.[11] The press and gamer cultures, however, were another story. There have been a number of stark examples of the idea that "Wii is for girls," from magazine articles on hosting "girls' night in" Wii parties ("Because isn't it about time we had something he wants, but can't get his hands on?") to a video for the G4 television channel that's a parody of the famous Apple versus PC ads, but in this case pits a skinny blond in a bikini ("I'm a Wii . . . just as cute as a button . . . cheap. And fun") against a fully clothed and bespectacled young woman representing the PS3 (she's interested in "World War II combat, karaoke, and tackle football").[12] Nintendo's own marketing has been less blatantly stereotypical, for the most part, which may indicate that market segmentation and gender stereotyping actually matter less in selling the Wii console than penetration into the homes of casual gamers, into the imagined space of the living room, by whatever means.

At any rate, there's good reason to try to sell the console to women. Starting a year after the release of the Wii, the company's own documents have repeatedly pointed to in-house statistics showing that over 50 percent of gamers using the DS and the Wii are now female.[13] The case of games and gender is just one way in which the Wii exemplifies the connections between platform technology and cultural and economic factors. Nintendo's niche marketing strategy based on certain assumptions about gender and the domestic space in which games are played led to certain design decisions. Those decisions about platform technology have in turn both constrained and enabled specific features of the creative and expressive works—the games created for the platform. And then the games have had an effect on the larger culture.

This view of platform and culture as deeply interrelated holds true historically for other media, of course, including print media, as we mentioned in the introduction. Books are a sophisticated form of technology for delivering texts, a set of platforms for cultural expression and communication. Since the fifteenth century, this has involved the technology of the printing press, including movable type, and later forms of typesetting, formes and frames for holding the type, and machines for pressing the image of that type on to sheets of paper, which then could be folded, cut, and bound into books. The discipline of book history studies print technology, but it also has to pay attention to the means of distributing the printed objects that it produces, the social institutions of copyright law, publishers, printers, sellers, libraries, monasteries, private collections, ways of getting books into the hands of readers or collectors, patronage, subscription, and (later) commercial marketing. The cultural contexts of particular readers completes the picture, including their social class, gender, level of education, tastes, and assumptions about the medium of print—what it can provide for them in the way of "cultural capital" or social status, say, as well as the contents of the books they read along with the knowledge and pleasure that books offer.

A video game platform like the Wii demands a comparable level of attention. If we want to understand it, we need to study the technology of the platform itself, but also the effects of the technology on the games produced for the platform. And the market for these games and the platform is more than an external economic consideration. It is a partly projected and partly measurable demographic reality, which is part of the larger system of expression that the platform creates—the outer edge of platform as it were. In fact, it's arguably one of the most important parts of that system, since in the end a video game system, unlike some other kinds of computing systems, is a media and entertainment platform, developed to engage an audience. It only becomes meaningful when it's played.

The Wii's potential audience is vast, as sales have shown. But Nintendo had to project that potential audience first in order to go on to construct it by way of the new platform. Its domination of the new market from 2006 to about 2010 has undoubtedly been enhanced by the form factor of the console—its unobtrusive, attractive presence in the living room. This design was in turn closely bound up with, and indeed made possible by, the decision to compete as a smaller, nimbler, lower-powered dinosaur in the console environment. Power isn't everything. Deciding to make it a secondary consideration was a crucial stage in the Wii's creation—one that has continued to have far-reaching implications, and one that has contributed to the identity of the Wii as what we are calling a social platform, defined as much by social contexts as by hardware and software considerations.

There are two large issues when it comes to the Wii's relatively low power: the constraints this puts on the system's capabilities, especially when it comes to graphics display, and the efficiencies in terms of power consumption that result. Both issues have to be understood not only in technical terms but also within specific cultural and social contexts.

The Wii's modest 729 MHz processor (the IBM PowerPC Broadway chip) contrasts starkly with the two major competitors' 3.2 GHz processors. For video, the Wii has an ATI (Hollywood) card, a 243 MHz GPU providing 480p maximum resolution, merely standard definition rather than the 1080p high definition (HD) of the other platforms, or the kind of graphics capability expected by hard-core players of highly cinematic games. Members of that demographic have continued to complain about the Wii's lack of HD (though in actuality, image *definition* has little to do directly with power). It's important to remember that power in a console—and computer systems in general—is always relative, and often a fuzzy concept, no more than a general sense users have of combined output effects, such as speed, image processing, and storage. Sometimes power is really no more than a marketing term with little precise technical meaning—as, for example, in the case of Nintendo's own slogan in the 1980s, in the era of the NES: "Now you're playing with power!" At any rate, the effects of power are always a matter of perception, relative to software needs and market expectations, which are set by the existing competition in a given generation.

Much more significant than raw numbers that measure graphics-rendering capabilities or processor clock speed is what software designers can do within the limits of a given system. Yet what software designers do is frequently affected by general perceptions, the market, and the technical specifications of the competing platforms. The determining connections between cultural and social factors and hardware or software decisions are in this way often indirect, highly mediated, and sometimes circular: projected expectations drive design, which in turn creates expectations that are fulfilled in later design cycles, and so on.

Consider the simple question of which games are developed and selected for release with a new system. Many of the first-generation games produced for the Wii were effectively ports or adaptations of games originally developed for the GameCube. In these cases Wii-specific functions were added, especially when it came to using the motion-sensitive Wii Remote controller, but usually without fundamentally altering the gameplay. *Wii Sports*, *Wii Sports Resort*, and *Wii Fit Plus* games, on the other hand, were developed from scratch entirely for the Wii, and so their creators were able to calibrate their design to the system's particular limitations. The sports games are highly abstract simulations that make use of selective features of game physics. *Wii Sports* consists of five sports simulations with Miis as player characters as well as NPCs.

With the sequel, *Wii Sports Resort*, however, user feedback and other data led to motion control being greatly enhanced, rendered more precise, thanks to the MotionPlus add-on (which we'll discuss further in chapter 3). This led to the inclusion in the new pack of Sword Play, actually a series of three sword-based games, in which you can battle single NPC opponents on an elevated platform above the water (Duel), methodically advance by cutting your way through an exaggerated number of opponents (Showdown), or slice your way through various absurdly oversize objects— fruit, pencils, and cake—at specified angles, showing off the ability of the enhanced controller to recognize vertical, horizontal, and diagonal swipes in fidelity to the relatively realistic make-believe motions that players make (Speed Slice).

In all of these games, the sword characteristically resembles a red or blue lightsaber as much as it does a traditional bamboo kendo sword. (Of course, the *Star Wars* Jedi weapon was based on martial arts swords in the first place.) As in kendo or Western fencing, competition is structured and formalized. Player avatars wear protective face-mask helmets and take hits in a methodical way, low or high on the body or head, depending on the opponent's parry, and finally collapse or fall off the high platform in the Duel game, when they fail to parry and are hit repeatedly in unprotected areas. These are sports rather than combat games, and they're not realistic, except in terms of the feeling they afford of wielding the sword via your controller. It *feels* fairly realistic, is the point, even though the sword is red or blue, and you're a cartoon caricature of yourself standing on a platform high above a giant pool. Although you can flail about with the Wii Remote to some extent, if only for fun or show, the possible effective moves are fairly limited by the program. In the Showdown game, where you cut your way through an oncoming horde, players seem comically zombielike as they approach methodically and wait their turn to be hit. The simplifications and compromises necessary to allow for intuitive swordplay are evident: true one-to-one fidelity of motion must be constrained within the limits of the game's cartoon world in order for the whole experience to be rendered entertainingly. Sometimes, as with the walking-zombie opponents in Showdown, the constraints tend to weigh down the gameplay. at other times the match is better, and it feels like realistic-*enough* weapon wielding.

In order to achieve some degree of fidelity in motion mapping, graphic realism in general was set aside on Nintendo's games for the Wii, or it was at least relegated to a much lower priority than it usually is on other game consoles. (Wii games by third-party developers, however, such as Electronic Arts' *Tiger Woods PGA Tour*, have often continued to attempt graphic realism on the Wii comparable to what's available on other platforms.) The most obvious example of Nintendo's strategy to make realism a secondary concern (at best) in order to concentrate on other features is the appearance of the Mii avatars. Their graphic design is simple in a self-conscious, cartoon way that calls attention to their simplicity. Like the various Lego video games, or the characters in Pixar's early animated films, from metal Luxo lamps to tin toys and the stars of the *Toy Story* movies, these sports games make an artistic virtue of necessity by limiting their environments and Mii avatars (which serve as both player characters and NPCs) to highly stylized caricatures, with their bodies glossy obelisks, all artificial-material surfaces and textures (see figure 2.2). This eliminates the need to animate complex texture-mapped hair, for instance, or flexing musculature, and avoids the need to have the avatars move in realistic, convincing ways. The advantage, besides savings when it comes to graphic processing, it that the Miis stay safely on this side of the "uncanny valley"—a metaphoric term for the anxious, disturbed reaction people have to almost lifelike simulated characters. They don't even attempt the kind of realism that can stand out so badly when it fails. When in play, the Miis sometimes don't have arms, say, but simply have tennis racquets, baseball bats, or swords protruding from the place near their polished-surface torsos where arms would be.

Nintendo designers have explained that the style of the Miis was based on traditional Japanese Kokeshi dolls with big heads and rounded, limbless bodies made from glossy painted wood. Their Kokeshi-, manga-, or anime-style cuteness (*kawaii*) has become the symbol of the platform's overall aesthetic. The prototype of the Mii Channel was first developed for the handheld portable platform the DS. Nintendo president Iwata recalls this history in a discussion with the head of the software development team. The DS prototype "already contained all the basic elements of what would go on to become the Mii Channel," he says.

> You could make faces with ease using the control system, and it had a very intuitive interface too. Miyamoto-san mentioned that he'd like to be able to create an "alter ego" that wasn't data-heavy and could be used to represent the player in lots of other games. And this was exactly what you'd made. . . . And now things have come full circle as the Mii Channel can be used with WarioWare: Smooth Moves.[14]

The radically simplified appearance and editable features of the Miis are actually native to a system even more minimalist and limited than the Wii is—the tiny screen and lower power of the pocket-size DS. Their small file size (they're anything but "data-heavy") and easy portability fulfilled

2.2 Miis

requirements that Miyamoto had expressed based on fitting into the planned limitations of the home-console platform.

This kind of design solution—deliberately limiting the data density, by limiting textures and surfaces that must be animated in the game's simulation, for example—has been Miyamoto's (and Nintendo's) strong suit for decades. Ultimately, as we suggested in the introduction, it goes back to the eight-bit era, when he created Jumpman, who became Mr. Video, who became Mario, with all his particular features meant for easy animating. It was an impressive design trick, to make a convincing character out of an eight-bit sprite. Nintendo's design ethos is still one of making something creatively compelling out of a limited palette of story and graphic elements. In the two recent *Super Mario Galaxy* games for the Wii (2007 and 2010), the hero is 3D, and the 3D environments (with their often-absurdly playful physics) are impressively designed, but still cartoons. The tradition persists in details such as the way that most grass on the planetoids that Mario explores is deliberately drawn and textured to look like bright plastic Astroturf instead of realistic organic vegetation. The stylized aesthetic of Nintendo's classic franchises is perfectly suited to the graphics-challenged configuration of the Wii and its standard definition images.

Comic artist and theorist Scott McCloud argues that cartoon abstraction causes the viewer to identify with the abstracted iconic image, to imagine oneself in the mask of the simplified cartoon character. This device, he says, is part of the traditional "national style" of manga (and anime) in Japan, making up "a long, rich history of iconic characters," thanks to the "seminal influence" of pioneer Osamu Tezuka, the creator of the classic manga *Astro Boy*, with its oddly proportioned, glossy-bodied hero.[15] It's no accident that Tezuka is an acknowledged influence on Miyamoto. Video game critic Chris Kohler cites McCloud's contention along with that of game historian J. C. Herz, who reminds us that this deliberately abstract manga style of drawing characters "translated easily into early video games, which didn't have the graphic resolution to represent characters with adult proportions. Small, stylized characters had fewer pixels per inch and were easier to use, and so video games borrowed, for reasons of expediency, what *manga* had developed as a matter of convention."[16] The stylized aesthetic of the Wii contains rich cultural allusions to all these conventional Japanese objects—manga, anime, and Kokeshi dolls—but it also grows out of earlier video game art and Nintendo's own history of video game design. The point is that it's not *only* a design aesthetic or marketing decision based on consistent "branding." It's also a practical move that makes sense "for reasons of expediency" given the technical limitations of the system on which the designs will be displayed. It bears repeating that this is not a one-way relationship. The platforms that Nintendo chooses to develop are made technically and commercially possible in part because of the design of the software destined to run on them, at least in the case of in-house titles created by Nintendo itself.

Besides the Mii-based *Wii Sports*, *Wii Sports Resort*, *Wii Play*, *Wii Music*, *Wii Fit*, and *Wii Fit Plus*, other Nintendo-made games for the Wii, such as *Super Mario Galaxy*, *Super Mario Galaxy 2*, *New Super Mario Bros. Wii*, *The Legend of Zelda: Twilight Princess*, and *WarioWare: Smooth Moves*, have been generally well received by both casual and more traditional hard-core gamers, in terms of their design and gameplay, both of which are results of their being optimized for the system from the start. But Nintendo has depended on third-party developers to produce more mature, action-adventure games, and the Wii has struggled to attract such developers in significant numbers. The company admits that this range of genres and styles is not its "key focus" or forte.[17] But it's also a circular problem of perception: insofar as the Wii is perceived as a system strictly for casual gaming, it becomes less likely to attract developers of more realistic-style software, and in turn this affects the perception of the platform's suitability for such titles.

The conventional wisdom among many critics and players, however, whatever its truth, is that the main reason for the lack of realistic action-adventure games on the Wii is limited graphics. Together with the depth of play, such games conventionally rely on high-resolution realistic graphics and cinematic effects, including prerendered cutscenes as well as robust online multiplayer modes, in many cases. In other words, they're better suited to the processing power and experience with online play provided by the Xbox 360 or PS3. Some reviews of a rare FPS exclusively for the Wii, publisher Ubisoft's *Red Steel 2* (2010), praised the game—and implicitly damned the Wii—by suggesting that it was the exception that proved the rule, approaching the graphic qualities of an Xbox or Playstation game.

According to comments by fans on numerous discussion boards, the relatively disappointing first-month sales for *Red Steel 2* were due to the hard-core audience having abandoned the Wii by spring 2010. Players who would have appreciated the game, this line of argument goes, had already stopped using or even gotten rid of the console. Conversely, the casual audience still devoted to the Wii would not be interested in an FPS of this sort. This was only anecdotal speculation by those who probably thought of themselves as hard-core gamers, and yet some of them had apparently already played the game, it would seem, so the story may not have captured the actual consumer reaction accurately. Nevertheless, this attempted explanation highlights the widespread perception that the Wii is too underpowered to support immersive action games of any depth—which it is assumed in turn must rely on the kind of realistic high-resolution graphics that require the greater "horsepower" of the competing systems.

Red Steel 2

Red Steel 2 makes a useful case study of what's involved in developing software for the Wii, and how the reality and perception of the system's power limitations affect that development process. The first game in the series and first FPS developed for the Wii, *Red Steel*, was a fairly realistic-looking action-adventure game with a Japanese yakuza crime mob theme, released by Ubisoft in November 2006 to coincide precisely with the launch of the console that same month. It received a flood of negative reviews, mainly focused on its clunky mechanics, especially the relatively crude synchronization of the Wii Remote gestures with in-game swordplay, for example—problems that obviously reflected the developers' lack of experience with the Wii's new controller technology. But there were also problems with skipping movement and occasional crashes that were probably the result of not anticipating the Wii's power limitations. In the game, you use the Wii Remote with the Nunchuk attached to handle both guns and a samurai-style katana sword. The possibilities for swordplay provided by a motion-sensitive wireless controller raised expectations in 2006 that were largely disappointed. *Red Steel* sold reasonably well—over one million copies in the end—undoubtedly riding on the popularity of Nintendo's new console and being the only ESRB T-rated shooter for the new system. Yet one review site said the game was "buggy" and "thoroughly unimpressive," because the sword fights felt more like "two cavemen hitting each other over the head with clubs," and it signaled widespread disillusionment, not just about this one game, but also about the new platform as a whole.[18]

The follow-up game, *Red Steel 2*, appeared in 2010 and was repeatedly referred to as a reboot of the franchise rather than a mere sequel. To make it, developers used an entirely new 3D game engine, Ubisoft's LyN, the same used for the company's *Rabbids Go Home* and expressly designed to exploit the full graphics capabilities of the Wii.[19] Most important of all, though, was Nintendo's improved motion control. Although development of the second game was already under way when the Wii MotionPlus accessory was announced, game design quickly centered on how to take advantage of the augmented control provided by the plug-in device, which uses a tiny gyroscope to increase the Wii Remote's sensitivity to rotational-axis movements. (We discuss this technology in detail in chapter 3.) The new game garnered much better reviews than the first one, including some that called it the best FPS game for the Wii.

The difference between *Red Steel* and *Red Steel 2*, between 2006 and 2010, was in part the improved mapping of player movements supplied by the MotionPlus device, especially during swordplay. But *Red Steel 2* also succeeded where the first game failed because the developers learned from experience how better to exploit the affordances and constraints of the Wii console as a whole. Jason Vandenberghe, the creative director of *Red Steel 2*, has said as much. According to him, the team "had spent the previous two years with the Wii, trying to learn what does and doesn't work with controls," the most difficult part of the process of making the sequel— "getting the inputs right," the calibration of the Wiimote and Nunchuk controllers with action in the game. The design process began with more complicated moves and button combinations, but repeatedly simplified them in pursuit of intuitive motion control. The goal was for the Wii Remote to feel like an imaginary gun when it's pointed at the screen—using the B button as a trigger—and an imaginary sword when you swipe in any direction. The elusive ultimate goal is a true one-to-one mapping of player motion and in-game character action. Still, when asked about developing later sequels for then-named Project Natal (later released as Kinect), the motion-sensitive system by Microsoft that makes use of cameras to capture the player's motions without a controller, Vandenberghe expressed skepticism:

> I mean, I would love to get hold of the Natal team and talk to them about it. Maybe I'm wrong, I could be completely wrong about this, but for me in first-person action games, you need a stick. I need clear, accurate input. . . . Maybe in ten years we'll be used to it; today I want a stick. So I hope with Natal there will be an option to hold a controller, or to use a one-handed controller of some kind that will allow me to have that analogue stick and then do the motion.[20]

We'll have more to say about Kinect in the final chapter. But in the context of *Red Steel 2* on the Wii console, it's interesting that Vandenberghe believes the task of optimizing the game for the Wii's constraints was actually furthered by having the Wii Remote as a prop or an object ("a stick") that promotes player engagement.

They may have thought that "you need a stick," but on the other hand, the *Red Steel 2* development team deliberately sought to avoid the problem associated with the Wii that has come to be known by players and developers as "waggle"—the tendency of certain games to allow relatively imprecise and uninvolved, weak waving of the controller to work as effectively as more mimetic gestures, a flick of the wrist instead of a full-armed stroke of a tennis racquet or sword. In *Red Steel 2*, swinging the remote harder and faster makes the character swing their sword harder and faster, and do more damage. Vandenberghe has trumpeted this feature, saying in interviews before the release, "We think we've defeated the waggle."[21] His remark echoes the claims made by the developer of the technology inside the MotionPlus device, Invensense: "No more playing 'lazy Wii!'. . . no more lying around on the couch and simply flicking your wrist to play Wii games. Sorry!"[22] An early reviewer of the game agreed, asserting that he quickly learned that you really have to stand to play effectively.[23] It's interesting that for reviewers and developers, the idea of motion fidelity and the system's tendency to promote full-body movement is recognized as a goal for Wii gameplay, and a kind of test of its success as a platform.

Adjusting the control system may have been the hardest part of designing *Red Steel 2*, but the decision that made that adjustment possible, that made it possible to take advantage of MotionPlus device without dragging down gameplay, was the overall graphic design of the game. Instead of realistic 3D graphics, *Red Steel 2* is drawn in the style of comic books and manga in particular, using cel-shaded images with distinct black outlines. The invocation of manga fits with the samurai-Western theme, and like the Miis, these differently simplified characters and settings allow for smoother polygon rendering; the game runs at sixty frames per second. Cel-shaded animation, or "non-photorealistic rendering," is also commonly referred to as "toon shading," and the cartoon effect is valued by gamers who fondly remember, for instance, the cel-shaded Link in *The Legend of Zelda: Wind Waker* for the GameCube. Cel shading is itself a kind of "retro" artistic back-formation, a complicated process that begins in most cases with a 3D model, and applies filters and lighting to achieve the "flatter" hand-drawn look. One important result, though, when it comes to the Wii is that designs can be made to require fewer polygons for detailed textures, because the design can suggest textures and details in a more abstract way via the drawing style itself. So this style of graphic animation is particularly suited to the limits of the Wii processors.

In *Red Steel 2*, perhaps the most noticeable manifestations of the style are the unrealistic streaking motion lines and reflective flares surrounding your moving sword or an opponent's oversize hammer, for example, both of which have a highly artificial look that fits into the context of the game's overall style. The action takes place in and around the fictional

Caldera, a surrealistic Western town of indeterminate era with some Japanese architectural features grafted on, including signs printed with Japanese characters. Building facades or city streets are treated in an abstract, simplified way, with relatively sparsely textured blocks of color suggesting stones or washes of shaded browns indicating dirt, but these gestures are acceptable within the conventions that are given. You play as a nameless gunslinger samurai (a member of a ninja clan of "protectors," the *Kusagari*), a hero in a wide-brimmed hat that often conceals his face entirely or only reveals the eyes (with pupils of two different colors), and a buckled collar on their long coat that hides the mouth and nose like an outlaw's bandanna. The result is not unlike the advantages of eight-bit Mario, in that little needs to be done in the way of animating the character's facial expressions. The physics, too, are straight out of the manga and anime traditions, or the related tradition of the martial arts film, with its exaggerated, larger-than-life fighting mechanics. One dramatic move allows you to strike an opponent with your sword so hard that they fly high into the air, to be shot in the moment they hang suspended or struck again with the sword as they fall.

The game has been characterized as a "first-person brawler," and repeated close combat and melee attacks make up most of its gameplay. You hold the A button to parry with your sword, for example, and most successful attacks involve using the buttons to get into the optimal position (frequently behind the opponent) before striking with your sword. In fact, after playing for a while, you get the sense that *Red Steel 2* was developed primarily as a reason to exploit the Wii's mechanics of swordplay and gunplay. The setting of the town, although attractively drawn, is most of all a map of squares and courtyards where encounters can be staged. The landscape is littered with an excessive number of crates and other receptacles that following a long-established video game convention, can be shot or smashed to collect money. The newness of the motion control means that early training sessions in Jian's Dojo, where you practice swordplay against mounted dummies and under the tutelage of a seated sensei figure, make no attempt to maintain any diegetic illusion. Not only are there the usual arrow indicators, pop-up text with button-indicating directions, there are demonstrations in full-motion video pop-up windows starring a modern young woman in a white T-shirt showing you how to hold the Nunchuk and Wiimote as well as make the various sword motions.

As game developers adjust to the Wii's constraints—and as their development cycle has coincided with the introduction of the retrofit improvement of the MotionPlus attachment in 2009—more effective software titles have emerged. One more example will help to illustrate what many of them have in common. *Monster Hunter Tri* (which was already a hit in Japan before its North American release), from the venerable Japanese developer Capcom, allows for multiplayer hunting missions against giant monsters that look like strange dinosaurs, across vast natural landscapes that sometimes look like otherworldly fantasy realms, in scenarios that can seem like a cross between *World of Warcraft* and Will Wright's *Spore*. When it was released, the game was heavily marketed as "the most beautiful game on the Wii," and in an interview, producer Ryozo Tsujimoto said of Wii games of this general kind, "You can [make them] within the limitations, but you need a sense of design." Like *Red Steel 2* (or for that matter, Nintendo's sports games), but employing a different aesthetic, *Monster Hunter Tri* leverages its design and artwork to offset the platform's technological constraints. In explaining this, Tsujimoto shares an instructive parable with his interviewer:

> He asked me to imagine a cluster of five trees that might appear in the game. Maybe the game can't render all five trees, so you're stuck with having to use four. How do you place them? That's the kind of thing focused on by his team. Their goal, from the start, he told me, was to develop the best looking game on Nintendo's system.[24]

The moral of this story, a variation on the strategy of using cartoon- and manga-style graphics, is that what can't be rendered by the system can be offset by effective, thoughtful, design—minimalist design. Four trees perfectly placed can look beautiful *and* avoid crashing the system. The limits of the platform ultimately determine design.

Power (Efficiencies)

The most notorious drawback of the Wii—its relatively limited graphics capabilities, which are considered the result of its relatively lower-powered processors—functions as a given, perceived limit that both Nintendo and third-party developers confront when designing successful games for the system. This has led to interesting creative solutions and successful software titles, from the in-house cartoon aesthetic of the Miis, to the related manga style of *Red Steel 2* or "primitive" fantasy style of *Monster Hunter Tri*. The most successful development strategy for Wii games has been to find ways to reduce the requirements for photorealism or other processing-heavy demands of the game world, in order to be able to direct computing resources to managing the mimetic interface of the motion-control system. This has so far worked to capture the casual market. But it has continued to provoke complaints among self-described hard-core gamers, who seek a deeper, more demanding kind of immersive game-play—one associated with photorealistic graphics and impressive cinematic effects (and increasingly, viewed in HD).

The split between these two markets can be illustrated by the appearance within months of *Red Steel 2* of another western-themed single-player action-adventure game, *Red Dead Redemption*, for the PS3 and Xbox 360. The two games have the Western genre in common, in a general sense (and coincidentally, the word red in their titles), but otherwise they could not be further apart. *Red Dead Redemption* is the product of Rockstar Games, the makers of the groundbreaking *Grand Theft Auto* series, and like those games, offers a vast sandbox or open world, a simulated geography to explore, as well as cinematic-looking 3D graphics. *Red Dead Redemption* was extremely well received, ending up on numerous year-end best-of-2010 lists. Reviewing it for the *New York Times*, Seth Schiesel describes the game hyperbolically in terms of the goal of total immersion: it "does not merely immerse you in its fiction. Rather, it submerges you, grabbing you by the neck and forcing you down, down, down until you simply have no interest in coming up for air."[25] This super immersive effect, we think, is often the opposite kind of experience sought by casual gamers in general and Wii gamers in particular. It nonetheless remains the holy grail of traditional hard-core games, so called triple-A titles that can take forty or more hours to complete, such as the kind of game epitomized in the GTA series.

This book is based on the premise (one shared by Juul's *A Casual Revolution*) that there has been a shift in recent years away from this kind of game as exclusively defining video games as a whole, with the rise of more casual or flexible modes of play along with the types of games that support those modes. The tale of these two different western games reminds us that the remaining division of hard-core versus casual gaming follows the division between platforms—at least in the Wii's own generation. Kinect and Move may have added a casual dimension across the board, but it remains a truth universally acknowledged that hard-core games belong on the graphics-capable Xbox and PlayStation, not on the Wii. Everyone agrees that a game like *Red Dead Redemption* could not run well on the Wii, with its minimalist, scaled-down, and admittedly limited processing power.[26]

But this limitation on the Wii's part can be seen in a more positive light, in terms of its notable success in helping to usher in the casual revolution—which we see as a general shift to the social nature of the platform.

And the Wii's limitations are no accident. They should viewed against the larger backdrop of recent developments in computing as a whole, including the rise of mobile gaming on platforms such as the iPhone and iPad or Android, all of which are creating new competition for Nintendo's DS (and now the 3DS), a market based on pared-down computing and display needs, for obvious reasons in the case of pocket-size battery-dependent platforms, and the social and economic fact of the rise of casual gaming. As consoles go, the Wii appears in retrospect to have come along at just the right moment, as a canny participant in the dual trends of casual gaming and lightweight, deliberately "underpowered" mobile platforms. Though it is thought of as a stationary object sitting beside the television, the Wii is itself actually highly portable, compared to larger, more complicated systems, and Nintendo has repeatedly stressed the fact that it can easily be carried to another room in the house or a friend's home. To the degree that a home console can do so, the Wii shares a number of goals with mobile platforms and recent trends in computing in general.

One important but often-overlooked aspect of these trends in computing is the shift toward the goal of lower power consumption. Remember that Miyamoto's living room marketing scenario, in which he imagines getting moms to buy the Wii console, includes not only ease of use, speed, and quiet but also energy efficiency—the idea that the console would be "not a huge energy drain." The relative energy efficiency of the Wii is indeed striking. A report by the National Resources Defense Council in 2008 compared the power use of the major consoles.[27] Sony's PS3 is the biggest power consumer, using about $134 worth of electricity a year (assuming, as the study did for all consoles, that it remains powered up). Microsoft's Xbox 360 is only slightly better, using $103 worth of electricity annually. By stark contrast, Nintendo's Wii uses only $10 worth of electricity a year. The greater power of the Xbox and PS3 is necessary to drive their high-end graphics and support other features. Though the details are frequently confused in popular discussions as HD, or in mere equations of power with better graphics, it is true that the high-end graphics of the larger systems are produced as high-resolution 3D images and animations. Added horsepower is needed to ensure that the Xbox and PlayStation can run the 3D volumes, and do the more advanced rendering necessary.

This power comes at a price. The competitor consoles basically cost more to operate over one to two years than the Wii currently costs to purchase. Energy and power consumption are functions of the host CPU, not just the GPU, and a computing system is only as powerful as its weakest link. To get an idea of what we mean by calling the Wii relatively energy efficient, consider its core CPU in comparison to that of its competitors. The Xbox 360's tricore 3.2 GHz PowerPC CPU is a member of the same processor family as the Wii's (the PowerPC), but obviously with more power and thus much increased power needs. The PS3 employs a CPU with a dual-core power processor element and seven synergistic processor elements. The seven synergistic processor elements are used to off-load major computational tasks using a model of parallel computation known as single instruction, multiple data. While the Xbox 360 and PS3 have some significant architectural differences, in both cases their CPUs are at the high end of processor speeds, even in the context of today's desktop and laptop PCs. It comes as no surprise, therefore, that the PS3's power-consumption footprint is the largest of the three. Actually, compared to the Wii, the PS3 is a veritable supercomputer, with a design reminiscent of vector-style parallel computers such as the Cray.

The difference in power use is significant. To put it in practical terms, the Wii can be powered for twenty years before its electricity costs match the price of the system itself. Even when following the National Resources Defense Council's green recommendations and powering down the console when not in use, the two higher-powered systems still use slightly more electricity when turned off, used minimally, or in standby mode than the Wii does when it's left on. Interestingly, the study rightly connects this difference to the different design constraints of the competing systems: "Using an average of just sixteen watts in active mode, the Wii is the juice sipper of the group. Attracting buyers with novel, interactive gameplay rather than power-hungry, high-end graphics, the Wii uses far less power to operate than its competitors."[28] So in the context of video game consoles, the Wii is the opposite of a huge energy drain, and this is directly tied to Nintendo's development of novel forms of gameplay.

Early reactions to the Wii's general profile were often right: it is a good deal like the original Mac Mini, which was deliberately designed by Apple to draw only a modest amount of power in order to perform its necessary functions (driving display graphics, for example, or acting as a home network server). More generally, the Wii can be seen as fitting into a larger trend in systems design over the past decade toward greater environmental and energy awareness, and more task-specific, "right-size" computing. Given that the opportunities at the high end of computing for energy efficiency are rare, the industry's tendency as a whole has been to miniaturize and specialize at the lower end of computing, and the Wii's overall design fits right into this trend. Small form-factor PCs, including the Mac Mini and popular lightweight netbooks, say, try to do more with less—but in the process, they thus multiply the number of such low-powered processors out there in the environment.

The real significance of the popular netbooks, in terms of energy efficiency, is that they have led to developments such as the Atom processor and Intel's i-series processors, which are designed to give you the highest performance when demanding tasks call for it, but relatively lower performance when it's not necessary. Unlike the Atom processor found in netbooks, which basically settles for lower performance in order to fit a lightweight form factor, with the added benefit of using little power in the process, the i-series processors behave much like the Atom processor in the nominal case, yet can increase their clock speed as needed for special situations. The i-series processors have found their way into successful normal-size notebook computers from just about every manufacturer, including Asus, the company that started the netbook trend, and even Apple, which has continued to refresh its notebooks to improve the battery life. Overall, a larger trend has emerged of computing systems aiming to do more with less power, and this has had an echo effect upward, as it were, in the realm of high-end CPU design as well.

Some examples of this larger trend that are especially relevant to a consumer device like the Wii in general and the console segment of computing in particular include the Mini-ITX framework, created by VIA Technologies in 2001. Since then, these systems have greatly increased in popularity for multimedia applications, especially for set-top boxes used for home entertainment, TiVo being the best-known brand of digital video recorder. There are also a growing number of users who employ solutions such as the open-source MythTV project digital video recorder and, recently, Apple's Apple TV. In fact, the Mac Mini took part in this trend, appearing early in 2005 at the moment the Wii was in the later stages of its development. It too had a strikingly minimalist design and notably small power footprint—only fourteen watts—and optimized its throughput in order to serve as a media computer, for instance, or drive relatively high-resolution graphics on a large monitor. It's worth keeping in mind that only the fact that the Wii must compete with other consoles providing impressive HD graphics, and of course the fact that games in the past decade have come to be defined by their high-end graphics, calls attention to its so-called limitations in this regard.

There has also been an increased interest in recent years in embedded systems, which is part of a larger trend known as "ubiquitous computing," the multiplication of appliance-like processors with low power needs that are nonetheless not necessarily *under*powered, given their targeted purposes. These include the WRT54G router by LinkSys, a popular consumer device aimed at home networking, or the Linux-based NSLU2 SLUG networked appliance (2004), used for wireless LAN and network attached storage services. A network attached storage device can be plugged into a network, and working much like a workgroup server, provides instant storage that can be shared with all the computers and devices (for example, smartphones) that can access Windows shares and other network services. A new category of "plug computers," such as the SheevaPlug, which serves as heir apparent to the NSLU2, consists of small machines the size of an electric adapter. These can be plugged in anywhere to serve as networked servers, and for distributed and targeted computing needs, including "cloud" services. Users can plug USB drives into them, for instance, which can be accessed as shares without being attached to any one particular computer (the primary drawback of having more conventional, "direct attached storage"). Again, low-cost and low-energy use are the key attractions here (the SheevaPlug uses only about 2.3 watts—about one-sixth that of the Mac Mini and about one-eighth that of the Wii when it's running), and these small plug-in processors are especially well adapted as media servers or storage and backup. And like the Wii, they are all about keeping as low a profile as possible to get the job done. The SheevaPlug and related GuruPlug, for example, are tiny—approximately three-inch cubes.

A theoretical question often taken up in computing circles these days is whether Moore's law is dead. Gordon Moore, a cofounder of Intel, famously noted that the number of transistors (or components) that can be packed into an integrated circuit roughly doubled every year from 1958 to 1965. From this, he extrapolated a prediction that the trend would continue—and it did for well over twenty years. While the precise end date for this upward trend is still unclear, it's notable that top CPU speeds, especially in available processors, seem to have peaked at around 3.2 GHz in recent years, and are no longer doubling every eighteen to twenty-four months. This has led to the emergence of multicore architectures, which effectively combine CPUs to achieve more processing power via multiplication. So a dual- or quad-core CPU featuring 3.2 GHz cores effectively has 6.4 or 12.8 GHz speed, respectively.

These speeds are of course seldom achieved in practice, since OSs and applications need to be optimized (and work collaboratively) to achieve optimal throughput. In many ways, we are witnessing the end of a long period in which CPU speeds continued to increase according to Moore's law. Even when gains are made, we also observe a "software lag," meaning that software is seldom able to take full advantage of the extra speed and additional cores. At the same time, paradoxically, we're also seeing the reemergence of Moore's law at the low-to-middle end of the computing spectrum, where the same processors that used to be large, hot, and therefore power hungry, can be built smaller, cooler, and more energy efficient, and then ramped up accordingly.

One way to understand the Wii's power is as an instance of this reemergence of Moore's law, through a system that operates within a set of design constraints on power needs as well as use. Purely in terms of MHz, the frequency of the latest CPU in the Wii is double that of the GameCube. In practice, this translates into two times or more improvement in performance over the previous-generation Nintendo machine. Meanwhile, at the other end of the spectrum, Moore's law is reaching its limit for the powerful processors in the Xbox and PS3, with the only way for continued increase being the addition of even more cores—and by consuming a lot more power in the process.[29] The Wii, by contrast, could continue to ramp up the clock speed and experience beneficial results. The PowerPC chip in its architecture can be increased to 3.2 GHz; all the designers have to do is expend more energy. Certainly for the present, that's precisely what the Wii developers seem to have decided not to do.

The Wii is the only major game console in its generation that exploits this paradoxical reemergence of Moore's law at the lower end of computing—the only one that could continue to increase its speed significantly in the current form factor (or an even smaller one). This is a direct result of design and engineering decisions at Nintendo. Kou Shiota, of the Integrated Research and Development Division Product Development Department, has described the aims for the console in this way:

> Normally when you decide to use new semiconductor technology, you do so solely for the sake of more extravagance and higher performance. In the case of the CPU, you try to progressively improve its processing power, which in turn raises its power consumption and increases its size. Sophisticated semiconductor technology is required to realize this goal. While you could use such cutting-edge semiconductor technology in order to facilitate this kind of extravagance, you can choose to apply this technology in other ways, such as making chips smaller. We have utilized the technology in this way so that we could minimize the power consumption of Wii. If the chip becomes smaller, we can make the size of the console smaller.[30]

Reducing the Wii's footprint—both in physical terms and in terms of its power use—while increasing performance over the immediately previous generation's system, the GameCube, was a primary goal of development, and Shiota even compares the Wii to hybrid gas/electric cars in this regard.

> When we were struggling to reduce the power consumption, there was a point in time when we simulated how power consumption would change in existing devices if we applied cutting-edge semiconductor technology to them. In the case of the GameCube, we discovered that the power consumption could be reduced to between one-third and one-quarter of the consumption of the GameCube's semiconductors. . . . Normally, when making new devices, companies compete with each other on the basis of "How much faster is the CPU, how much more memory is there, and how many more polygons can be displayed?" But Nintendo posed the question, "How much can we decrease power consumption and maintain performance?"[31]

This is the complex background to Miyamoto's later public remarks, characteristically understated, that "power isn't everything in a console."

A video game console is a computer specifically designed for playing games when hooked up to a television. Historically, the dedicated video game console (after the Magnavox Odyssey or Atari VCS in the 1970s) emerged more or less in parallel with consumer-model PCs. At various times and in specific instances, it was designed to compete directly with the PC. The other consoles in the Wii's generation, the PS3 and Xbox 360, are massive, multipurpose machines that go the PC one better. In one sense, the Wii took a deliberate turn off that path, off that engineering "road map," and at the level of its processors aimed instead to be a dedicated games machine in the most targeted, efficient, and low-cost way that it could. Yet given economic realities, Nintendo has continued to feel the pressure to make its console compete with other machines in the same generation by offering some relatively limited forms of online play, for example (and with new pay structures for the privilege), as well as introducing Netflix access via the Wii in 2010. (Since Nintendo's console cannot play DVDs, this was seen as a significant move.) These compromises are clearly part of a balancing act based on pragmatic imperatives of the marketplace as much as on any desire on the company's part to loosen the constraints built into the console itself.

In the end, however, the Wii console's limitations and affordances alone have not defined the system in the public imagination, except as these have been translated into design, and then marketed as such. Iwata may have held aloft the small and newly efficient black console at the E3 conference in 2005, but the more socially significant preview came later, at the Tokyo Game Show in September, when he introduced the new Revolution controller. It's telling that Vandenberghe, *Red Steel 2*'s director, originally pitched that game as using *two* Wii Remotes like two samurai swords, or a shield and a sword, one in each hand (thus passing over the actual control system, which used the Nunchuck extension controller). The Wii Remote has become the widely recognized symbol of Wii gameplay. In the next chapter, we take a close look at the small rectangular device that has become synonymous with the Wii as a platform and started a whole new cycle of cross-platform development of motion-sensitive controls: the celebrated, satirized, but undeniably iconic Wii Remote.

At the Tokyo Game Show, September 2005, Nintendo president Iwata stood at the podium to deliver the keynote and asked, "How can we expand the gaming population and how can we develop the market?" Holding an imaginary control pad in two hands in front of him, thumbs up, he added, "Since the days of Famicom, the game control mechanism has become more and more sophisticated," with so many buttons and requiring such skilled two-handed control that it has turned into a barrier to "novice" players. There is a need, he continued, to make gaming much more accessible, to entice "everyone" to want to "touch" the controller.[1]

Then on the giant screen to his right, a video showed the crowd the new Nintendo controller for the first time—a rectangular piece of white plastic tilted at an angle and slowly emerging from what appeared to be molten white plastic, like a kind of industrial-design primordial soup. Buttons appeared and swam around into their proper configuration. A hand reached out and grabbed the controller, and the video shifted into what has become the signature motif of Nintendo's marketing campaign for the Wii: a montage of players of many ages and types (though at this stage, all or almost all were Japanese), singly or in groups, shot as if from the television out, pointing and moving the new controller around in a variety of gaming situations. Watching the video, viewers at the conference had to imagine what might be on the screens in front of the actors, just based on sound effects and the mimed motions of the players: fishing, cooking, swatting flies, and (with the addition of the curved extension controller with an analog stick for the other hand) shooting a gun or swinging a sword. The sequence ended with a slide showing five vertical controllers in different colors arranged in a row like candy bars. "This is the Revolution controller," Iwata said, holding up the actual device in his right hand as the cameras flashed.[2]

One live blogger immediately posted his reaction: "looks like futuristic television remote."[3] Indeed, Iwata himself has explicitly compared the controller to a television remote, in terms of both its form factor, because Nintendo wanted it to be small and attractive enough to be left out on the "living room table," and its accessibility, the goal being for everyone to think that it's "something relevant to them," and actually pick it up and use it intuitively. The aim is clearly to achieve an "emotional design," to use Donald Norman's phrase—one that gives people pleasure and enhances their perception of the controller's affordances.[4] That pleasure and those affordances were designed to be as domestic, familiar, and tested as turning on a television. Later, the developers would recall that it was Iwata who insisted the new controller be called a "remote," for just those reasons. Iwata wanted a design that would encourage immediate accessibility. As he later explained:

> The TV remote in your house is something that always sits within reach and is picked up and used by everyone all the time. Since I wanted the controller to be used in the same way, and since it ended up looking like one in the end, I strongly believed that it should be called a remote. And also because one of the most fundamental questions behind Wii's development was why some people use the TV remote all the time, but hesitate to pick up a game controller. So I really insisted that it be called a remote.[5]

The official name for what developers had been calling the core controller became the Wii Remote, and the nickname Wiimote quickly caught on. From its association with the television remote, the Wii Remote borrows certain key themes and affordances, and these tell us a good deal about Nintendo's goals for the platform as a whole: accessibility and intuitive simplicity, and the implied comforts of the domestic space in which it's supposed to be used. Of course, the simplicity of the one-handed controller was immediately qualified with attachments and augmentations, but in interesting ways that explain much about the relationship of players to the intentions of the platform's designers. And the imagined family living room was revealed to be an abstract possibility space, from the point of view of the platform's designers—a space bounded by measurements made by tiny machines. This is the actual as opposed to theoretical HCI at the Wii's heart, the give and take of intention and reception enacted in the player's living room, a possibility space defined by design and use.

Form Factor and Technology

The Wii Remote is actually smaller than many modern universal television remote controllers, measuring approximately 5.81 by 1.43 by 1.12 inches, so that it can fit comfortably into the palm of your hand (see figure 3.1). And when compared to many television remotes today, it also has a radically simplified interface: a power button at the top (or front, when held in a horizontal position and pointed away from you), a cross-shaped directional pad, and an oversize and translucent A button below that (the B button is a trigger on the reverse side, set into a curved surface along the back of the controller). Across the device's center is a row containing the minus and plus buttons on either side of a small home button (labeled both on the button with an icon of a house and beneath the button with the word "home"). Below that is a small speaker grill, then one and two buttons arranged vertically above a horizontal row of LED indicators, and the Wii logo printed in gray. In total, there are eight buttons on the top, including the on/off power button, but not counting the B trigger on the reverse side. The battery compartment on the reverse side also contains a tiny red button for synchronizing the controller with the console.

The controller's profile actually feels more like the handle of a lightweight tool or an umbrella than like the standard universal cable-DVR-television remotes many of us have become used to. It even has a wrist strap like an umbrella's, added to prevent the device from slipping out of your hand during active gameplay, and now ships with its own stretchy protective plastic case. Every gaming session on the Wii begins with a warning screen with safety diagrams, reminding the player to tighten the strap to prevent accident or injury.

But this rectangular wand-shaped pointer is only the most basic core controller. For many games—especially back-catalog ones downloaded via the Virtual Console or played on GameCube media, or traditional action-adventure games or FPSs—the Wii Remote alone is inadequate. So Nintendo developed a plan to treat the Wii Remote as a hub for various extension peripherals, starting with an extension device that plugs into the remote's base and rides on its wireless connections, using a three-foot cable, a controller shaped like a curved pistol grip with Z and C buttons on its underside, and an analog control stick on the top, to be operated with the thumb (see figure 3.2). This controller allowed for two-handed play, and was codenamed Nunchaku or Nunchuk, after the martial arts

3.1 The Wii Remote

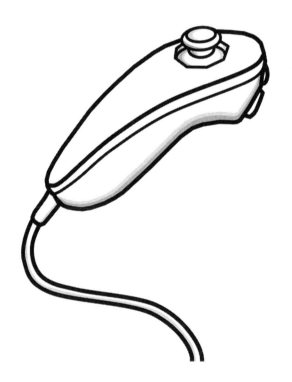

3.2 The Nunchuk extension controller

weapon made of two short clubs attached by a chain or cord. The name stuck right through to release, and when Iwata debuted it, he showed one attached to the Wii Remote at the Tokyo Game Show.

The creator of the Nunchuk, Kenichiro Ashida, has explained how the asymmetrical design of the two connected controllers came about: "At first, I also considered a design similar to that of the remote. But since it was so obvious that the right and left hands are used differently, I realized that making the designs similar would just make it harder to control."[6] So the Platonic ideal of the one-handed controller was in fact immediately altered in a design compromise in order to enable two-handed play. Reportedly there were even requests from within Nintendo's own software development teams, such as those responsible for the *Metroid* franchise, for such an extension, based on concerns about how their own games would translate into the environment of the new one-handed controller.

Connecting the Nunchuk to the base of the remote does usually signal a shift in gameplay style or game genre. Using the two-handed double-controller setup with the lightweight cable connecting the Wii Remote and Nunchuk still feels relatively simpler or freer, however—at least more nimble—than using, say, a two-handed DualShock controller for Sony's PlayStation. The D-pad controller is heavier and generally more substantial feeling. Everything—the buttons, triggers, and sticks—is arrayed in front of the user for rapid, heads-up, two-handed play. The DualShock is more like a serious, stationary control panel with an industrial feel, something like an aircraft controller or high-performance steering wheel; it could in most cases be mounted on a stand in front of the television and still function (so long as the user could reach all the triggers). Whereas the lightweight Wii components, separated into two hands, allow for and even encourage improvised mimetic gestures on the player's part—such as one- or two-handed waving, poking, swinging, punching—while retaining the basic array of necessary buttons and at least the one analog stick.

The debut keynote video mentioned above showed a young woman playing what sounds like a Mario game and flicking the remote upward to make the character jump (though we cannot see what she sees on the screen, we can hear the familiar jumping sound effect), and Iwata's keynote suggested that Mario might be made to jump by moving the remote.[7] But in fact, once the system was ready for release the following year, it became clear that older Mario games would be played either with the Classic Controller—another extension peripheral, a kind of abstraction of earlier two-handed control pads with two analog thumbsticks and the basic traditional array of buttons—or by turning the Wii Remote horizontally and using it as if it *were* an earlier controller, using two hands, controlling the D pad with one hand, and the one and two buttons with the other. Using the Wii Remote in this position makes it suddenly obvious to an observer that in its button layout and perhaps a more general spirit as well, this purportedly revolutionary rectangular plastic controller is a direct descendant of Nintendo's first breakthrough home-console controller for the NES (Famicom).

The Wii Remote is a motion-sensitive device. This means that it measures, at over two hundred signals per second and in three dimensions, the movements the player makes with it, using a combination of infrared and wireless Bluetooth channels to transmit the movement data, and then map the movements onto the game space. So if you swing the remote in a sweeping backhand gesture, your Mii avatar swings their tennis racquet the same way on the screen. The measurements are made by Analog Devices' ADXL330 triple-axis accelerometer, a machine inside a tiny, square integrated circuit in the Wiimote. The accelerometer—a small piece of hardware much like those found, for example, in the iPhone and iPad—is a self-contained machine with moving parts known as a MEMS device. A column on Nintendo's Web site usefully and simply defines MEMS as "micro fabrication techniques that use applied semi-conductor technology to produce extremely small mechanical structures."[8]

The Wii Remote's accelerometer is only one of the myriad forms that MEMS can take, and there are a number of ways to make these microscale machines. In the case of the accelerometer, its extremely small moving parts work in concert with etched circuits in the system, translating analog physical motions into electronic signals and thus digital data. The Wii Remote MEMS consists of a sliver-size plate of polysilicon, a "proof mass" that's mounted with springs to float suspended over a substrate. Air in its patterned channels acts as a cushion for the plate, allowing it to float just barely above the substrate and react to subtle changes in acceleration, both magnitude—how much movement—and direction. In relation to a second layer of polysilicon, the device measures acceleration on an X-Y-Z grid. Electric voltage shifts with the shifting relation of the parts, and minute changes in voltage, caused by the accelerometer's movements as the Wii Remote is tilted, allow for measurements along three axes: up and down, side to side, and forward and back.

The basic physics behind the accelerometer can be explained by Hooke's law (formulated by British scientist Robert Hooke in 1660) on the relationship between force exerted on a mass and the position of that mass, which is seen, for instance, in the displacement of a mass attached to a spring with its acceleration along a particular dimension. Although it's easy to demonstrate by experiment in a physics lab, it's much more difficult to picture in the case of a tiny MEMS device, and it's extremely difficult to actually build such a device. Great care must be taken to ensure that the entire proof mass doesn't come into contact with the substrate; only parts of it can touch the base that it floats above. This is easier said than done, given the microscopic scale of everything in the MEMS, not to mention the amount of testing that must be done before something like the version in the Wii Remote could have been completed and made available to the public. A teardown or act of reverse engineering by ChipWorks revealed that the proof mass has stiction bumps that prevent the mass from ever coming fully into contact with the substrate. To measure each of the three axes, the proof mass has to be "rapidly constrained and released."[9] The current is then measured and translated into a digital reading for each axis. The actual measurements are done when the proof mass and substrate align to form the equivalent of a transistor.

These accelerometer measurements are beamed to the console via a Bluetooth connection, where they're coordinated with data about the position that the Wiimote is pointed to on the screen. A complementary metal-oxide semiconductor (CMOS) sensor in the pointing end of the Wii Remote determines this position. This is a device like the sensors used in digital cameras, which "sees" the light emitted from the LEDs in the sensor bar mounted near the television at over two hundred signals per second. (The Nunchuk also contains a motion-sensitive accelerometer as well as its small analog joystick, but lacks infrared and Bluetooth capabilities, since it's designed to piggyback on the Wii Remote.) The measurements are compared to a database of possible moves in a given game situation, such as swinging a tennis racquet backhand or a sword with a downward vertical slice.

This complicated multipart and multidirectional controller system, partly wired and partly wireless, is what makes possible the Wii's mimetic interface. Indeed, a good deal of "cross-mirroring" is going on in the setup, as LEDs are sensed from one direction, motion is sensed and beamed from another direction, and feedback on the screen guides the controller's pointing and movements in relation to all this. Ironically, it takes the intricate MEMS, two kinds of communication channels, including one that relies on strapping a sensor bar to the television set, and constant coordination with software running on the console in order to produce the *illusion of* a "simple," "accessible," and "intuitive" interface. The purpose of this elaborate and largely invisible technology is to ensure that rather than relying on difficult-to-master button combinations, the player can just pick up the Wii Remote and wave it around. It captures the relatively intuitive movements of the player's miming, or imitating with bodily motions, a wide range of in-game actions. This is what Nintendo meant when it called the Wii Remote a revolutionary controller, and it's true enough that this particular combination of technologies *as a system* has never been used before, although its basic idea—motion control—is now no longer unique.

Four years after the Wii's debut, 2010 saw the release of imitations by the two large competitors in the console market: Sony's PlayStation Move, using Wii Remote–like wands (but with colored balls on the ends of them), and on November 4, 2010, Microsoft's Kinect, a controller-free system that uses cameras and depth sensors aimed at the player to capture and recognize motions. The Wii was first out of the gate in this competition—in fact, to apply a more appropriate metaphor, it *created* the field of motion-sensitive controllers in the first place as a way of moving into the "blue-ocean" segment of the market, away from the competitors, which have since then joined it and are busy turning that part of the ocean "red" with the blood of the struggle for dominance.[10]

But the idea for Nintendo's motion-sensitive controller system didn't emerge from nowhere. There's a multilayered history behind it at Nintendo and elsewhere, and placing it in context helps us understand both what's truly new and not so new about it, and its particular affordances and constraints. A research and development manager at Nintendo has been quoted as saying that the company worked on a motion-sensitive controller of some kind as far back as the mid-1990s, during the development of the Nintendo 64—a console, incidentally, that was originally codenamed "Project Reality."[11] The company built a prototype of the device, apparently meant to be worn like a wristwatch, and then applied for a patent, but the patent was dropped because the device was too difficult for players to use. Afterward, there was the Pokémon game *Pocket Pikachu*, which resembled the popular Tamagotchi virtual pets and incorporated a pedometer to measure motion when you took it for a walk. (Interestingly in anticipation of the Wii, the color version released in 1999 also included an infrared system, allowing for the exchange of data between two games.) *Kirby Tilt 'n' Tumble* for the Game Boy Color handheld platform (2000 and 2001) was an even closer precursor. It had an accelerometer built into the game cartridge that you actually tilted to make the character move in different directions, not unlike many games for the iPhone and iPad today.

More generally, anyone who spent time in video game arcades knows that the idea of controlling a system with your body's movements has been around for some time.[12] *Dance Dance Revolution* is the best-known example of a controller that prompts the player to move their whole body (though, to be precise, the placement of the feet is all that's really being measured). Atari first introduced the pressure-sensitive controller to the home-console market, with its the Foot Craz control pad made by Exus for the 2600 (VCS) platform. This controller supported jogging and exercise games. The same basic technology, produced by Bandai, was used by Nintendo for the Famicom (NES), with the *Family Trainer* (in Japan) and *Family Fun Fitness* (in the United States) games, and then purchased by Nintendo and named the Power Pad, to be used for a later track-themed sports game. Namco Bandai later brought back a control mat for the Wii, for use along with the Wii Remote to play its *Active Life: Outdoor Challenge* (2008).

In the next chapter, we'll say more about this somatic form of control in relation to the Wii Balance Board. Like music and rhythm game controllers, bongos, drum pads, and guitar controllers, the actual input of such devices—foot pressure, hitting a color-coded drum pad, pressing buttons, and strumming the lever of a guitar—is only a small (if obviously crucial) part of the experience of using them. They are also props for a playful performance—dancing, running, or playing music. The games usually do not really require full-body actions, but the props encourage them in the spirit of engaged gameplay. Somatic controllers are part of a mimetic interface. They provoke the player into performing as if they were playing rock music or jumping hurdles. This is why players of *Rock Band* are rewarded with graphic decorations for lifting the neck of the guitar controller. In this way, somatic controller games bear a family resemblance to party games such as *Twister*, which was essentially a set of markers and tokens that served as a pretext for a social party game, or a way of encouraging players to contort their bodies and interact in silly ways. Nintendo's Power Pad was not only the precursor of the Balance Board, as we'll see; it's also related in a more general sense to the idea behind the Wii Remote—that the player's bodily motions are the main point, the main focus, of playing a game.

The Wii Remote's CMOS sensor and LED system is a new instance of an old idea, with a long history at Nintendo: that of using light and light sensors of some kind to connect games with their controllers. Even before its first home-console system, in the early 1970s, Nintendo repurposed abandoned bowling alleys in Japan as shooting galleries using a system of light guns aimed at photovoltaic cells mounted on targets. Players shot at projections of clay pigeons at the end of the alleys, down where the pins had been. The first of these laser clay ranges opened in Kyoto in 1973. In 1974, a similar system allowed you to shoot at an image from a sixteen-millimeter film projector of a "Wild Gunman" at the end of an alley (there was a sensor mounted on the screen). That title inspired a video game version for the NES home console in the 1980s called *Wild Gunman*, a clear descendant of the weird bowling-alley proto–arcade game of the early 1970s. The first light gun for use with the Famicom version of the game was a realistic-looking plastic revolver. For later markets, the device took on the futuristic shape of a ray gun and was known as the Zapper. It was also used for the popular shooting game titled *Duck Hunt*. In fact, the use of light as a channel of communication between the screen and peripheral controllers was also the basis of perhaps the most notorious peripheral device in console history, the R.O.B. This was a move on Nintendo's part to position the NES as a toy-based "entertainment system," rather than merely a video game system, in defensive reaction to the video game crash of 1983.[13] But it can also be seen as an experiment in controller systems at Nintendo of the same general kind that eventually led to the Wii.

The R.O.B. communicated with the game software by way of flashes of light on the television screen, thereby causing a red LED on the robot to light up. On-screen, the player moved a character to jump onto buttons that prompted the robot to stack up colored disk-shaped blocks on posts around their platform (*Stack-Up*). In another game, *Gyromite*, the R.O.B. is made to place actual spinning gyroscopes on small buttons, depressing levers that in turn push the buttons on the NES control pad that has been inserted into the base of the robot's platform. In this way, the robot can raise and lower barriers in a side-scrolling platformer game, allowing on-screen characters to run and jump.

Seen retrospectively, in the context of the Wii's development, the R.O.B. seems less frivolous and more like a harbinger of creative ways of conceiving of the video game interface, such as the Zapper with its own beams of light. It's interesting that the direction of the light can go from the screen to the device, or the other way around. The idea is to establish a communication-and-feedback link between a controller and what the player sees on the screen, or an instance of what Norbert Wiener first called "cybernetics," the science of control (from the Greek word for steering).[14] The use of an infrared LED beam in the Wii is different in its design and level of sophistication, but at a certain level of abstraction and in a historical context evident over twenty years later, the Wii too can be seen as a composite cybernetic system of control and feedback, making use of interoperating light-based, electronic, and mechanical components. The levers and spinning gyroscopes of these earlier games were just reminders of the role played by mechanisms and material objects of one kind or another in all video game controllers, whether in the form of buttons, triggers, joysticks, pads to stand on, or tiny accelerometers.[15]

The MotionPlus Attachment

Interestingly, the Wii ended up using gyroscopes as well, though of a different sort than those stacked by the R.O.B. Nintendo released an expansion component in 2009, or what it marketed as an "accessory" that "takes the motion-sensing controls of the Wii console to new levels of precision"—but that might also be seen as a kind of belated hardware patch for the Wii Remote—the MotionPlus accessory. It's an extraordinary example of industrial design, just in terms of the commercial and technical risks that it represents. MotionPlus is an extension that plugs into the base of the original controller. It adds 1.25 inches to its length, plus additional weight—as well as some practical headaches when it came to the wrist strap and the connector port at the Wii Remote's base—along with a new, longer elastic jacket for the controller. In exchange, it significantly adds to the Wii Remote's ability to measure player movements, including a new set of rotational movements measured by the gyroscope.

This additional MEMS device is a dual-axis rate gyroscope, the IDG-600, made by InvenSense. Although there was a cruder form of gyroscope used in Nintendo's *WarioWare: Twisted! 3* for the portable Game Boy Advance platform, Nintendo has said that the MotionPlus gyrosensor developed from a modification on the kind of sensor used to stabilize handheld video cameras. The combination of the Wii Remote's accelerometer with the MotionPlus gyrosensor allows the combined two-part controller to measure movements along six axes, not only along straight lines (up and down, left and right, and forward and back) but also twisting and rotational movements (pitch, roll, and yaw), thus moving the system much closer to a one-to-one ratio of player movements to in-game actions. According to Kuniaki Ito of Nintendo's product development, the sensitivity of the Wii MotionPlus gyrosensor was increased from the approximately three hundred degrees of movement per second possible in video camera sensors to about sixteen hundred degrees of movement per second, or about 4.5 complete rotations.[16] The gyrosensor is reportedly much more sensitive than the accelerometer in the Wii Remote. For example, software corrects for "temperature drift," or the tendency of the sensor to react in response to ambient conditions of temperature or humidity, and the gyro is tuned to run in two different modes, basically at two different speeds, in order to allow for different kinds of measurements—one mode for fast movements by the player, and another for slow movements.

The core technological improvement of the MotionPlus is to offer a "tuning fork" gyroscope implementation—again using MEMS technology—which effectively works by suspending two proof masses instead of one and being able to measure various rotations, amounting to a spherical as opposed to rectilinear measuring system. It is easy to see how this would supply more responsiveness in many situations than could the original accelerometer, which must do its sampling of each dimension in rapid succession. There's a real question as to whether both systems are truly necessary now, strictly from a technological point of view (as opposed to the economics of manufacturing and retail sales), or whether the gyroscope could theoretically do all the work. If any rotation can be measured, there is an equivalent (x, y, and z) measurement that can be obtained by a straightforward transformation of coordinate systems. So what the Wii Remote used to measure could be measured by the MotionPlus as well. At any rate, the original accelerometer was not precise enough as it was configured, so adding precision required a literal extension of the controller.

In 2010, Nintendo released an integrated Wii Remote with "Wii MotionPlus INSIDE" (as the letters embossed on the device read), thus concluding the development process, uniting the iconic controller and its extension in a single new device. The combined controller with integrated MotionPlus marks a kind of recognition of the original design's limitations. In response to the question of why this added precision came so late to the system—as what gyroscope manufacturer InvenSense rather revealingly refers to on its Web site as "The Missing Piece of the Puzzle!"—Nintendo engineer Junji Takamoto claims that the company considered adding the gyrosensor to the original controller, but the idea was rejected in the service of optimal design and easier marketing, in order to keep the Wii Remote small and hold down the cost. He implies that rapid advances in MEMS made it feasible a few years later to add it to the controller via the MotionPlus, but he doesn't say how much early complaints about the inaccuracies of the accelerometer-based Wii Remote also might have led to this decision.[17]

The engineers and designers at Nintendo celebrated the MotionPlus as more than merely an incremental increase in sensitivity. Yet not surprisingly, the most effusive description comes from Keizo Ota, with the Entertainment Analysis and Development Division, who was in charge of developing the software developers' kit (SDK) for Wii game makers. From his perspective, the increased sensitivity provided by the Wii Remote with MotionPlus will be a huge improvement attracting new software to the system, since it will supposedly "allow game developers to get a sense of the player's feelings."[18] This odd way of putting it sounds at first like a rather mystical interpretation of sensitivity, but Ota seems to mean that something close to a one-to-one real-time correspondence of player motions and the movement of objects in the game can offer a kind of objective correlative or operational definition of the player's affective responses. The game knows how the player *feels*, because the system measures what the player *does*—and with what velocity and intensity, and at what precise angles. Using the gyrosensor to augment the accelerometer's measurements, and using the accelerometer to correct and supplement the measurements of the gyrosensor, offers a motion-mapping system that captures player's responses and even in effect their intentions to respond, whether expressed as a rapid sword swipe or mere flinch.

It's this elusive data that Ota characterizes as providing software developers access to what the player is feeling at any given moment. He describes watching his daughter play *New Super Mario Bros. Wii* and stretching her whole body in response to the game, and his realization that MotionPlus allows the system to capture those natural responses on the player's part, to "detect how the player is feeling and respond accordingly."[19] Actually, this sounds like a vision of the interface that could well incorporate the much-ridiculed peripheral Nintendo has hinted at for years and shown in limited ways, the Vitality Sensor, which could pose radical new challenges to software development, since it's apparently meant to be a device for measuring the heart rate and the skin's electric charge—more traditional indicators of the body's (and mind's) internal state.

As we saw in chapter 2, the increased sensitivity of the Wii Remote with MotionPlus has led directly to some game design decisions in the third-party exclusive title *Red Steel 2*, for example, including allowing the player to crack a safe by rotating the Wii Remote close to their ear as if it were the dial, holding down the C button, and listening for a click. Refining the swordplay that's at the heart of that game was, of course, more important. In that case, the gyrosensor not only allows for measuring the angle at which the player twists their wrist when aiming the sword (the degree and rate of rotation) but also allows for measuring how hard they swing, and a good deal of gameplay is built around those combined measurements. Some enemies (especially those in armor) require hard hits. Mere flicks of the Wii Remote won't kill them. As the InvenSense product Web site says, "No More Playing 'Lazy Wii.'"[20] The player really has to swing their arm wide, miming a powerful slicing motion. This allows *Red Steel 2* to capture (and respond to) the player's response or feelings at that moment in the battle—feelings in this case being reductively and operationally defined as their somatic manifestation, as how hard and fast the player reacts to swing the sword at the approaching enemy.

The most extensive tests of the Wii Remote with MotionPlus are gathered in Nintendo's own *Wii Sports Resort* collection, the sequel to the proof-of-concept games that shipped with the system in 2006, *Wii Sports*. The MotionPlus accessory was bundled with the new game, and an instructional video accessible from the introductory title screen shows the player how to attach it to the base of the Wii Remote and then calibrate the new controller device.

The game is set on the fictional WuHu Island, apparently somewhere in an imaginary Pacific. The island may be based in part on Nintendo's company resort, purchased in 1991 on the Big Island of Hawaii, where employees could rent a house or apartment at subsidized rates.[21] The real resort offers access to the Mauna Lani golf course, and the fictional WuHu Island also contains a lush golf course as well as a Hawaiian-looking volcanic mountain, but also has an odd, quaint European-style village on it along with lots of fields, trails, pathways, and coastal waters where the twelve different resort-themed sports are located: Swordplay, Wakeboarding, Archery, Frisbee, Cycling, Golf, Table Tennis, Bowling, Basketball, Canoeing (which is really more like kayaking, except for the paddles), Power Cruising, and Air Sports. The original *Wii Sports* had five games, only two of which were updated for the sequel. In each *Wii Sports Resort* game you play as a Mii, and Mii NPCs show up as competitors or observers, sometimes to comic effect.

The system's fidelity is less precise than is often claimed, but motion mapping is nonetheless the point in the end, and the results can be surprisingly satisfying during many of the games. These nonrealistic sports simulations deploy the near one-to-one mapping provided by the motion-sensitive controller to make your mimed actions *feel* fairly realistic, rather than attempting to make anything look realistic. The rest of the game's pleasures are found in the cartoon artistry and entertaining design, including the comic use of Miis. In a bit of interesting metacommentary on the mapping of player to the game, the instructional diagrams in the manual show a blue-silhouetted Mii for in-game illustrations and a blue-silhouetted, normally proportioned woman (with her hair in a topknot) for all player illustrations. The human player, two kinds of helper representations, and the Mii avatar are all transparently, almost allegorically related. You're clearly meant to enjoy their interlinked correspondences as a design feature as you move among them during gameplay, as opposed to losing yourself in anything approaching a realistic immersive game world.

The first time you play, the introductory cutscene begins with a flyover of the island from the vantage point inside an airplane, from which you skydive to start the game, getting some basic training in the correspondence of your Mii to the Wii Remote as you fall. One of the most striking images in this sequence is a translucent Wii Remote that's briefly superimposed over your free-falling Mii to make the point that your Mii is essentially a visualization of the coordinate position of your controller in your hand, in space, in relation to gravity. The image tilts and tips, moving in six different ways as you move the Wii Remote with the MotionPlus attached—a literal visualization of the correspondence of player motion and in-game action. The remote becomes not just a controller but also a material object conjoined to the avatar, and as you manipulate one, you manipulate the other. In this skydiving game you aim at clusters of other Miis, and link hands with and collect them for a higher score. A skydiving photographer appears to snap group pictures when you do, and you can see the pictures at the end of the ride. You can encounter and collect a mixture of user-created and Nintendo-provided Miis, from those made by your friends and family to, say, a little green alien or Mario himself in a skydiving suit and helmet. In your final approach, you have to aim accurately in order to fly down through a series of targets formed by other skydivers in ring formation, reminiscent of the star-shaped targets in *Mario Kart Wii*, for example. Then the parachutes open in a final brief cutscene, followed by the stats and photos.

After you've played this game, however, you always begin down on WuHu Island, with camera shots of Miis at various locations, and their recent game stats in a horizontal crawl displayed beneath them. There's a button to select instructional videos on connecting and disconnecting the MotionPlus and Nunchuk, and recalibrating the MotionPlus when it gets out of sync. Initially, the system has to be told whether your sensor bar is above or below the television set in order to calculate the angle at which you're pointing. As with the first version of the controller, resyncing is sometimes necessary: you put the Wii Remote upside down on a flat surface, such as a table or the floor, and the system ticks off ten seconds as it recalibrates the starting position of the gyrosensor and level of the accelerometer. Radio frequency wireless signals as well as changes in temperature can interfere with and throw off the calibration. Once again, a fairly complicated system is required to create the illusion of an intuitive interaction with the game.

The games repeated from *Wii Sports* offer improved motion tracking, including the ability to see whether your golf club addresses the teed-up ball at an angle, for instance, or how your wrist is twisted while bowling.

Some of the new games contain obvious demonstrations of the capabilities of the MotionPlus gyrosensor. You twist the Wii Remote like a hand throttle to get a burst of speed and surge forward on your Jet Ski in power cruising, and your surging personal watercraft interacts with the physics of wakes that you happen to be crossing, for example, or targets at which you're aimed. And as we mentioned in chapter 2, the Speed Slice activity in the swordplay game calls on you to model the direction and rotational angle of your stroke as you race to cut through a series of comically gigantic objects, such as a watermelon, sushi, pencil, egg, candle, and cake. When playing golf, the Wii Remote must be held level during the swing to avoid a slice. A swing meter to the left of your Mii shows the strength of your swing, but also bends and twists to one side or the other if you are twisting the remote and not swinging straight. In a pop-up window, an animated blue silhouette of the topknotted woman from the printed manual demonstrates the proper form.

Games for the Wii, and Nintendo's own titles in particular, necessarily include more instructional and practice materials than is usual for most other platforms, at least before the advent of Move and Kinect. Prompts about how to hold the controllers, or telling you to plug in the Nunchuk or place the Wii Remote on a flat surface for syncing, accompanied by some-times-animated diagrams, are a common part of the experience of playing games on the platform. In *Wii Sports Resort* alone, some games require only the Wii Remote with MotionPlus (Golf, Bowling, Canoeing, Skydiving, Swordplay, Frisbee, Table Tennis, and so on) and others require the two-handed Wii Remote and Nunchuk combination, held either as handlebars (in Powercruising, Biking), or when using the Wii Remote as a bow and the Nunchuk with its Z trigger in the arrow hand (in, for example, Archery). Mostly, these prompts, diagrams, and videos are well designed and well integrated into the games, but their ubiquity is a reminder that you are using a new and probably unfamiliar control system.

This is presumably even more the case for players in the casual demographic that the Wii targets. By definition, such players are statistically less likely to have played video games before, so familiarity with even the use of the conventional directional or D pad, for example, cannot be assumed. In addition, relatively more casual gamers are by definition less likely to have time to devote to learning any system of controls, whether it involves button combinations or the meaning of particular symbols in a heads-up display. Players must be able to pick up and play for relatively short sessions with little or no preparation.

One kind of response by software developers to this situation has been to make the gameplay interface so intuitive (pointing or shaking with the

Wii Remote) that training is unnecessary. Another response, as seen in *Wii Sports Resort*, has been to build in various carefully designed tutorials and helpers, some popping up during gameplay. Though many games offer such materials in a limited way, Wii games obviously must make a special concerted effort in this regard, and often as a result, learning to use the controls becomes part of the gameplay itself, in a Wii-specific variation on what Alexander Galloway has called "nondiegetic operator acts"—configurative actions such a setting up, or pauses in which a game world hangs suspended.[22] Close to the system's launch, proof-of-concept titles for a new platform like the Wii necessarily push such acts further into the foreground of normal gameplay, or what players actually spend their time doing as they interact with a system.

Just to cite one example from a classic Nintendo franchise: development of *The Legend of Zelda: Twilight Princess* in its ported form for the Wii was well under way when Miyamoto intervened to insist that the traditional first day in a training village—where you explore and learn how game mechanics work, such as how to use the control system to control your avatar, Link, to navigate, talk to NPCs, find jewels, and so on—should be expanded to three full days in order to give Wii players more time to get used to the game and practice with the controls.[23] This seemed necessary, no doubt, for the two related reasons that Wii players, defined as casual gamers, would be statistically less likely to be familiar with the game world and gameplay of a game like Zelda, and because the Wii controller itself was new and different for any player who encountered it. So the developers increased the time spent (marked by scale-model periods of sunrise to sunset) in the first village by a factor of three.

In the same franchise, *Link's Crossbow Training* was released in 2007, packaged with a white, curved, molded-plastic peripheral shell that allows the Wiimote and Nunchuck to be clicked into place to serve as the barrel and a stock with a trigger of a stylized rifle (or crossbow). In an apparent homage to the 1980s' light gun, it was named the Zapper. In fact, the game was first titled *Introduction to Wii Zapper*, and it's essentially a simple and relatively brief shooting-gallery style FPS game based on the maps and enemies of *Twilight Princess*, in which you complete levels by shooting at targets and enemies. Nintendo's Web site advertises the game in a straight-forward way as training for the new controller(s): "After a few rounds of *Link's Crossbow Training*, players will be more than ready to pick up any of the future Wii Zapper titles, like *Medal of Honor Heroes 2*, *Ghost Squad* and *Resident Evil: The Umbrella Chronicles*."[24] Though it's explicitly couched as training for the Zapper, to some extent the game also trains players to interact with the world of *Twilight Princess* in particular and the Zelda universe in general from the perspective of the Wii control system.

We've seen how *Wii Sports Resort* includes a variety of training modes based on the use of MotionPlus, but the creation of software to test and train the player in using Wii controls began with the first version of the Wii Remote, most blatantly in *Wii Play*, released in Japan (2006) as "Introduction to the Wii." This is a bundle of nine minigames, some of which overlap conceptually with *Wii Sports*, and others of which served as precursors to games in *Wii Sports Resort*—games like Shooting Range, Table Tennis, Laser Hockey, Fishing, Billiards, Charge!, and Tanks!, as well as the more casual Mii-based games, Find Mii and Post Mii. Some of the games seem to have been featured conceptually in the early videos that Nintendo showed of players using the system, and one gets the sense from them of a short and direct line leading from experimental research and development on what the new Wii Remote might do to the boxed software for the retail market. It's almost as if the player gets to play test a range of possible applications of the new controller.

WarioWare: Smooth Moves

The most creative example of a game that incorporates training and proof-of-concept uses of the Wii Remote into actual gameplay is *WarioWare: Smooth Moves*, a series of over two hundred fast-paced, timed microgames (much faster and shorter than minigames, at about five seconds each) that train the player in various possible gestures using the Wii Remote. Many of the microgames seem as if they could be dadaist, self-aware ports of alpha or beta tests of the new Wii Remote, in keeping with the spirit of the fictional *WarioWare* franchise itself. Released in 2006 as a launch title for the Wii, *WarioWare: Smooth Moves* was produced by the Software Planning and Development Division. Designer Yoshio Sakamoto has said that the team immediately came forward with a software proposal once they saw the concept for Wii Remote, thinking, "This was made for WarioWare!"[25]

The feel of *WarioWare: Smooth Moves'* microgames is summed up in its slogan, which Miyamoto himself approved and insisted be written on the game's packaging: "More! Shorter! Faster!" Reportedly, the team solicited brief ideas for microgames from Nintendo employees, who wrote about a thousand such ideas on yellow sticky notes and stuck them up on a wall. The team winnowed it down to the two hundred included in the game when it was released. Somewhat oddly, the developers suggest that "female staff" in particular kept coming up with fun ideas for microgames, but the team was concerned that players wouldn't know how to hold the Wii Remote in each case.[26] So they decided to include (very) brief instructions before each microgame on how to hold the controller. These became ironically exaggerated when someone noticed that the instructions were reminiscent of a traditional Japanese dance and manners manual, which teaches proper "forms." (The Japanese title of the game makes this theme explicit: *Dancing Made in Wario*.)

In the game, the player has to learn nineteen different forms using the "mysterious Form Baton" (a comically pretentious name for the Wii Remote; some forms also require attaching the Nunchuk). The voice instructions were designed to sound over the top, recorded using a Canadian staff member with what sounded to the Japanese Nintendo employees like a "funny accent" in the spirit of foreign television show Japanese-language courses. You're timed (the image of a fuse burns along the screen's bottom) as you quickly run through one approximately five-second game after another: holding the Wii Remote on your nose like an elephant's trunk ("Elephant"), holding it on your head ("Mohawk"), balancing it like a tray ("Waiter"), setting it down on the actual floor or table and then snatching it up at just the right moment ("Discard"), holding it vertically ("Umbrella") or out in front and horizontal ("Tug O' War"); then these are applied in a range of funny microinteractions. So the "Discard" form is used to pick up and answer the phone, for example (and the built-in speaker in the Wii Remote actually says in your ear, "Hey! What's up?"). In what is surely a kind of inside joke at Nintendo, holding the Wii Remote in the standard way, horizontally pointing forward, is ironically called simply "Remote Control."

Indeed, besides testing the Wii Remote, and training the user in pointing and waving at the game interface, *WarioWare: Smooth Moves* applies its vivid graphics and the self-conscious irony already associated with the series to the Wii Remote itself, offsetting some of the pretentious aura built up by Nintendo's marketing rhetoric about the Revolution controller. The game's creative energy and spirit of wild invention is especially appropriate in a party title, and particularly for the Wii, which we would suggest is a social platform in that it's designed to be played in a social setting with other people. It provides a "mimetic" interface in that the game mirrors your motions, but also in the sense that watching others play makes it easier to imitate them and learn the forms.[27]

There's a loose, comical story connecting the microgames, set in various houses in Diamond City. It starts with Wario's discovering the mysterious Form Baton among the "ancient artifacts of an ancient civilization" in the "Temple of Form," and after the levels have been successfully completed, uses the train as a transitional device to link you to the unlocked multiplayer mode. But the story is clearly a joke on itself, and in keeping with Wario game tradition, is also a joke on other Nintendo games, such as *The Legend of Zelda: Wind Waker*, which was tellingly called *The Legend of Zelda: Baton of Wind* in Japanese. In that game for the GameCube (2002–2003), Link wields a slender white device—the magical Wind Waker of the title—that the game's official Web site describes as "part conductor's baton, part magic wand." This is clearly an imaginary precursor to the actual Wii Remote, and allows the elfin hero to control the wind and "affect the natural world in many other ways."[28] In turn, Wario's mystical baton in this game for the Wii is an obvious parody of the Wind Waker, but also, whether intentionally or not, a parody of the revolutionary new controller that the game is meant to showcase. The story is so absurd that it serves as a kind of commentary on the absurdity of all video game backstories, and their tendency to be arbitrarily constructed and ultimately beside the point of the gameplay, except insofar as they can enhance the tone—which in this case is one of playful absurdity.

In fact, the whole *WarioWare* series works as a kind of punk spoof on itself and the process of software development, or perceptions of that process. Wario is an antagonist of Mario (to whom he bears an obvious inverted relationship marked by the first letter of his name and the associations with a Japanese word, *warui*, meaning "bad"), a greedy antihero or dark Mario, and in this series he's determined to enlist friends in his game development company to crank out and sell as many slapdash video game products as possible. The first game in the actual franchise was for the handheld Game Boy Advance platform in 2003: *WarioWare, Inc.: Mega Microgame$!*—created by the Nintendo research and development team behind the Game Boy itself. One result of this satire is a reductio ad absurdum of the popular cliché about games being content-free exercises in eye-hand coordination with questionable cultural values—in *Smooth Moves*, picking your nose becomes one of the forms taught by this "manners" manual—and perhaps promoting attention-deficit/hyperactivity disorder. Unintentionally, however, the story can also be interpreted as a prophetic satire on the emerging catalog of titles for the Wii that were rushed out quickly to capitalize on the system's popularity.

A five-second game would seem to be the very definition of shovelware in the traditional view, from which the Wii might be seen as encouraging shallow and brief bouts of casual gameplay, instead of core-style, difficult, and extended, serious efforts. By accident or design, *WarioWare* on the Wii is an especially potent combination that calls attention to a whole range of anxieties provoked by the Wii platform's advent.[29] In this case the connections between the affordances of the Wii, with its motion-sensitive controller, and the creative software meant to run on the platform are clear and direct. With *WarioWare: Smooth Moves*, Goro Abe of the software development team tellingly observes, "The process of applying new technology to the software means that whatever we do becomes a game in itself."[30] It says a good deal about the importance of the franchise that the domain name of the official Web site of the real Nintendo Software Development Support Group is warioworld.com.

The Wii Remote as Magic Crayon

Developing software for the Wii involves programming for its particular affordances and within its particular constraints. This includes first of all programming for the intuitive interface provided by the Wii Remote controller. In fact, Nintendo's SDK, which a third-party developer can purchase after being successfully accepted and registered as an official Nintendo developer, ships with a tool called LiveMove, made by AiLive, which offers a graphic user interface (GUI) for "training" a new game to recognize a repertoire of motions by the Wii Remote. The programmer turns it on, repeats a series of named sample motions (flipping a pancake, say) in various speeds and at different angles, and the program then captures those and automates the code for integration into a game under development (in this case, it might be a restaurant game). With the Wii control system, game creation itself has to leverage the intuitive interface.

This is a case of a major console system enabling what game developer and theorist Chaim Gingold has called a "magic crayon." Magic crayons, in Gingold's definition, are representational languages that combine art and computation, or basically software tools for authoring computational works such as games in an intuitive way. According to Gingold, a magic crayon should be "accessible" and "sketchable" as well as "computational" and "expressive."[31] It's a term for an intuitive interface from the authoring side that approaches some of the same goals Nintendo has expressed for the Wii from the player's side, including most of all accessibility ("for everyone").

From either the authoring or player side, pointing and marking objects are among the most intuitive and powerful actions one can perform with the Wii Remote. This is made vividly clear in the success of third-party games for the Wii that involve such controller actions. Even a game ported from earlier systems such as Capcom's *Okami* can illustrate this power, since it involves using the controller to paint as if it were a calligraphy brush (a mechanic that was to return several years later in *Disney Epic Mickey*, as we will show in chapter 7). Drawing a circle in the sky makes the sun appear, for example, or drawing a line across a chasm can repair a broken bridge and allow you to pass. These mimetic drawing or swiping actions on the Wii had previously been accomplished much less directly, using the analog sticks and button combinations of the PS2 control pad.

Similarly, a WiiWare title aimed at younger players, *Max and the Magic Marker*, exploits the relative "naturalness" of drawing with a pointer controller. It's a kind of literalization of Gingold's magic crayon metaphor, and in this case, highly reminiscent of the classic children's book *Harold and the Purple Crayon*, in which a little boy creates objects and settings in his environment by drawing them. *Max and the Magic Marker* is a platformer puzzle game in which a boy gets a (literally) magic marker in the mail. He draws a monster and himself, and then chases the monster across the platforms of the game world. You use the Wii Remote as if it were a drawing tool, and it moves Max's giant magic marker image on the screen. The game's physics enable what you draw to take on substance, so that a line sketched quickly during gameplay behaves like a bridge, rope, barrier, or lever, allowing your character to negotiate obstacles in the landscape. It's a brightly colored game world that invites participation and makes the player feel like a collaborator in the game-making process (a much simpler version of the kind of engagement afforded by *LittleBigPlanet* for the PS3). But the key feature is the intuitive and accessible convention of drawing with the handheld controller—moving it just as you would an actual magic marker.

Or compare this to the acclaimed independent puzzle game *World of Goo*, which was developed by 2D Boy for the PC but also WiiWare, and quickly came to define the standard for that "channel" on the Wii (we'll offer a detailed analysis of *World of Goo* in chapter 5). Of course, neither *World of Goo* nor *Max and the Magic Marker* was developed exclusively for the Wii. Their interfaces are in some ways as native to the standard PC mouse as they are to the Wii Remote. You point and click, trace, draw, and grab and drop on both platforms, which serves to remind us that despite all the talk of revolution, in many ways the Wii Remote is a return to the earliest ideas of interface in the 1960s—which led to developments first at Xerox PARC, then Apple, and finally Microsoft, based around the GUI controlled with the mouse. *World of Goo* works so well on the Wii because you use the Wii Remote intuitively to grab, move, and arrange goo balls—the same intuitive actions that were originally codified in the mouse's design. The game even refers to this process as "drag and drop," just as it is referred to in Windows or OSX. Basically, the game just uses the Wii Remote as a big wireless mouse: you point and click. Now, the change of scale of the controller and size of the television screen when played on the

Wii, among other features of the console, undeniably change the feel of the actions, but this pointer-based use of the Wii Remote is in some ways the simplest, most accessible application of all.

The Wii Remote as Mouse

Douglas Engelbart and William K. English, in a famous 1968 paper and demonstration, called the controller they had invented an "SRI [Stanford Research Institute] cursor device . . . used for screen pointing and selection." They go on to describe the "mouse" (which notably, still required quotation marks around it) as "a hand-held X-Y transducer usable on any flat surface."[32] It worked by using a system of wheels to measure changes in analog voltage, converting the rolling of the wheels over the tabletop in mapped proportion to the X or Y coordinates, and using an analog-to-digital converter to control what was displayed on the screen. The mouse coordinates are translated into instructions for the computer.

Until the introduction of touchpads for PCs, and then the touchscreen for mobile phones and Apple's iPad, the mouse had become the default interface for most day-to-day computer users, replacing the command line for all but the most technically savvy (many of whom continue to prefer the command line for programming and data-centric tasks anyway). It's important to notice that unlike the command-line interface, the mouse involves tracking user movements in physical space, and converting those (analog) movements to digital data in the computer that can (but don't have to) result in graphic representations. Engelbart and English compared it to the available alternatives, such as light pens (the mouse was "generally less awkward and fatiguing to use") and joysticks, for functions like efficiency and speed. The original mouse even employed three buttons for "special controls" to digitally supplement the analog input provided by the moving wheels, not unlike the Wii Remote's use of buttons in addition to input from the accelerometer, gyrosensor, and infrared sensor. The Wii Remote could be seen as modeled as much on the mouse as it is on the television remote. Both devices are essentially "X-Y transducers," as Engelbart and English refer to the mouse, but with the Z axis added for the Wii.[33] They convert movement on a Cartesian grid to represented actions in the possibility space of the video game. (In the Wii's case, the X-Y and Z grid is also augmented with spherical coordinates by way of the MotionPlus accessory.)

Obviously the joystick is also an X-Y transducer, and one that goes back to the beginning of the twentieth century, in digital form first—say, either on or off, left or right—and then analog form, with more precise mapping of player motion. If the Wii Remote seems designed to work like a simple wireless mouse, in the case of many games the Wii does not do away with the joystick or two-handed controls in general. The Nunchuk with its analog joystick ships with the system for a reason. As we've said, the slender white Wii Remote has become a useful marketing icon. But this icon has in practice always required various additional layers, technological qualifications, and supplements—from the Nunchuk, to allow two-handed play and analog-stick control; to wrist straps and translucent protective jackets (which Nintendo distributed free once the decision was made to add them), to prevent accident or injury; to the MotionPlus add-on (and eventually the integrated controller with MotionPlus built in), to increase the sensitivity of motion control. Within Nintendo, the idea of a one-handed controller was an ideal, the insight that marked the Wii's departure from previous game systems.

In an interview posted on Nintendo's Web site, Kenichiro Ashida, of the Integrated Research and Development Division, explains his own shift from hard-core to more casual gamer as he got older, had a family, and had less time to play traditional games. His sense that the traditional multibutton joypad had reached the limits of its design in his view accompanied a kind of division between his creator self and player self. The traditional controller and the style of gaming it represented had come to seem incompatible with his life, and it was this that finally brought home to him the need for change, convincing Ashida that "it might be time to reconsider the entire gameplay style of grasping the controller with two hands, sitting glued to the TV until morning." In response, Miyamoto, laughing, recalled his own hard-core resistance to giving up that paradigm, confessing that ten years before he had said, "People who want to play Mario with one hand needn't play at all!" [34] Ashida, however, speaks for the massive demographic that Nintendo has successfully tapped into with the Wii, as Miyamoto came to understand. Over ten years later, many people are playing Mario on the Wii, of course, often using two hands (the Nunchuk plus the Wii Remote, or the Wii Remote turned sideways like an NES controller).

Other games have been developed that use only the Wii Remote, but more significantly, the one-handed controller that looks like a television remote has become an icon that stands for "Wii" (even the lowercase, sans serif i's in the logo look like two Wii Remotes, and some advertising prints them that way). The little white rectangle is in the end a symbol of the desire for a more casual mode of gaming, or a kind of material synecdoche, the part that stands for the whole, of the Revolution console. In the next chapter, we zoom out from the Wii Remote to look at perhaps the most radically different extension device for the Wii: the Wii Balance Board, which you control with your feet, or actually, the weight of your body. More than just another peripheral, it's also a kind of symbol that in this case signifies the continuing aspirations of Nintendo to engage the player's whole body in gameplay in order to expand the definition of what counts as a video game while also taking control of the living room.

In a crowded auditorium at the E3 2007 conference, Nintendo senior executive Miyamoto and Nintendo of America president Reggie Fils-Aime demonstrated a new peripheral, the Wii Balance Board.[1] After Fils-Aime stepped up on what looked like a double set of slim white bathroom scales and weighed in (joking about his hefty body mass index), the two executives played a quick bout of Soccer Ball Heading, leaning from side to side on their Wii Balance Boards (as their Miis followed suit) in order to return balls—and avoid the occasional cleated shoe or, even weirder, stuffed panda head—that came flying at their heads. Fils-Aime won, but the real point of the demo was for the audience of game developers and marketers, and everyone who watched it later on YouTube or read about it in the press, to see the world's most famous game designer, the creator of Mario and Zelda, standing on the Balance Board in his stockinged feet, evidently having fun, using his body to control what he made a point of calling a new *game*. It's not at all obvious, even several years later, that *Wii Fit is* a game, properly defined, or that the Balance Board is much more than a gimmick. But the purpose of this chapter is to look closely at the reasons for the introduction of this peripheral in the first place along with the contexts in which it might make sense as part of the system and ask what the Balance Board tells us about the Wii's nature as a platform.

Earlier at the same E3, Fils-Aime had introduced the *Wii Fit* software—which he also referred to as a game—by tying it to the company's strategy of "audience expansion." The first and most obvious reason that *Wii Fit* and the Balance Board were introduced was to advance Nintendo's plan to increase the overall number of video game players by targeting untapped segments of the market. During his portion of the presentation, Miyamoto said (through a translator): "When we first were thinking of the concept for the Wii, this is what we thought"—in other words, that the Balance Board grew out of the core vision for the system. Miyamoto stressed that the living room was the intended location of the Wii and all the activities it encourages. The point, he explained, was for the platform and video games in general to be made "relevant to everyone in the household." This is an obvious allusion to the "moms"—that gendered and age-specific Nintendo marketing construct—who would find *Wii Fit* relevant when they might not feel that way about, say, *Mario Kart Wii*. And here was the connection: in order to be family friendly in this way, Miyamoto remarked, Nintendo had to pay attention to the topic of "health," the very thing that video games were often blamed for ruining.[2] Like the Wii in general, the Balance Board was introduced in an attempt to undermine stereotypes about the negative social effects of gaming.

The original codename for *Wii Fit* was "Health Pack," one-third of an overall strategy reportedly sketched out by Miyamoto at the start of Wii development, along with "Party Pack" (which more or less became *Wii Play*) and "Sports Pack" (which became *Wii Sports*).[3] In other words, from Nintendo's point of view, the Balance Board was not merely a gimmicky new peripheral. It was part of a larger plan to conquer the home market on every front and to redefine gaming. Its role was to head off critics by associating Wii gameplay with health, exercise, and fun family activities pursued in the social space of the living room. That's a lot of weight for the Balance Board to carry, metaphorically speaking. We'll begin with a look at its literal form and function, which as it turns out, is to carry and measure the distribution of weight.

Form Factor and Technology

As a piece of hardware and an example of industrial design, the Balance Board is solid looking and monolithic (see figure 4.1). A rectangular white plastic platform with two textured-surface footpads on top and slightly curved corners that flare in a kind of pillow shape, it's approximately 20.1 by 12.4 by 2.1 inches, with four small round feet. It measures the player's weight and, given user-provided data, center of balance. The most mundane of household objects seem to have supplied the design ideals for all the Wii platform's components. The console was imagined as a stack of 3 DVD cases standing near the television, with the Wii Remote as a standard television remote control on the coffee table, and the Balance Board was designed to resemble a set of bathroom scales. (In fact, one designer early in the process briefly imagined its being located in the bathroom, with the player carrying data into the console via a USB drive.)[4]

Nintendo says that the Health Pack originated with Miyamoto's idea— not the most obvious one, on the face of it—that weighing yourself daily could be "fun" (as opposed to being pathologically obsessive or tedious). During development, the bathroom-scales idea was expanded when the developers noted that sumo wrestlers have to use two scales because of their size, or one for each foot. A physical trainer consulted later in the process also used two scales to measure and improve their clients' balance, since the combination of scales can measure which foot you're putting more weight on. This led the developers to focus on center of balance, not merely weight, as something measurable by the console's technology— data that could be correlated with health—and this led to the Balance Board's final form as a kind of bifurcated digital scale with four sensors.

Miyamoto insisted at every stage that they hold down the Balance Board's cost. So the developers explored various existing, commodity-component solutions, including using actual off-the-shelf bathroom-scales technology. But even sophisticated electronic household scales only measure weight four or five times per second, and a game controller has to keep pace with the rate at which images are processed—sixty images per second. So early ideas for building rapid sensors into the device included

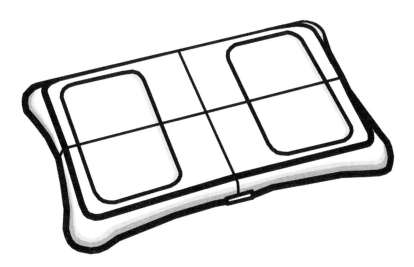

4.1   The Wii Balance Board extension controller

repurposing an optical rotary encoder that had been used in the Nintendo 64 controller, and one prototype involved using a single sensor of this kind. Another idea was just to attach the Wii Remote to the Balance Board using a cable and special slot, and in that way gather data on the tilting motion of the board.

In the end, however, concerns over cost as well as safety and liability (the Balance Board when configured in this way would be too high or might tilt too much when a player was standing on it) led to the adoption of a different kind of load sensor—strain gauges in each of the stubby feet. In each strain gauge, tiny sensors measure the stress put on the small pieces of metal to which they're attached, as the strips are deformed ever so slightly by the player's shifts in weight from one foot to another, or by leaning forward onto one's toes or back onto heels. The strain gauge is a relatively simple sensor with almost no moving parts, so it's a robust technology for a peripheral on which players will be standing and stepping (sometimes harder than they need to). As if to make a point, Nintendo went so far as to have it officially certified as a standard-observant bathroom scale in Japan, and Japanese models include a sticker testifying to that certification. Electric resistance is increased in the metal wire as it's stretched or deformed, and the changes in voltage are thus converted into data about player movements, using the peripheral's onboard processor. The data is sent to the console via Bluetooth at sixty signals per second, where the results are translated into on-screen actions.[5]

Once it became clear that the designers would not be tethering the Balance Board to the Wii Remote as an extension controller, an independent wireless module giving the Balance Board its own Bluetooth link had to be included.[6] This was a first for the Wii; all other controllers are extensions of the Wii Remote, piggybacking on its wireless connection. One of the developers has pointed out that this new independent wireless module opens the door to any number of future Wii peripherals that might be developed, revealing a concept of platform as extending out into the living room indeterminately, through a series of peripheral devices scattered like furniture, just like the coffee table, remote control, rug, or scales, and one can perhaps imagine others—the platform as the whole LAN of communication and control.

Wii Balance Board as a Game Controller

It may be an interesting piece of hardware, and may fit into a larger business and design plan on Nintendo's part, but is the Balance Board really best understood as a working *game* controller? And does software like *Wii*

Fit even qualify as a game? These are of course semantic questions with no obvious final answers. For Nintendo's part, rather than defining games in strict terms, Iwata has said that with the Wii, the company has begun to think in the less restrictive terms of just making "things that respond in fun ways to human input."[7]

In 2006, the same year that the Wii launched, this sort of expanded purpose led to the launch of the Touch Generations brand of games within Nintendo for the DS and Wii platforms. These games were targeted to the broadest-possible audience, first in Japan, with extremely popular titles such as *Brain Training* and *Nintendogs*. The software with which the Balance Board was bundled, *Wii Fit*, goes even further afield from traditional games than these do. Yet as we've seen, Nintendo executives were careful in the year of its release to refer to it repeatedly as a game—perhaps worried about losing Nintendo's core audience as a result of expanding its mission too broadly too quickly. *Wii Fit*'s logo shows the word "fit" right up against "Wii" and leaning a little to the right, like a player standing on the Balance Board. It's essentially a collection of exercise and health-management software programs with the addition of some balancing and aerobic games. These *Wii Fit* games use the Balance Board as a motion-sensitive controller—though in a different way from the Wii Remote—or use the Balance Board and Wii Remote in combination. Or in one anomalous case, jogging, the Wii Remote alone is used. You hold it or put it in your pocket in order to jog in place and make the Mii avatar jog through the game's on-screen environment. There are gamelike elements in several of the activities, but most of *Wii Fit* clearly falls on the exercise side of the "exergame" genre.[8]

Within Nintendo, there seems to have been a division between those working on the core franchises—Zelda and Mario—and *Wii Fit*. Even with Miyamoto backing it, *Wii Fit*'s team evinces a certain self-consciousness about working on something so far from traditional gaming—something, as one staff member in the Software Development Department says, that's at the "opposite en[d] of the gaming spectrum" from Zelda games.[9] A similar response can be seen among gamers once *Wii Fit* was announced and released. A video that Nintendo executives showed during presentations to introduce the game was later remixed by a user for the Web site sarcasticgamer.com and posted to YouTube. In it, we see the official video of a series of actors demonstrating the Balance Board's use over a soothing sound track, intercut with on-screen clips of the game, but in the place of Nintendo's narration, a parodic voice-over says:

The makers of *Wii Sports* now give you a little white thing you stand on.

For far too long video games have limited themselves to being fun and entertaining. But with *Wii Fit* the sky's the limit as you explore exciting new exercises like . . . *Leaning Side to Side!* . . . And don't miss *Sticking Out Your Leg!*[10]

The voice-over mocks the console as a piece of interior decorating for your living room ("goes with anything from Ikea") and satirizes the relatively light exertion required by many of the *Wii Fit* games ("combines the perfect balance of barely moving and doing mundane things"). It claims that it will take kids away from playing outside and put families back in front of the television, and makes fun of the idea that "people all over the world think they're getting exercise" by pointing to the mundane peripheral that symbolizes this aspect of the platform—the "little white thing you stand on."[11]

Behind this ridicule is the recognition that historically, peripheral devices like the Balance Board have frequently been introduced primarily to market new software, and more often than not with the whiff of gimmickry about them. This may be an uncomfortable reminder for some of the roots of game creation in hacking and hobbyist communities, resulting in insecurity among some members of the gaming and development communities about anything that looks uselessly geeky. From the beginning, when people placed translucent plastic filters over the television screen to play Magnavox Odyssey games "in color," new kinds of home game systems—but especially new controllers and peripherals—have often seemed merely newfangled consumer gadgets.

In the 1980s, a kind of ancestor of the Balance Board was released for the NES, the Roll 'n' Rocker, a plastic board with a rounded bottom that served as a D pad for almost any game on the system when plugged into the console.[12] A regular NES control pad was attached to the board to make the other buttons available by hand, but you stood on the board (that is, you could stand on it if you weighed under a hundred pounds—a clear indicator of the age of its target market) and leaned from side to side to control the direction. It quickly gained a reputation as an ineffectual gimmick.

Or take Nintendo's Virtual Boy, the gargoyle-like head-and-shoulder-mounted display released in 1995. A control pad was attached by cable for playing red-tinted monochrome, lo-fi, simplified 3D games—the effect created using parallax optics. In retrospect it clearly looks like a conceptual precursor to the 3DS, but in its own time it was treated with a good deal of skepticism. Virtual Boy was created by Gunpei Yokoi, legendary for inventing the more successful handheld platforms Game Boy and, before that, Game & Watch. Even earlier, however, he had made one of Nintendo's first toys, the Ultra Hand, an extendable mechanical grabber, and was later responsible for the light-powered Ray Gun that grew out of the Laser Clay Range shooting galleries.

Yokoi's work is a reminder of the fine line in the historical commercial market between video game systems and toys. Before the commercial failure of the Virtual Boy, Yokoi had a reputation at the company for the pragmatic marketing of toylike devices. Interestingly, he's also famous for establishing a company doctrine that has returned to prominence in the Wii era: "lateral thinking with seasoned technology," meaning thinking creatively, outside the box, about how to use what has already been tested, is readily available, and by implication, is relatively inexpensive—the opposite of working at the cutting edge.[13] Miyamoto himself credits Yokoi with shaping Nintendo culture in this direction, for establishing that "Nintendo-ness" is not about "the tech edge" but rather about redefinition by way of lateral thinking.[14]

In this spirit, for example, the Wii made use of the existing GameCube chip architecture, and the Wii Remote used relatively mundane, nearly off-the-shelf commodity technologies such as infrared sensors, LEDs, and Bluetooth to create its new control system. The fact is that game controllers, peripherals, have historically always been open to the charge that they are just toys, mere gadgets. The Balance Board in fact spotlights long-lasting tensions surrounding game gadgetry—tensions still present under the cool facade that high-powered game systems, with their multibutton control pads, have acquired in recent decades.

Wii Vitality Sensor: Capturing the Player's Internal State

Here it might be useful to compare the Balance Board to the most ridiculed peripheral for the Wii so far, the Wii Vitality Sensor, which has not yet even appeared. It was first glimpsed in prototype when Iwata himself presented it at E3 2009, and has been mentioned publicly on numerous occasions since, but the Vitality Sensor has still failed to materialize as we complete this book. One prototype looks like a small bean-shaped pod into which the player inserts a finger so that it can measure the player's pulse and then send the heart-rate data to the system as feedback. Iwata has placed the device in the context of the push to expand the audience for video games and suggested it was a way to "visualize something which is otherwise invisible"—the internal state of the player's body: "Traditionally, video games have been developed to give an increased sense of excitement or stimulation. But it may not be long before games are also used to let people unwind, or even make it easier to fall asleep."[15]

There has been a constant trickle of jokes in the press and on the Internet about the promised Vitality Sensor since then, though, and it's hard not to see it in the way many on the Internet have: as a gadget in the line extending back in Nintendo history as far as another arcade device (not really a game) invented by Yokoi in 1969, the *Love Tester*.[16] This was essentially a coin-op toy that pretended to measure the love or attraction between two people when they held hands while holding onto its electrodes, with a meter that reacted to electric resistance in the two bodies. Yet this device, which playfully defined love in a pragmatic and operational way as combined electric current, was also treated semiseriously by Yokoi, who claimed that the couple's emotional state would in fact be reflected in the measured increase in electric current—an argument that sounds much like Iwata's suggestion, now forty years later, that the pulse-reading Vitality Sensor might measure something significant about the player's internal state. As we've seen in the discussion of *Red Steel 2* in chapter 3, Nintendo has viewed even the reactions and physical motion captured by the Wii Remote with MotionPlus as measurements indicating the player's feelings during gameplay.

The Vitality Sensor is an indicator of how Nintendo developers think about controllers in general—as haptic-somatic feedback loops in the tradition of rumble packs (vibration) and in-controller speakers as well as the newer accelerometers and strain gauges. This view of the platform as a kind of PAN for gaming has also led to the development of Microsoft's Kinect. Indeed, Nintendo has expressed ambitions for the Vitality Sensor that go beyond the Health Pack mandate into more traditional game franchises. Iwata has suggested, for example, that it might be possible "to incorporate the Vitality Sensor into Zelda so that as you become more scared, the enemies become even tougher." One can imagine action games in which measurements of the player's increased pulse become a factor in the way the game's artificial intelligence shapes "excitement or stimulation," to use Iwata's terms.[17] But the Vitality Sensor garnered an endorsement from the American Heart Association presumably because of plans to do the opposite—to help users learn to manage their heart rate in a feedback loop through software that would be the antithesis of stimulating action games. Perhaps in protective reaction to the publicity surrounding Microsoft's Kinect as well as defensiveness about the device itself, Nintendo chose not even to mention the Vitality Sensor at E3 2010. Nevertheless, at the same conference the game developer Ubisoft demonstrated its own meditation or concentration game for the PC based on biofeedback, *Innergy*, which uses a Vitality Sensor–like finger cuff along with cartoon visualizations to train the user in synching their breathing and heart rate.

Actually, there is a history of using such peripherals as meditation aids at the boundary of gaming. In 2008, theorist and game developer Ian Bogost created a game written in 6502 Assembly language for the Atari VCS system (available on the original format cartridge media) and also for the iPhone (and later, the iPad), called *Guru Meditation*.[18] It's a kind of art game—one might even say antigame—in which you try to remain as still as possible (either by holding the iPhone or iPad level or sitting on a control pad with the VCS) until a sitting guru levitates and a timer records your score, which goes higher the longer you concentrate in an unmoving position.

As Bogost explains it, this game is a tribute to an earlier legendary hack—which may or may not have actually taken place—by the developers of the Amiga computer OS. The story goes that frustrated with the system's tendency to crash, the programmers created a kind of game that required them to still cross-legged and still, balanced on an early Atari peripheral, the Joyboard, a controller made by attaching a joystick mechanism to a platform so that you could control it by standing on it. The legend serves as a kind of origin story to explain a particular error message on the Amiga system, the "Guru Meditation" fatal software error. But the Joyboard is also a clear precursor of Nintendo's Balance Board. Bogost points out that you could even play a skiing game that shipped with it, *Mogul Maniac*, which is not unlike the ski jump in *Wii Sports Resort*, and in fact *Wii Fit* includes an unlockable meditation game of its own, oddly like Bogost's (although *Guru Meditation* was essentially completed and had been publicly presented well before *Wii Fit* shipped).[19]

In the *Wii Fit* game, you sit still on the Balance Board (just as the programmers were rumored to do on the Joyboard) and breathe deeply, while watching a burning candle in the middle of a dark screen. The candle flickers more the more you fidget, and it goes out if you move too much. Part of the objective is to ignore the potential distractions that the game provides, such as the sound of crickets or human voices, and if you sit long enough, insects that come close to and sometimes end up in the flame. If you turn your head to look or flinch in response, the candle flame wavers or goes out. The game encourages the "just sitting" of Zazen practice, letting distractions in the environment pass by while you remain undisturbed. It's about as far from the excitement or stimulation of action games as you can get. Such applications in effect work as experiments. At the periphery of normal game control conventions, they test the limits of what can count as interacting with a game system, but in doing so, they're always open to the charge of being silly. It's a fine line.

Partly to offset the charge of gimmickry and avoid having the Balance Board become a historical oddity that goes the way of the Atari Joyboard,

Nintendo has worked to develop and has encouraged the third-party development of software that would exploit it as a legitimate game controller. In one published discussion, *Wii Fit* producer Takao Sawano says, "Sometime during development, I started looking at the Wii Balance Board as more than just an accessory that could weigh players and more like a controller used with the feet. I think there's a lot of fun stuff you can do by applying human balance to gaming, and I hope lots of different people step up to the challenge."[20]

Looked at another way, the satirical video remix we mentioned earlier may suggest something seriously threatening about *Wii Fit* and the Balance Board—not to mention the Vitality Sensor. When the latter was introduced, one prominent game site, 1up.com, referred to its debut as the primary "WTF moment" of E3 2009.[21] Many anxious comments on discussion boards likewise reflected a general sense that Nintendo's Health Pack initiative for the Wii fundamentally challenges what counts as a video game in the context of the vast new consumer market that the console has opened up. It's interesting that despite all the ridicule, in the end a good many critics on the blogs or in the game press gave *Wii Fit* and its immediate sequel *Wii Fit Plus* good reviews. Even 1up, which mocked the Vitality Sensor, for example, awarded *Wii Fit Plus* an A-. And the game has continued to sell well. By March 31, 2010, *Wii Fit Plus* alone had sold 12.65 million units worldwide in less than a year since its release.[22] Peripherals for exercise games are objects that signal an ongoing redefinition of gaming— a process with a long history, but continuing with new prominence in the wake of the casual revolution.

Wii Fit Plus ("Measuring")

Wii Fit Plus was released in 2009 either alone or bundled with the Balance Board. As a sequel, it offered the original *Wii Fit* games along with fifteen new ones, plus additional strength training and yoga exercises. There are more actual gamelike games than in the first *Wii Fit*. You can run an obstacle course that's essentially a 3D platformer (you walk, run, or jump in place on the Balance Board); you can tilt a board with holes in it (you lean on the Balance Board) so that balls fall in the holes without falling off the edge; and you can flap your arms to make your Mii (in a chicken suit) fly and stop flapping to descend on to targets, leaning into the direction you want to travel (in this case, remarkably, the Balance Board detects the rhythmic motion of your arm flapping). With the exception of jogging, all of these make use of the Balance Board; for some you stand on the board but also hold the Wii Remote.

Outdoor-themed activities take place on WuHu Island, the same location as in *Wii Sports Resort*. A map in the manual shows the topography and landmarks you see during gameplay. (When the first title, *Wii Fit*, was released, the setting still had the unfortunate name of Wiifity Island.) When jogging, your semitranslucent first-person Mii follows a Mii guide, or as you learn, you can follow a dog who runs past you in order to go to other trails on different parts of the island. Six classic Nintendo icons from Mario games appear in various locations around the island as Easter eggs to be discovered. You can also cycle around the island, using a two-handed control, locating and riding through flags in a winding course. A certain degree of freedom—you can run off trails and through the grass—cannot help but recall by contrast the different experiences of bike exploration in open-world games like, for instance, *Grand Theft Auto: San Andreas*.

One of the new features in *Wii Fit Plus* allows for the creation of customized workout routines. A locker-room interface offers a shortcut to favorite activities accessible from the Calendar menu. Once you've created your profile using your Mii, you start the game in Wii Fit Plaza, a bright, pale, abstract space with grid markers on the ground receding to the horizon, and graphs, charts, and icons hanging overhead—graphic reminders of the conceptual heart of this suite of games and gamelike activities: measuring and plotting fitness data. At the welcome screen you're greeted by an animated Balance Board character, which makes remarks based on your recent workout history, time of day, and so on. The rubbery little Balance Board is a fully imagined character that behaves like a Disney cartoon, waving with one of its corners as if it were a hand, bowing formally, jumping around, and running on a treadmill in the background.

During its early development, the Balance Board even had a tail based on the cable that connected it to the Wii Remote, but when the Balance Board was redesigned to be wireless, it lost this feature, even though Nintendo animators complained that it made it harder for the board to express emotion.[23] It's a cross between an artificial intelligence personal trainer and the kind of traditional helper characters—often small fairies or sprites like Navi in Zelda—that accompany your own character, offering hints, directions, or encouragement. In that context, it's interesting to note that this helper character is a cartoon personification of the actual controller you're physically standing on, or a way of integrating the physical Balance Board peripheral into the game and rendering it friendlier for the player, though it may inadvertently suggest, partly in contradiction to this user friendliness, that the controller is in control of the gaming experience.

The Balance Board coaches you in your workout routines, but since it can hardly demonstrate body positions (for that matter, neither could the unreal-proportioned Miis, which are also minimalistic cartoons in their own way), a more anthropomorphic and proportionate NPC was required. The developers reportedly imagined an odd backstory scenario in which the Balance Board "hires" more human-looking personal trainers to demonstrate activities and teach the players. Two male or female trainers are available for the player to select. The trainers are reasonably realistic looking; motion capture and live models were used to create the animations. The way they wear their hair changes from month to month, or during the week versus on the weekend. In yoga, the trainers coax you back onto the Balance Board if you step off while exercising, exhibiting the kind of artificial intelligence that the developers say sets them apart from a yoga instructional DVD, for example, because in effect they are more like true video game NPCs.[24] The first version of the game had only a female trainer. The male trainer was added as an option later, and the male and female trainer characters subtly exhibit some traditional gender differences, as the developers understood them, in their styles of coaching.

The whole issue of gender was more central to the development of this particular title than one imagines it might have been for many traditional Nintendo games. Iwata connects the push to include games that might be attractive to women to the fact that female gamers reportedly make up more than 50 percent of the gamers playing the DS and Wii.[25] The *Wii Fit Plus* development team included two women, and one, Mari Shibata, who also worked on both *Wii Sports* and *Wii Play*, attended a Nintendo youth program called the Game Seminar, where she says that she heard a good deal from the company about its push to develop diversity in gaming as a way to "increase the gaming population." Shibata notes that she was also told, "It was important to put more effort into games that appeal to female users." Yet Shibata reveals as well that a fairly pronounced kind of gendered division of labor persisted in the case of creating software for *Wii Fit Plus*. It was primarily the women on the team who came up with the Hula Hoop game, she says, in order to offset the early emphasis on sports games made by the men. And she jokingly adds, the women insisted on its "sparkly" aesthetic, which according to her is even reflected in the background music for the game.[26] Given this developer's backstory, it's interesting that Nintendo made a point of having male executives demonstrate Hula Hoop onstage in one early demo.

After being greeted by the Balance Board you go to a Calendar screen, from which can conduct a Body Test—establishing your center of balance, measuring your body mass index, and weighing in—with the results showing up on a graph, or you can go straight to training activities. For the Body Test, you're prompted to put the Balance Board on the floor and turn it on. Then, when it's ready, a high-pitched, robotic voice says to "step on." A small Mii-like wireframe silhouette rotates off to the screen's side as the system repeats: "Measuring . . . Measuring. . . . " Scan lines sweep up the Mii figure as it rotates, suggesting that your body is actually being scanned—when of course it's really just being weighed and its center of balance determined. That image—the rotating wireframe Mii body being scanned by the system—is a visual metaphor for what's essential about *Wii Fit Plus* and its Balance Board controller as well as what's ultimately essential about the Wii, at least from the point of view of the designers and software developers at Nintendo. It's a figure for the idea at the heart of the Wii as a platform—the idea of focusing attention on the player's active body out in physical space, rather than on the virtual presence of an avatar in an imaginary game space. And the technology that makes the shift of focus possible is located at the platform's periphery, in peripherals like the Balance Board.

Player Space ("Adequate Space Required")

Warning screens on the Wii always remind players with diagrams and text to attach the Wii Remote with the wrist strap and use the protective jacket, but also to "clear the space around you" before you begin. In the diagram, the iconic living room containing the blue silhouette demonstration player-figure is standing facing a television, and a coffee table has been moved to one side. In the *Wii Operations Manual*, an overhead-perspective diagram shows a television screen to the left and a player extending a Wii Remote to the right. A box between the screen and the player with a graphic warning symbol reads: "CAUTION—Adequate Space Required."

Although this warning is of course a legal disclaimer, from the perspective of the platform it's hard not to read it as a suggestive description of the invisible key component in the Wii as a system—the physical space *between* the components, and between the player and the display.[27] Like white space in typography design, this negative space is crucial for the operations of any platform, but the Wii maps it and makes it an integral part of its design, even its primary purpose, because of its reliance on a mimetic interface and support for more casual games.

The diagram from the *Wii Operations Manual* is reminiscent of another recent image from Juul's book, *A Casual Revolution*, in which a silhouetted player-figure stands in front of a television. Video game play involves three different kinds of spaces, Juul argues, and any given game can stress one of these spaces more than another: the 3D *game space* of the imaginary game world, "behind" the screen; the flat *screen space* that serves as a window on to that world; and *player space*, the physical space occupied by the player's body. Whereas "traditional three-dimensional games force players to imagine a bodily presence *in* the game world, mimetic interface games"—such as Wii games—"allow players to play from the perspective of their physical presence in the real world." The Wii controllers "support the illusion that the player space is continuous with the 3D space of the game."[28]

If we superimpose Juul's three spaces on the *Wii Operations Manual* image, thinking about how the player space of the Wii is usually imagined, it becomes clear why "adequate space required" is a phrase so ripe with meaning. For the Wii, player space is the most important space—a crucial component in the platform. It's usually imagined as a middle-class living room, in concrete terms, but it's also an abstract possibility space for designers and software developers to think about and create for. In the diagram in the *Wii Operations Manual* it takes up the most space of all, as a loaded empty space in the center of the image that's intended to be a possibility space and, most of all, a social space.

Before the Wii was released, some speculated that it would be a 3D projection system, using augmented reality technology to actually beam the game world out into your living room all around you, much like the *Star Trek* holodeck.[29] They were wrong. But they had the right idea about the Wii's shift of attention away from the screen and out into the physical space of the player. Rather than immersing you in a realistic virtual bowling alley, say, the Wii allows you to imagine you are bowling while also remaining aware that you are standing in your own living room. Juul maintains that it "gives the impression that player space continues into the 3D space of the game," that the lane extends straight from your feet (player space) to the screen and beyond into the virtual game space.[30] What it actually does, however, is encourage a kind of make-believe bowling *without* any truly immersive illusion at all. The whole idea of the Wii's new controller system—whether the Wii Remote, the Balance Board, or both in combination—is that the peripherals are parts of the platform. You always play at the platform's periphery. Total immersion is not required.

The Wii Sensor Bar beams infrared LED signals out into the room in a fan-shaped grid that the Wii Remote sensor picks up, allowing the system to read where it's pointing. Meanwhile, the accelerometer and gyrosensor in the Wii Remote with MotionPlus tells the system (via Bluetooth) how the player is gesturing. If the player is standing on the Balance Board, the system learns from the stress gauges where their center of gravity is and where their body is leaning. With a Vitality Sensor attached, should that device finally emerge, the player's pulse and the galvanic charge of their body could be added to the mix. A picture starts to emerge here of the Wii in action as a kind of local network of things—to borrow a term from ubiquitous computing or augmented reality—where the things or objects in question are prosthetic devices attached to the player's body, as well as the player's body itself.

As we'll develop further in chapter 7, this is fundamentally different from the way that Microsoft's Kinect aims to achieve its otherwise-similar mimetic-interface gaming experience. Kinect seeks to erase any sense of things or objects cluttering the space between player and game, so that the player can get lost—immersed—in the game space. All motion-sensitive platforms work by redefining physical game space as the center of activity. But the Wii, first and still most of all, uses its modular components, its peripherals, to openly take discrete measurements of the player's body and bodily reactions in a dimensional play space, and makes this process an open part of the platform's experience. The grid of play space, extending outward into the real world where the player stands, is "required" for the Wii's network of things to function in the way they were designed. And part of the design is the space they need, imagined simply and named the living room, but this is a kind of localized, culturally specific code for "player space."

The Wii was the first game platform in recent years to openly acknowledge and foreground the importance of this space as part of the game experience, after an extended period in which systems competed to produce greater and greater realism in a virtual 3D game space—greater immersion—by way of ever-escalating power and graphics capabilities. All of this is aimed at taking your mind off the physical space of your living room and helping you disappear into the virtual world of the game. A device like the Balance Board is a material embodiment of the opposite tendency in the new generation of consoles (or at least console additions, in the cases of Sony and Microsoft).

Game designers often think in terms of creating possibility spaces, arrays, or grids, based ultimately on a mathematical, algorithmic visualization of actual possible moves and states within a given game. Such a grid of possibilities is the practical engineer's alternative to the much-cited notion of the "magic circle" within which games are played—a concept borrowed from Johann Huizinga's anthropological work in 1938 on the role of play in human culture, *Homo Ludens*.[31] On the one hand, the magic circle simply means that players agree to abide by the rules; on the other hand, it also suggests they draw a circle around the game for its duration, creating a kind of alternate reality, a space apart.

Games and game platforms that stress immersion focus on the circle's inside. But actual play frequently takes place in a metaphoric space more like the literal chalk circles, for instance, that players draw for marble games. The player stands just *outside* the circle, or *on its perimeter*, half in and half out. Similarly we can think about video gameplay, from the point of view of an engaged player, as taking place along the edge of the magic circle, at an imaginary border *between* the game world and the physical world outside the game. If games are played in an imagined magic circle, a device like the Balance Board blatantly sits on the circle's circumference, as a peripheral working at the periphery of the game's grid, as an object whose technology magic (like its measuring of your data) is not hidden from view as you step onto it and lean from one side to the other. As an example of design, the Wii says that it takes a network of components, peripherals like the Balance Board, to bring the grid of player space to life, and the periphery is where the action is.

The Magic Circle and Miniature Garden

Video games have always been played at the threshold between game space and player space, and skilled players move easily from Hyrule to the health meter to the Z button and back, linked together by the technologies of platform: displays, haptic feedback, and controllers. What the Wii has done is to shift the conceptual balance from imaginary game space to player space. Games using the Balance Board make this vividly clear because the device so blatantly focuses on the player's body. But to some degree this is true of any game designed for the Wii that takes it seriously as a platform.

Take *Super Mario Galaxy*, for example—a 3D platformer that takes place, after the opening scenes and practice level, in a version of outer space. You navigate along a fairly linear path of possibilities, moving from one whimsically surreal planetoid to another. But the use of the Wii Remote—shaking it to make Mario spin into objects, say, or using it to point at and grab stars and other objects, or (in *Super Mario Galaxy 2*) target objects for Yoshi to eat—heightens the sense of hands-on manual engagement when compared to traditional button-combination controls. Whereas an earlier side-scrolling platformer like *Super Mario Bros.* played with the boundaries of the screen by allowing you to run and jump continuously in a scrolling view of a 2D world, *Galaxy* simply hangs the vividly colored and textured planetoids out in the imaginary space in front of you, as a series of globes receding into the distance in an undefined space, which you are convinced to treat as a possibility space mapped onto your movements as you stand in the physical space of your living room.

Inside the game, each planetoid in *Super Mario Galaxy* is a miniature world with its own rules (such as avoid moving tracks or circular saw blades, spin into and then kick Goombahs to find coins or keys, or avoid the sucking black hole). In this way, each planetoid is a miniature world, though with some bizarre features as well as pleasant miniature gardens, plants, hills, lakes, and cottages. Chaim Gingold notes that Miyamoto has repeatedly described his aesthetic ideal in making games such as *The Legend of Zelda* as an attempt to give the player a "miniature garden that he could put inside a drawer." Gingold proposes that Miyamoto probably had in mind "*penjing*, miniature landscapes in containers"—or bonsai, in Japanese, and we think that the link between Miyamoto's games and the bonsai aesthetic is quite suggestive.[32] For one thing, such stylized miniature gardens and trees are often deliberately out of proportion, relying on simplification and abstraction to suggest rather than copy to scale the dimensions of objects, so a branch that's larger than normal can suggest, for example, the trunk of a full-sized pine tree. It's not hard to see now this traditional aesthetic of exaggerated features and playing with scale might have influenced the look and feel of the Miis as well as the self-contained world of Link's adventures in Zelda.

Gingold argues further that the idea of building scale models links miniature gardening with video game design. "This simultaneous play at micro/macro scales is a key pleasure of models. . . . Miniature gardens are scale models of bigger phenomena."[33] But his remark on penjing and bonsai indicates an important qualification: unlike in proper *scale* models, in creative works such as games, scale is always flexible and manipulable in order to achieve particular emotional effects—for instance, the accessibility and *kawaii* of the Miis. With that qualification, however, the idea that mapping the relationships between micro- and macroscales, between virtual and real worlds, so that, as Miyamoto says, the player can experience the pleasures of controlling a miniature garden, turns out to be particularly useful for understanding the Wii, its interface, and its most characteristic software titles to date. As we've seen, the whole idea of the Wii's motion-sensitive control system is that a nonrealistic, nonimmersive game space can be productively linked to the player's physical space by treating the player space—the living room—as a critical part of the equation, a grid for possible moves that can be mapped onto the game. For the Wii, player space is not something to be transcended or wished away in a headlong plunge into immersion in the imaginary game world. Player space is instead a place to remain aware of while being engaged in active play.

This is what Will Wright means when he says that the Wii takes advantage of "an instinctually mapped bandwidth," and that it's all about "non-immersive gaming."

> We used to think of, like, the best games are the most immersive. I really dive in . . . I live in the monitor. The world around me ceases to exist as I'm playing the game . . . immersive gaming. When you think about the Wii, you know, you're sitting in a room with your friends playing the Wii. Most of the entertainment is not happening on the screen. . . . So basically you're breaking away from this idea of an immersive game.[34]

Unwittingly anticipating the key feature of the still-to-come 3DS, Wright goes on to observe that mobile gaming is moving in the direction of augmented reality, and that it's "the intersection of the real world and the virtual world that gets really interesting."[35] Gingold recognizes that Wright's own games—*The Sims* in particular, at the time that Gingold was writing—"use the interplay of micro/macro to map the player into the simulation and encourage participation."[36] This is a useful way to understand the key affordance of the Wii Remote and Balance Board: as enabling the scalar mapping of the player's reactions into the game world, from small twitches to larger whole-body movements, twisting a wrist or rotating hips, leaning forward, lunging into a virtual enemy, or jogging in place. In this way, the Wii encourages a physical play in excess of what is strictly required by the control system, or a form of play that's close to childlike make-believe (playing "swordfight" or "jogging").[37]

On the surface, this seems to be the way that Microsoft's Kinect works as well. But in fact, in our own experience playing games on the system, it offers a fundamentally different kind of mimetic interface. It proudly does away with peripherals (like the Balance Board) and captures player movement in order to try to make the room disappear in the player's consciousness, to pull the player all the way into the game world, using motion control to produce a new version of that old ideal: a sense of total immersion. The Wii, by contrast, as a result of its "lateral thinking with seasoned technology," is more self-conscious, sometimes awkwardly so, about the role of its peripheral objects. As a platform, its gameplay is dependent on the controllers, focusing the user's attention on the peripherals and what one does with them—which is to say again that it shifts attention to the platform's periphery, the boundary where the body meets the system's various devices.

The Living Room as Player Space (Wii no Ma)

Since May 2009, Nintendo has offered something called the Wi no Ma Channel to Wii owners in Japan, which the company says "will let you use your Wii to take back the living room."[38] It's actually an advertising-supported streaming video-on-demand and television channel for the Wii, or something like Netflix or AppleTV and iTunes, but with a more eclectic mix that includes exclusive content for Nintendo as well as a special advertisers' room where Mii-embodied corporate representatives present ads along with special content—since the channel was developed in collaboration with the Dentsu advertising agency. We think, however, that the interface for the Wii no Ma Channel is rich with symbolism about the system as a whole.

A 3D Mii-based model of a family living room, perhaps in a Tokyo high-rise, the channel is meant to represent an idealized view of the family's relationship to the Wii as an entertainment hub. Miis interact in the virtual living room, and through them you can access the channel's family-oriented entertainment, movies, instructional videos, quizzes, children's programming, and anime. Content can be transferred to the DSi for mobile viewing. There is a calendar and message board, and viewers rate the videos after watching them (thus providing user data for the advertisers). In fact, the houseplant in the corner turns out to be a link to the separate room in which marketing Miis tout their corporate products, politely sitting down at a table with your own Mii and introducing video commercials for you to watch. It's your choice whether or not you visit the room, and hence whether or not you look at the ads, but it's hard not to notice the metaphoric significance of Nintendo's having brought into the space of the virtual living room a doorway to this kind of targeted direct marketing.

The living room is sparsely furnished in the Japanese style, and the centerpiece is a round, modern, blond-wood, Eames-style coffee table (or in this case, tea table). An abstract version of the table appears as an icon in the channel's logo—where each letter **i** in the word Wii is at first sitting on either side of the table like little glyphs of Miis—and as the "home" icon on various menus. Posters are hung on the walls advertising software titles such as *Wii Fit*, and there's also a little flat-screen television in the corner of the room on an elegant stand with, unsurprisingly, a slim white box standing vertically beside it. Of course the Wii no Ma virtual living room contains a tiny virtual Wii console. Videos on the Japanese Web site thus create a kind of infinite regress as you see a real-life family in their living room using the Wii to watch the Wii no Ma Channel on which their Mii family uses their tiny virtual Wii to watch television or play games. It's a perfect illustration of the aesthetic effects that Gingold attributes to Miyamoto's miniature garden—the playing with the relationships among various levels of micro- and macroscales in a virtual living room that's like a domestic container garden, a sort of bonsai version of the room in which the Wii is actually meant to be played.

The name of the service combines Wii with *ocha no ma*, which is a word for a traditional Japanese family living room, where Miis representing a family can assemble. When announcing the channel, Iwata suggested that the spread of large flat-screen televisions at just the moment when the Wii was introduced offered an opportunity for Nintendo to return entertainment to a central viewing location in the era of mobile devices and the Internet, a way to reclaim the living room—while also, thanks to *Wii Fit* and *Wii Sports*, transforming that traditional living room into a new kind of game space. According to Iwata, Nintendo research showed that most people had the Wii attached to the largest screen television in the house, and he interprets this as a cultural opportunity to "revitalize" the living room, to encourage family members to "smile" as they watch videos or play Wii games together.[39]

As we've seen, Nintendo's revolution is inherently Janus-faced: it looks forward, while also looking back. In this way it attempts to redefine gaming and the audience for gaming. The Wii claims to offer a new style of gaming to a new audience for games, but it does this in part by looking back with reassuring nostalgia to an idea of entertainment associated with the company in its earlier heyday in the 1980s. Wii no Ma is so far a localized Japanese version of the side of the console that seeks to return to Nintendo's roots in family entertainment and (re)occupy the living room. In that context, the white rectangular Balance Board is a platform of another sort—the kind you stand on—that signifies the importance of the game platform's social function out in physical space. It's a peripheral at the active periphery. It does look like another a piece of streamlined furniture, along with the round coffee table, designed for the real-life version of that tiny miniature living room, like a yoga or tatami mat, but with technology inside. It is an object at home in the idealized family space, the social space occupied by the player's body, where the Wii as a social platform is designed to be experienced.

When you switch on the Wii, the first screen you see is an array of twelve smaller ones, the initial interface for the system, known as the Wii Menu (see figure 5.1). The twelve small screen icons with slightly rounded edges contain dynamically updated content-specific animations representing different Wii Channels (there are four television screens containing twelve screen icons each, for a total of forty-eight Channels), each of which, when used or filled, offers a service or content stream from Nintendo (for weather, news, shopping, or the Mii Channel), a game downloaded from the Virtual Console or the WiiWare service, or games loaded from discs in the optical drive. You select one of these Channels to do almost anything on the system. Thus the collection of Channels on the Wii Menu is the GUI to the console's system functions, in addition to being a set of portals to services and software. The Channels interface represents real channels of access, distribution, and transmission for the platform. In this chapter, we want to use the Wii's Channels as a way to talk about the wider network technically outside the platform itself, beyond its boundary, but that defines its content and the way users experience it.

That interface runs on top of an embedded firmware operating system known in the Wii hacker community as "IOS" (I/O subsystems, or internal operating systems). As is typical of many embedded computing systems, the Wii firmware is in effect a resident OS that unlike in typical desktop computers, is intended to be as lightweight as possible. The IOS is so lightweight, in fact, that it only focuses on the barebones needs of an OS: I/O, memory management, and process scheduling/dispatch. It runs on the ARM portion of the processor (that is, separately from the PowerPC),

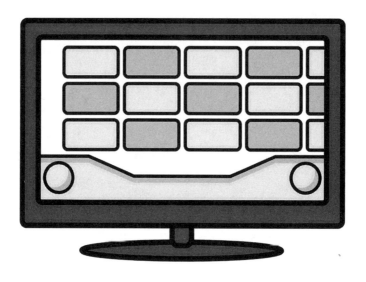

5.1 The Wii Menu with Channels

and therefore does not have access to the graphics subsystem. Hence, it doesn't directly affect the display.

As an OS, the IOS is designed to be regularly updated via an always-on Internet connection called WiiConnect24. Games for the Wii on discs are often distributed with the software updates included, however, because a given console may or may not be connected to the Internet, or may not have WiiConnect24 enabled. Each disc-transmitted update is applied when the game is started, if it hasn't been applied previously. (This also allows Nintendo to apply new security patches and disable illegal home-brew software.) Individual games and system software such as Wii Channels run as applications on top of the IOS—an architecture that is reminiscent of dedicated application scheduling found in the earliest of computer OSs. In a game system, this makes sense because the game really is "in charge" of the system at any given time while it's running, until the user quits or switches to another application. Like Apple's apps on the iPhone, iPod Touch, and iPad, Channels works by simplifying the user's relation to the system, and then representing it through GUI conventions in terms of discrete functions, services, and games, one at a time.

The simplicity of the Wii Channels interface clearly stands out when you compare it to the Xbox 360's Dashboard Menu, for example, with its many layered "blades" or panels receding into the 3D distance that you flip through one at a time, and on which detailed and complicated settings as well as options are displayed, or the PS3's XMB Menu, with its vertically and horizontally scrolling menu icons and lines of text floating over an abstract animated graphic, a complex screen that resembles a busy PC desktop running Windows 7 or OSX. By contrast, the Wii Menu looks extremely pared down. Nintendo's strategy of accessibility begins with these menus.

The Channels obviously look like an array of television screens, such as one might see in an electronics store (Nintendo says this was an inspirational image) or a shopwindow, especially back in the mid-twentieth-century heyday of television. This is an apt symbol of the Wii's aspirations to be a home-entertainment hub with the broadest possible appeal. The company Web site declares, "Wii is revolutionizing how people play games. But the Wii is far more than just a game console. Explore Wii Channels and you'll find them packed with entertainment and information and that the whole family can enjoy."[1] The Channels are the graphic signs of the system's channels of distribution, pathways through which the user gains access to games and other content, including especially the Wii Shop Channel, which directs users to the Virtual Console and WiiWare services.

This chapter is about the Channels interface as a top-level representation of low-level system functions. But it's also about Nintendo's software publishing and distribution channels, and how the design and implementation of both kinds of channels have affected the games created for the platform. This involves taking a brief look at the social symbolism of the television, and at how nongame Channels ("entertainment and information") fit in with game Channels on the system to shape the player's overall experience of using the Wii.

The Television Metaphor (a Menu of Channels)

A cross-departmental system function team at Nintendo was created to develop the Channels interface. The design and wide variety of different kinds of channels was a direct result of the aim of offering different things to different kinds of users—every member of the family—to show that the Wii was capable of providing "quick and frivolous entertainment, as well as something in-depth and serious."[2] The metaphor of television channels is significant in terms of broader cultural associations that at least older users have with television as a medium. Think of the Wii no Ma Channel, which we briefly described in the previous chapter, where the family's

Miis gather around a central coffee or tea table with a remote controller on it (along with a tea tray) and a television in the corner dominating the idealized family living room (*ocha no ma*). The traditional television set is a conceptual focal point for that virtual living room.

The television metaphor also inspired the Wii Remote, as we've seen, and we find it represented again in the nostalgically shaped, cathode-ray screen icons of Channels. Just as Nintendo wanted users to leave the Wii Remote out on the coffee table in the living room, and wanted the console to be attractive, small, and power-efficient enough for "mom" to want to have it sitting out in that living room, so the organizing metaphor of channels harks back to a still-powerful cliché—the family watching broadcast television on a central hearthlike set—rather than finding and viewing modular media objects on mobile devices, personal laptops, or tablet devices, which is after all the increasingly more likely scenario today.

Even the word channel invokes the idea of a more unified time when stations provided programming over licensed portions of the radio spectrum. Sociologists have described the importance of the idea of "home electrification" in postwar Japan in particular, when modernity was associated with ownership of symbolic household appliances, but especially the television set. In the United States during the same era, the head of NBC in 1954 described the television as he wished it to be: "the shining center of the home."[3] The Wii's television symbolism still has that kind of ideological resonance, perhaps especially for the older consumers that Nintendo has targeted as buyers of the system, suggesting that this new kind of video game console can re-center the family's entertainment.

In reality, however, although the Wii's Channels may have a uniform look, they represent a set of different *kinds* of pathways for data, mostly depending on the Internet, after all, whether via WiFi or a hardwired Ethernet connection, some streaming and some downloaded to memory, some arriving quietly during standby time via WiiConnect24, and some being channeled to the user by way of games inserted in the optical-drive slot and accessed via the Disc Channel—and some of those bringing with them encoded system updates as well as the games themselves. Nintendo's DS also can be linked to the Wii wirelessly for downloading and uploading content, including some user-generated content.

The word channels implies order and downward flow. It is thus a deliberately archaic term for what is actually a fairly diverse set of pathways to the user—and to some degree from the user, since some Channels afford upstream or shared data, whether game states shared in online play, Miis that are set to mingle with other users' Miis, accessing the Web using the Opera browser on the Internet Channel, or purchasing software via the

Wii Shop Channel, either more Channels (which are basically application loaders, after all), or Virtual Console and WiiWare games. In what follows, we consider a selection of the Channels in turn in order to demonstrate some of the diverse kinds of services and system functions that the user can access behind the illusory facade of the unified Channels interface and to illustrate how the boundaries of the videogame console as a platform are being tested and sometimes redefined as a result.

Channeling the System

From the small screens on the Wii Menu, Channel Preview screens are one level down. Once there, you can select a Channel or scroll through all Preview screens. The Wii Menu and Channels interface was designed to further Nintendo's blue-ocean strategy and make the console something various family members, including nongamers, would want to access every day. So the Forecast Channel, for example, was created early in the process as a kind of utility widget that might be accessed every morning—a demonstration that the system was always on and being updated overnight with fresh weather data. A zoomable globe, like Google Earth but provided in this case by the National Aeronautics and Space Administration, can be grabbed and spun using the Wii Remote to show locations around the world that you can zoom in on for weather forecasts for specific cities. Each Channel's screen icon on the Wii Menu has its own dynamically updated sound effect and animated image, offering a top-level glimpse of the content without having to open the Channel.

The Disc Channel is basically the interface for the optical drive. Fixed in place at the top-left corner of the Wii Menu, it's the only one you can't grab and drag to reposition—a sign that games loaded from optical discs still have a certain assumed priority in the Wii's conceptual architecture. On the other hand (and this is an important point, conceptually), the Disc Channel icon is exactly the same size and appearance as the other Channels, suggesting that playing games is the first among equal options, finally only one of the many uses of the console, which was expressly designed to appeal to nongamers as well as gamers. Accessing *Super Mario Galaxy 2* via a DVD-ROM inserted into the Disc Channel looks and feels exactly like accessing the Mii Channel, say, or the News or Forecast Channels. It becomes just one more little screen in the array of possibilities.

The Mii Channel is at the other end of the spectrum, marking the Wii's special character as a casual, social platform. It was added relatively late in the development process, borrowed at the suggestion of Miyamoto himself from caricature-editing software being developed for the DS. In chapter 4, we compared the Miis to traditional bonsai container gardening, and following that analogy, the Mii Channel is their top-level container, their own miniature garden on your system. Indeed, when you think about it, much of what you can do on the Channel resembles the arranging, pruning (editing), and rearranging that are typical of such gardening.

Newly created Miis start out on the Mii Plaza, a radiating grid of gray and white paving stones where all the Miis made on the system gather and stand or walk around making small gestures, as if to remind you that they are in fact animated. They may talk to one another (as signified by *Sims*-like or chat-space word bubbles above their heads with tics appearing in them in place of text). Sometimes they doze off. All the while, cheerful orchestral music plays in a loop. The Miis can be rearranged and sorted in various ways using the whistle icon. When not in use, the heads-up icons disappear so that the Miis moving around on the Mii Plaza fill the screen. You can grab the Miis, by pointing and using both the A and B buttons of the Wii Remote, for closeup viewing or to edit their features, mail them to other users, or transfer them to a Wii Remote's onboard memory (each controller can hold up to ten) so that they can be physically carried to another Wii. As you continue to use the system over time with WiiConnect24 turned on, any number of Miis made by other users can visit your Mii Plaza, and your Miis can show up on other users' Wiis anywhere in the world, assuming each of you has adjusted the settings so they can mingle.

The Mii Plaza can hold a hundred Miis at a time. The Mii Parade is a kind of transitional space (which has pastel rainbow-colored stones instead of gray and white ones)—a temporary space for Miis out of commission or in transit, not active in games. Both for Nintendo-made and third-party games that are so designed (this option is apparently part of the SDK), Miis can show up as player characters or avatars as well as NPC opponents, team members, or in crowds of spectators. When playing *Wii Sports Resort* or *Wii Fit Plus*, for example, one of the many Miis created on your system or downloaded from another user to your Mii Plaza may appear on the beach watching as you play Frisbee, or cheering you on in a bike race, challenging you to a sword duel, or jogging past you on an island trail.

These little cartoon avatars might seem easy to dismiss, but they are an integral part of the platform's design as a whole and do in fact impact the user experience in significant ways. They establish its essential aesthetic, the look of the platform, and serve as primary avatars for the signature games created by Nintendo. The Mii Channel is a way to manage, edit, and share your collection of Miis, yet it's also itself a kind of software toy with gamelike features: collecting, manipulating, and watching their simple emergent behaviors. It's not so different in design from some popular online so-called social games on Facebook, say, or like a good deal of the activities engaged in by players of the popular franchise and global phenomenon from Nintendo, *Pokémon*, which as everyone knows is about collecting and trading as much as it's about traditional gameplay, and which is also a card game with deep connections to the traditional ones with which Nintendo got its start.

The Wii Channels often (by design) blur the line between entertainment, information, and games. Even something as straightforward as the Photo Channel, which is essentially like the image organizing and viewing programs on every PC and many mobile devices these days—with thumbnails, albums, and customizable slide shows, for instance, but viewable on the television screen—also has some gamelike features, from comic editing and doodling on photos for sharing, to a "puzzle" filter that cuts a still image or video up into pieces, then scrambles them to make a kind of slider puzzle that when correctly reassembled, rewards you with sound effects like those in video games and reports your time to a score board. A small, animated black cat moves around the screen and meows while you're editing or working puzzles; a kind of distant relative of the notorious paper clip in Microsoft Office, the cat also opens a tips menu when you catch it with your Wii Remote cursor. These features presumably form a gateway to gameplay for the more casual Wii users.

The control panel along the bottom of the Wii Menu contains an SD card icon, which provides access to any installed SD memory card via a separate SD Card Menu. Early on, this feature was not enabled for launching games, only for limited backups, and the system's lack of storage and dependence on the 512 MB of internal flash memory was one of the most frequently voiced complaints about the Wii after it was released. This was perhaps not noticeable to many casual players, who tended at first to use only the Disc Channel to play one game at a time from optical media. It became a growing problem, though, as downloadable games became increasingly available via the Virtual Console and WiiWare services, and more people began to download them.

At first it was impossible to download the initial nine games made available with the WiiWare's launch without deleting some games from Channels that had been earlier downloaded from the Virtual Console, and an early review stated it as plainly as possible: "What WiiWare really, really needs is more storage."[4] Shortly thereafter, on March 25, 2009, Nintendo responded to the complaint with the 4.0 Wii Menu system update, which enabled the full use of SD cards and secure digital high capacity (up to 32 MB) cards, and also mini- and micro-SD cards with adapters. (GameCube games have always been savable on specific GameCube memory cards.) After the update, you could store saved game data as well as load games and Channels from the SD card menu, which looks like a dimmer, shadowy version of the Wii Menu, with the same array of little television screens representing placeholders for downloaded software. Some games can be backed up to the SD card in their entirety, but some prevent this using digital rights management (DRM) software. You can use the removable cards to share saved game data with other consoles but you cannot share downloaded games or Channels.

The SD Card Menu was a way of expanding the available system memory. For the purpose of simplifying system management for the user, the system's internal memory is translated initially into about 1840 "blocks," much as currency is converted into Wii Points for purchases on the Wii Shop Channel. Each block stands for about 128 MB of storage (as determined by a quick calculation). In actual practice, the SD Card Menu is most important as a way to make room for software downloaded from the Virtual Console and WiiWare services, and not insignificantly, to put launching that software on a par, visually and practically, with launching a game on the Disc Channel or any other Wii Channels.

Two of the Wii platform's key features, the Virtual Console and WiiWare service, are accessed from the Wii Shop Channel. They are Nintendo's way of attempting to leverage its own back catalog and distribute smaller, more independent third-party games online. On the Shop Channel's start menu, a receding stack of the iconic television screens sprout handles and turn into shopping bags. A "Start Shopping" button takes you to the Channel Menu, where you can access the Virtual Console or WiiWare as well as other Wii Channels for downloading. You can also add Wii Points (by credit card or the code on a purchased points card) along with account management links and a shopping guide. The number of Wii Points currently in your account shows up in the lower center of the screen.

Signified by a small, curved Classic Controller icon, the Virtual Console is the service that allows you to download games from earlier systems for playing on the Wii and then play them via emulation. These systems include Nintendo's own NES, SNES, Super NES, and Nintendo 64 as well as Commodore 64 (in the United States and Europe), Sega Master System, Sega Genesis, NEC Turbographics 16, and SNK NeoGeo. The Virtual Console Arcade gathers a variety of emulated arcade titles. The Classic Controller, a kind of Platonic ideal of a joypad with analog sticks and buttons, works with all Virtual Console games, which is decidedly not the case with the Wii Remote. It's difficult to overstate the importance of the Virtual Console to the concept, design, and marketing of the Wii as a platform. At the first demonstration of the new console at Nintendo's press conference during E3 2005, Nintendo of America's Fils-Aime recited various numbers by which game consoles are assessed, including graphics image resolution and processor speed, and then added "one more number to the mix"—two, as in two billion games sold by Nintendo over the course of its twenty-year history.[5] However impressive on its own as an estimate, the point of the number was briefly to shift attention from the console hardware to the catalog's depth, which is always Nintendo's strategic advantage as one of the most important game developers and publishers in history.

President Iwata's talk followed later and included a claim that the Wii would "redefine" the term "backward compatibility." The Wii (which at that point was still called Revolution) was designed, he asserted, "to be a virtual console, capable of downloading twenty years of Nintendo content."[6] With that phrasing—"to *be* a virtual console"—Iwata deliberately blurred the line between hardware and software in a way that emphasized the significance of the emulation service to the new system. Iwata showed a slide—to loud cheers and applause from the audience at the conference—with the new Revolution (a black version) surrounded by previous Nintendo consoles. Then an animation began on the giant screen in which the other systems shrank and got sucked into the blue-lit drive slot of the new machine. This was followed by the image of multiple game boxes from the past systems appearing in successive clusters and getting sucked in as well. The symbolism clearly said that the small black console would be able to ingest Nintendo's deep, historically crucial back catalog—an image meant to persuade the audience that the Revolution would indeed be a virtual console. This idea was later manifest when the software channel for the Virtual Console service was released.

Distribution: The Virtual Console

The Virtual Console's download service within the Wii Shop Channel is a way to access a collection of software-based emulated consoles. These in effect translate a series of earlier platforms, allowing older games to run on the Wii in a simulated NES or Sega Genesis environment, for example. Not surprisingly, users have noted some differences between the original games and emulated versions, including some enhanced graphics, newly translated text, and a few name changes of objects and references in games due to intellectual property issues.[7] And earlier games originally published before 1994 now have to be reviewed and categorized by the Entertainment Software Rating Board, an institution that didn't exist before that date.

Perhaps the most common changes reflect the use of new controllers. Even the Classic Controller, produced for this purpose, cannot perfectly duplicate button arrangements and the rumble-pack force-feedback effects of some earlier system controllers. Some games can be played with the Wii Remote turned horizontally, using the buttons as if it were an NES controller. The advertised idea is that the Virtual Console gives you access to past games; the reality is that emulation re-creates some though not all the conditions of earlier platforms, and always requires certain adjustments and translations—literal language translations, but also translations from one hardware-and-software environment to another.

As with other aspects of the Wii, in this case a retro revolution is a carefully constructed experience, involving reconstructed contexts as well as software emulation. It's one way to understand what Nintendo means by redefining backward compatibility—with the emphasis perhaps on the word redefining. When downloaded, each Virtual Console game in effect occupies its own separate Channel—reportedly a deliberate design feature to avoid the user's having to sort through menus to start a game. It's also a way to expose more casual users to the games that others download. But another effect of this decision is, again, to treat each emulated title with equal status on the system to any new game or Nintendo Channel, if only in terms of how it is accessed and where it sits on the menu.

Distribution: WiiWare

Next to the Classic Controller icon on the Wii Shop Channel menu is the logo for WiiWare, which launched in March 2008 (in Japan) and May 2008 (in the United States). Like the Xbox Live Arcade and Sony's PlayStation Network for the PS3, WiiWare is a digital distribution channel for original games, which in this case cost from about five hundred to fifteen hundred points (about five to fifteen dollars). Because points are available in increments of a thousand, you often have a balance of remaindered points toward the next purchase—a cause of annoyance for some users. Earlier in the system's life, users couldn't download demos of WiiWare games before they bought them. They had to go to Nintendo's WiiWare Web site to view screenshots and videos in order to learn about and preview games.

Expectations were inflated early on for the WiiWare service, and there was widespread hope that it would be an open gateway for small, independent developers, even individuals. But by 2011, Fils-Aime was quoted as saying that, though the company was "reaching out" to independent developers, it was "not looking to do business today with the garage developer" or "hobbyist," clearly a reaction in part to the explosion of app-based games for mobile platforms.[8] The barriers to entry for WiiWare are lower than for traditional professional development, but they are still prohibitive for true amateurs or individual creators with limited funds. The same SDK that's provided to accepted disc-based Wii game developers is provided to WiiWare developers, who must first apply and be accepted by Nintendo, then pay between approximately two and ten thousand dollars for the kit, sign a nondisclosure agreement, and meet certain baseline requirements, such as having a commercial office space in which to work (no developer with only a home office is certified). This is purportedly to ensure the security of the SDK materials during the development process, but it also works to establish a certain required professional status for WiiWare developers and their titles.

Although there have been conflicting reports about this, the size of WiiWare games seems to have been limited to about 40 MB. Nintendo has said that part of company policy for approving WiiWare games is to encourage smaller games, for many reasons, including responding to the desires of the casual market, and to ensure that they download easily and run smoothly on the Wii. It's also the policy to limit how frequently a particular developer can release a game on the service. Again, Nintendo sees this as a matter of quality control, a way to prevent shovelware on a platform that already faces some criticism about its cheap and easy content. In one interview about the limitations that Nintendo has imposed on WiiWare developers, Tom Prata, the director of project development, stresses the positive fact that the company allows third-party WiiWare developers the "freedom" to take advantage of the full range of features supplied by the system, from motion-control peripherals and WiiConnect24 to Mii data, on an equal footing with the developers of disc-based games. The purpose, he says, is to "encourage creators to focus development resources on areas that matter most to consumers: gameplay."[9]

A number of successful developers have responded positively to the policies, though of course they are under nondisclosure agreements, and by the very nature of having been successfully licensed by Nintendo, have an interest in emphasizing the positive side of WiiWare development. Dan Muir of Legendo, for instance, is the creator of *Pearl Harbor: Red Sun Rising*. When asked about what makes marketing WiiWare games difficult on a limited budget, he blamed the fact that many reviewers don't take the service seriously enough to pay attention to it. Although he admits that the Wii does have "some limitations with regards to space and graphical power," which made it somewhat difficult to make the appearance of animated water effective in his own game, and that the team had to compress the game's missions and varied aircraft options into the 40 MB limit, overall he notes that the development process "has been pretty smooth so far."[10]

Frontier Development's David Braben, the creator of *LostWinds*, says that WiiWare was chosen over Sony's or Microsoft's digital delivery services because the whole point of the game was to exploit the motion-sensitive Wii Remote, which in this case the player uses like a wand to control the wind, directing it in order to manipulate objects in the game environment. The game is designed so that the Nunchuk and the Wii Remote each controls a different character, one of which is the wind, with one controller in each hand. When asked about the size restriction or the constraints of the console's memory, Braben said these weren't really issues for development of *LostWinds*. All games work within the limits of their given systems, and early in the history of gaming, good things were done with games running on 2K platforms. Moreover, he observes, the constraints of the Wii have served to "focus" the development team. "In a sense, any limitations, and there are always limitations, do help. It's just part of the creative process."[11]

Developers balance the Wii's affordances as a platform against its constraints when they consider whether to apply for authorization—and these affordances include its motion-sensitive control system, but also, equally important, its providing an entry point to the potential mass market of casual gamers. Just after it was released in 2006, the Wii was still largely an unknown for many third-party developers. By the time WiiWare was introduced in late 2009, however, the Wii Remote and the system as a whole were better known and had been tested. Choosing to make and distribute a game for the Wii was both a better business risk and a better creative risk. After the introduction of Sony's PlayStation Move and Microsoft's Kinect in 2010, the same risks applied to these new systems, though perhaps in a less extreme form, since Nintendo had by then tested the waters of motion-control gaming for four years. Since their release, all three platforms have had to compete not just for players but also for developers.[12]

Every platform has to attract third-party developers if it wishes to expand its library. Fils-Aime admits the problem. Nintendo knows how to create games for "younger consumers" and "more casual players," but it wants to provide "core" gamers with content as well, "something like *Bio-Shock 2*. . . . And we also recognize that we don't create that type of content ourselves. We're not good at it and it's not a key focus area."[13] *Nintendo Week*, the streaming review and advertising program available on the Nintendo Channel (which can be added to the Wii Menu), includes a comical character named Dark Gary (really just one of the hosts, Gary, in costume), a slapstick parody of the stereotypical hard-core gamer. He's dressed all in black from watch cap to jeans, and has a soul patch as well as a snarky attitude. The character is probably meant to offset the somewhat-chirpy qualities of the two hosts, Gary and Alison, while also poking fun at pretentious "core" gamers in the Nintendo fanbase. Dark Gary is often brought on to review and market third-party games such as Capcom's *Monster Hunter Tri*—a game widely seen as helping to bring core gamers to the Wii. It's precisely the kind of game that Fils-Aime has in mind: not what Nintendo itself is good at making but rather what the company knows the core portion of its audience expects.

But besides occasional heavy-duty titles of this sort, Nintendo has counted on its WiiWare service to produce a diverse catalog of shorter games, closer to the casual side of the spectrum, yet also identified as independent or artistically creative, or aesthetically experimental in ways that its own catalog usually is not. This serves to illustrate how any platform is a social platform, in the sense that it's shaped by the creative works that run on it but also the social contexts within which it's defined, and these social contexts include projected and actual audiences along with their expectations.

One example of the cultural cachet that the WiiWare service aims to establish is its inclusion in 2010 of a much-respected independent game, *Cave Story*. Originally an action-adventure platformer with a retro look and Japanese story elements (such as the Mimigas, which look like anime-style rabbits or creatures from a Hayao Miyazaki film), it was released as freeware for the PC in 2004, and designed and created by a single auteur-like artist and coder, Daisuke Amaya (aka Pixel). It became a cult hit, and was ported by fans and modders to multiple platforms, including Linux, Mac OSX, and Sony's PSP, but none officially or for commercial release.[14]

Starting in 2008, an independent development company, Nicalis, worked directly with Amaya to bring the game to WiiWare. The point in this case was not so much to use the Wii Remote and motion-control system. The Wii version comes with some enhancements, including options to toggle on better-resolution graphics and a rearranged sound track—or toggle on original graphics and music. For controls, the Wii version just uses the buttons on the Wii Remote or the Classic Controller, and according to Tyrone Rodriguez of Nicalis, the designer Amaya himself "personally chose the button configuration for the Classic Controller."[15] The decision to use Nintendo's platform and its distribution channel seems to have been based less on the Wii per se and more on the general aura of Nintendo as a brand, its affording the developer a conduit to the right kind of ready players, a suitable audience for the game. Fans have noticed that *Cave Story* resembles classic-era games for the NES from the 1980s.[16] Rodriguez says that there is just "something about *Cave Story* that seems perfect, specifically for a Nintendo platform and also for WiiWare." He adds that "Nintendo has been 100-percent supportive of this project."[17] As this example illustrates, WiiWare is an important part of the Wii as a platform for all sorts of commercial reasons, but those reasons are themselves necessarily bound up with the historical and cultural aura of Nintendo as a company as well as a brand.

World of Goo (via WiiWare)

One of the most praised titles on the WiiWare service is 2D Boy's puzzle art game, *World of Goo*, which might be said to share some general "indie" DNA with *Cave Story*. It was created by Kyle Gabler and Ron Carmel, both former EA employees who advertise their independent status on their Web site by joking that their "swanky San Francisco office" is "whichever free wi-fi coffee shop they wander into on a given day."[18] (But this may be a bit of an ironic fiction; unless they received a waiver from Nintendo, they would have needed a stable office space in order to be authorized as Wii developers and receive the SDK.) The two principal developers produced most of the quirky artwork, which sometimes resembles Edward Gorey drawings or a Tim Burton movie, and music, based on Astor Piazzolla's dark *nuevo tango*, and also coded the game. *World of Goo* was released more or less simultaneously (without DRM) for the PC, the Mac, Linux, and the Wii, via various digital distribution channels, including Steam, for example, as well as on WiiWare.

During a talk at GDC 2009, Carmel ran through the costs of developing the game: four thousand dollars for the hardware, one thousand dollars for the software, five thousand dollars for quality-assurance testing, five thousand dollars for localization, and five thousand dollars for legal fees.[19] In spring 2009, the game's publisher, Brighter Minds Media, went bankrupt—but not the development company, 2D Boy. The estimated revenue from only the WiiWare version of *World of Goo*—which amounts to about 60 percent of the overall revenues—is over two million dollars.[20] The choice of WiiWare as a distribution channel has proved successful in less tangible ways as well. *World of Goo*, which would likely have been a critical success on any platform, turned out to be perfectly designed to appeal to the audience that the Wii has tapped into.

Choosing to develop on the Wii as well as the PC has helped to shape the game in multiple ways, from controls to imagined audience. The developers claim that "the Wii remote was the only controller other than the mouse that made sense for this game. If we tried to make the game use a dual-shock style controller players would end up feeling like they're in a straightjacket."[21] They say that the game is a generic hybrid of physics-based puzzle games combined with thematic and story-based adventure games, but they also reveal this interesting bit of history: "We originally thought we were making a casual game, like bejeweled." It's clear that the casual audience was targeted from the beginning, and this is likely one reason the Wii (and the particular distribution channel embodied in WiiWare) was right for the game.

> Playtesting was still showing that people who don't normally play games aren't getting the game quickly enough to stay engaged. We first tried to address this by adding a tutorial system that you can see in this revision. It sucked. It was complicated and cumbersome and we eventually dropped it when we got the connection logic to feel intuitive enough and it was replaced with a single signpost: "drag n' drop to build the pipe."[22]

This explanation for how the diegetic in-game Sign Painter's sometimes witty tips came to stand in for tutorials also makes it apparent that in play testing *World of Goo*, the developers were trying to reach "people who don't normally play games." In 2006–2007, Nintendo's digital delivery channel, WiiWare, must have looked like a pipeline (pun intended) to the untapped market.

As we suggested in chapter 3, in this game the Wii Remote is used essentially as a mouse. You point and click, drag and drop, select menu buttons, or just scroll around in the levels that are just slightly larger than one screen (and that imply connections at their margins to the other island levels as glimpsed in the opening game world silhouette). Rumble in the Wii Remote sometimes offers feedback to your actions. Just as a game such as *LIT* makes use of the Wii Remote as a flashlight, and *Max and the Magic Marker* exploits its resemblance to its eponymous implement, *World of Goo* recognizes that the simplest intuitive Wii Remote gestures for the casual gamer may be tied to the use of similar handheld interface devices—in this case, the mouse.

An early prototype Flash toy posted on the 2D Boy blog is a simple improvisation on the point-and-click interface.[23] You click to create "goopy bubbles," black circles that then behave in surprisingly emergent ways when you click on them again, splitting in two, bouncing into one another, and resembling artificial life games from an earlier era of creative computing. Clearly ancestors of the goo balls, these bubbles are in a sense just visual manifestations of the act of pointing and clicking at its most primitive and pleasurable—like popping the cells in plastic bubble wrap. Enhancing the physics by which the bubbles interact with one another must have seemed like the next logical step toward making the game. The pleasures of pointing and clicking remain integral to gameplay—for instance, in the feature that allows you to click on little fireflies (which make a satisfying pop and flash when you do) to "go back in time" and reset the game state by undoing the latest move. It's worth taking a close look at the story and gameplay of *World of Goo* in order to see how the control system and distribution over WiiWare channel subtly affect the experience of playing it.

The goo balls are sticky and alive, making the act of catching and manipulating them more challenging. They have little animated eyes and are constantly moving until the balls are stuck in place, at which point skinny struts appear between them and hold them in formation, so that making progress in the game is like building virtual geodesic or Tinkertoy structures, and the laws of physics apply. The designers have created a series of four chapters and an epilogue, each containing multiple levels, suggesting a larger story about corporate greed, environmental exploitation, complicity and responsibility, and climbing toward a goal. These themes, along with the usually black and viscous goo itself, and all the pipelines everywhere, made the game seem like a dark satire on the oil industry, among other things, but perhaps also on its own industry—the game industry. Players find themselves in the position of helping the goo balls reach the pipelines and be gathered up—in other words, more or less on the side of the World of Goo Corporation—for a point-of-view effect not entirely unlike that of the *BioShock* games. But the story is only obliquely told and remains in the background for several levels. It's perfectly possible to play the game for its puzzles, more or less ignoring the story altogether. As one reviewer puts it, the game

> touches on a variety of important themes and does so with such tact and subtlety that those who simply want an amazing puzzle game will find it and be content, but for those of us willing to look . . . there is something more.
>
> Beneath, we will find not simply a game, but a work of art that can touch us in ways many outsiders don't think a game can. The game covers themes that highlight not only the tragedies in our lives and our world, but also remind us to not despair, but to keep on pressing on, into the unknown.[24]

Though it seems likely that many relatively more casual players simply have fun with the physics of the puzzles, the atmosphere created by the music and artwork as well as the loaded referentiality of the Sign Painter's texts add a kind of contextual depth to the experience, even if any given player does not fully understand it. This makes *World of Goo* the quintessential casual art game, perfect for WiiWare distribution, since it can be picked up and played flexibly, according to varying schedules, while still intriguing even casual players with the overall game experience. Twenty minutes of goo ball maneuvering can be as satisfying in its own way as the roughly ten hours it takes to beat the game as a whole.

The fourth chapter is titled "The Information Superhighway," and offers a satiric look at information technology and the Internet as a kind of parallel and potential counterforce to the dark industrial world that dominates the rest of the game. The Sign Painter's welcome to this chapter is signed with the traditional test message, "Hello World," and is even more sardonic than usual:

> Welcome to the Information Superhighway! A land of beauty! A land of science! Philosophy! Architecture! Fan fiction! Everything you see, from the water to the leaves are made from sweet free flowing information. See if you can catch some information on your tongue! Of course . . . the whole place was abandoned years ago. This must be all that's left.

Here the palette changes at first to *Tron*-style green and black, and the goo balls look like squares (in this environment, eight-bit graphics and pixels come to mind). Later, you are supposedly able to improve the look with an upgrade to "256 stunning colors" (though things actually remain fairly monochromatic). Without entirely spoiling the game's story, suffice it to say that this chapter in *World of Goo* is a crucial step toward the conclusion and turns on parodic representations of email (and especially spam). A reviewer even suggests, perhaps somewhat mischievously, that this drab look may be "a commentary on modern video game systems, which wield more horsepower than so many consoles before them, yet we keep seeing games that stick to such drab and limited creativity."[25]

This seems a plausible source of inspiration for the game, except the focus would appear to have been on the development and publishing side of the game industry, the channels through which creative works go out into the world and reach an audience. 2D Boy's Gabler has said outright that the "overarching story of *World of Goo* is a big metaphor for the development process":

curious and naive little goo balls, encountering a large international corporation and its global pipe distribution system. Meanwhile, we're a curious and naive new indie studio, eager to explore, encountering large international publishing corporations with their global distribution systems. Or, more generally—hope, ambition, curiosity, etc., collide with a cold bitter reality. World of Goo Corporation, in particular, is a giant metaphor for some of the absurd experiences we've had along the way with publishers so far.[26]

This may be a bit disingenuous (or perhaps just tongue in cheek). At this point at least, 2D Boy is hardly naive and has negotiated the channels of distribution for its intellectual property better than any independent developer in recent memory. But this interpretation of the game's thematic content indicates the persistent and fundamental need for creative developers to connect with "large international publishing corporations with their global distribution systems." As for Nintendo, 2D Boy says that particular company has been "amazing to work with . . . [and] completely hands-off when it came to the game and went out of their way to help us promote the game and get it through lot check quickly."[27] *World of Goo* is not only one of the most critically acclaimed games distributed via WiiWare. It has become one of the proof-of-concept games for the Wii's digital distribution channel. The two partners making up 2D Boy have become the poster boys for the idea that the Wii can be a welcoming platform for independent developers, providing a channel of digital distribution through WiiWare to the new audience for games in the casual revolution era.

WarioWare D.I.Y. (for DS and WiiWare)

Those without the ambition or resources to apply for authorization from Nintendo and pay for the SDK can get at least a limited as well as playful sense of what it's like to develop games for the Wii by playing *WarioWare D.I.Y.* for the handheld DS. As we've already said, the game is a collection of typical *WarioWare* microgames, yet more important, it includes a fairly sophisticated editor with tutorials for making your own microgames (hence the DIY). You start with a menu of premade assets and objects, but you can also draw on the DS screen with the stylus to make backgrounds and new objects, then program their rules, actions, and behaviors using a selection of game action or assembly instruction scripts associated with your objects, all accessible from a friendly Wario-themed GUI in an editor that resembles *Mario Paint* (SNES). You're taken through the tutorials in the WarioWare Inc. section along with the irascible Wario himself, and both he and the tutor, Penny Crygor (the granddaughter of the mad scientist Dr. Crygor), refer to you by name ("Would you draw the spots on the ladybug, Steve?" or "Were you listening to all that, George?").

The parameters of the end product are severely limited, to say the least. Like other WarioWare games, each game lasts about five seconds, repeats and speeds up until you lose four lives, and then it's game over. Within those parameters, and given the preset palette of behaviors and effects (and combinations thereof), it's still possible using the tutorials to make a fairly interesting little microscale capsule of gameplay in about an hour.

We made some *WarioWare D.I.Y.* games while working on this chapter, just to test it out. As mentioned in chapter 1, we called the first one *Make Room!!!*, and its motto and imagery are taken from the *Wii Operations Manual* diagram that we discussed in chapter 3: "Adequate Space Required." The setting represents a living room, with a television set and a round coffee table (inspired by the Wii no Ma Channel) along with a player avatar viewed from above, holding a Wii Remote in one outstretched hand. You have to tap quickly with the stylus (or click with the Wii Remote, if you're playing on the Wii) on the table to move it out of the way in time, or else the television explodes. If you win, the table scoots off to one side and a tiny eight-bit Mario pops up on the television with an appropriate power-up sound effect. Then you repeat, faster and faster. We drew the art "by hand" (except for the Mario and the fire flower on the table)—which is to say, using familiar digital paint tools.

The final steps in making the microgame were to invent a name for our "company" (we called ours EvertInc.), package the game in a virtual "cartridge" that we "designed" (by selecting options), and then "ship" it. For that stage we got to see an animation of the game-making machine, the Super MakerMatic 21, spitting out a stream of cartridges (like goo balls) into a truck to be distributed to stores. You can share the game from DS to another DS, or send it to the Warehouse for someone whose Nintendo Friend Code you know to pick it up later via WiFi Connect.

WarioWare: D.I.Y. is a parody game about how games are made. There's even an Assembly Dojo where you can play puzzles involving completing parts of games. It manages to be fun because it exploits the irreverent humor and radical miniaturization of the game form in the WarioWare series to give players a kind of microscale model experience of some features of real game development (as far as we can understand them, not being developers ourselves)—from concept and design, to production, to distribution.

User-created microgames can then be shared through a number of channels, including beaming them directly from one DS to another via WiFi. But they can also be uploaded to the Wii via a game called *WarioWare D.I.Y. Showcase*. Once that's purchased (for eight hundred points) and installed on your Wii, you can access premade and some user-generated microgames, and play them on the Wii using the Wii Remote in place of the DS stylus. (On the DS, of course, you tap with the stylus to interact with the game.) Not only does this offer a fruitful channel for truly amateur game making (within the severe constraints of the microgame format and the game's editor) but it also closes a development circle: the Wii—with its lean profile, efficiencies, and Wii Remote controller—was partly inspired by the success of the DS, with its miniature form factor and stylus controller. Both systems are based on and promote casual gameplay.

Nintendo deliberately connected *WarioWare D.I.Y.* to professional independent game development and leveraged the cultural cachet of some of the most acclaimed third-party developers for WiiWare in order to advertise the game. Full-length trailers, viewable on YouTube, feature Carmel of 2D Boy and Alex Neuse of Gaijin Games using the DS to make *WarioWare D.I.Y.* microgames that are somewhat more sophisticated than our test case game (to say the least), and are based on their own WiiWare games, *World of Goo* and *Bit.Trip Runner*.[28]

Wearing a 2D Boy T-shirt, Carmel creates a single pipe and a single goo ball that interact dynamically with a timed tap of the stylus for a microgame called *Suck Goo*. We watch as he draws the background, a hill, sky, and clouds with the digital tools, then adds an overhead pipe in sections, rounds out the elbow joints, and adds highlights to make it look like a cel-shaded 3D object. Then in the pixel editor, he draws a goo ball and adds cartoon eyes something like those in *World of Goo*. He uses the "Maestro" function in the editor to generate a micro–sound track and then demonstrates the finished game, which somewhat disappointingly requires you only to tap on the goo ball in order for it to get sucked up—all timed of course, while the patented bomb fuse burns along the bottom of your screen. The goo ball doesn't move. You just have to click increasingly quickly as the game speeds up in repetition. On the video, Carmel celebrates *WarioWare D.I.Y.* as a "game about making games"—significant praise from the creator of what many have called one of the best WiiWare games available.[29]

Neuse's demonstration microgame is a bit more satisfyingly gamelike. The trailer starts with the indie developer of the retro rhythm-game franchise welcoming you to the development studio of Gaijin Games in Santa Cruz, California. Neuse then makes a microgame based on the retro challenges in *Bit.Trip Runner*, featuring the pixel-art avatar Commander Video. He invites both an artist and a programmer from the series over to judge the results. In his finished microgame, successive fires sweep across the screen, and you have to tap to make Commander Video jump over them. Neuse praises the tools and interface as "easy" and "intuitive," and says to his colleagues, "Dudes, we're going to have to use this to make our games."[30] This is just a joke, obviously, but these advertising trailers—like the game as a whole—blur the distinction between commercial third-party developers (whose games are available in the *Showcase* under the category "Big Name Games") and amateurs (with or without serious design aspirations).

Just as in its fiction *WarioWare D.I.Y.* includes the opportunity to design a cartridge and watch it being shipped from the factory, the *Showcase* on the Wii is also industry themed. When you download fresh content via the Wii WiFi Connection service, the graphics suggest that the "product" is being "shipped" to you in a box as it's downloading, and you use the Wii Remote to grab each box and stock it on your shelves in a kind of warehouse or library. The point of many of the big-name games seems to be in part to cross-promote *World of Goo* or the next *Bit.Trip* and *WarioWare D.I.Y.* But they also work conceptually to close the gap a bit between amateur gamers and their indie heroes, to imply that anyone can make something instantly playable—and that to some extent is at least something like a professional WiiWare game—that can be uploaded and accessed via the WiiWare Channel of distribution.

Internet Channel

Another option for more professional and commercial development is to make small, Web-delivered Flash games, customized for the Wii Remote instead of a mouse, and advertised on the Web as "for the Wii." Yet their coding means that even if they are truly meant to be played on the Wii, using the Wii Remote, Balance Board, or other Wii controllers, they cannot be downloaded via WiiWare but rather can only be accessed via the Wii's so-called Internet Channel—which is basically a built-in Wii Opera Web browser with menus. The Channel was free when the system first shipped, but Nintendo began to charge five hundred points for it a year later (and then made it free again in September 2009).

It's meant to be a convenient way to access the Web on the television screen, but it's far from offering a comfortable user interface. A virtual keyboard pops up when needed for input, much as it does on many touch screen mobile devices, although you have to push the keys by poking at them and clicking using the Wii Remote. And the Opera browser can't always handle all the features of most normal Web pages. So a layer of Wii-purposed Web sites meant to be accessed using the Opera browser via the Internet Channel has grown up to make browsing on the console a less unpleasant experience. WiiCade, for example, offers Flash games in a format that works on the Wii and uses the Wii Remote. Similarly, MapWii offers system-customized maps linked to friend codes, and MiiTube has a Wii-optimized interface for watching videos from YouTube, with large-type menus and search form, and with pages set to avoid the need for horizontal scrolling. The Internet Channel in theory makes the console a place to access Internet-published games, some portion of which could be designed to optimize certain features of the console. At least so far, however, this particular channel of distribution and access has remained mostly theoretical.

Homebrew Channel: The Platform's Edge

Finally, even further outside official channels for the platform is the Homebrew Channel. It is not a legitimate Nintendo service but instead a special kind of exploit in which an "unlocked" Wii console can in effect create a pirate channel in the Channels menu for loading unauthorized applications built from user-generated code, so that users can run unlicensed games and other software on the platform. Nintendo updates to the system, provided automatically via WiiConnect24, block this channel, of course. The Homebrew Channel is essentially a rogue clone of the official Wii Channels, and it includes emulators for other platforms, somewhat like the Virtual Console. After "jailbreaking" the Wii, Homebrew users download and install a .WAD file (a game file format descended originally from *DOOM* and reportedly meaning "where's all the data?"),[31] an archive to create a channel much like the official ones. From that new channel with its own GUI, users can see listed and launch their own or other users' Homebrew applications from an SD card or USB drive.

The Wii Homebrew Web site claims that the Channel also allows for applications to be launched via TCP or a USBGecko device from a PC.[32] Indeed, this site and others like it remind us that the Homebrew Channel is itself the manifestation of a larger network of fans, hobbyists, hackers, and modders, who make use of deliberately "broken" Wiis to piggyback their own version of the Wii platform on Nintendo's official and legal version. In this way, even a closed proprietary platform can always be pried open.

That even a tightly controlled and dedicated computing platform like the Wii, with its use of DRM and various security measures built in, would be open to such hacking is also a reminder that no platform is ultimately defined entirely by its manufacturer or licensed uses. Every platform is a combination of hardware and software that is in part defined by the possibilities that lie outside what it was designed to do, because every platform is a site of sometimes-unpredictable transactions with users. Author William Gibson famously had a character remark that "the street finds its own uses for things."[33] Video game players, as users go, tend to include an activist or hacker segment that engage in the more extreme kinds of creative uses, whether or not they are licensed.

As we will explore further in the next chapter, however, even perfectly legitimate, authorized, and licensed uses can test the boundaries of what was originally intended for a platform by its creators. Playing video games is the kind of activity that always to some degree depends on such boundary-testing uses, since gaming encourages clever and ingenious moves to overcome barriers and obstacles of many kinds, and the line between an "exploit" and an extremely clever move—and more generally, the magic circle of gaming and what's outside its perimeter, out in social space with all its unpredictable interactions—is often difficult to define.

About a month after the Wii's release, a video appeared on YouTube titled "Wii-diculous."[1] In it, a group of three friends, young men in their twenties, play *Wii Sports* after hours in a big empty movie theater. The camera begins in the projection booth and then aims at the front of the theater, where the Wii Bowling alley fills the almost-thirty-foot screen (a caption reports the dimensions). People stand on the stage and bowl as their friends' cheers blend with those of the in-game Mii audience and the game's sound effects, piped over the theater's sound system. The friends run through various sports as the video shows them playing Wii Tennis from out in the aisles or within rows of red velvet seats, and Wii Golf from the stage, chatting and joking as if they were playing in their living room. Their life-size shadows show up on the screen, of course, looming between them and the now-towering Mii avatars. They end with a round of Wii boxing, one of them playing up close, right on the stage, and one out in the aisle. The digital projector light glows, high above in the back of the theater.

This was a stunt with resonance (the video was still garnering comments several years later). Nothing symbolizes recent changes in the broad media landscape better than an empty movie theater (old media) being taken over by a video game (new media). Regular comparisons of movie ticket sales with those of games attempt to chart the rise of one medium during the fall of another, although it's a complicated relational calculation, and DVRs and cable certainly have done much more than games to reduce theater ticket sales. But the common idea is that going out in public and being entertained in a dark, crowded roomful of strangers is declining, and with it, one more social activity that takes us out of the house, away from the television, like bowling in leagues.

Looked at this way, the theater stunt was a way of breaking out of home-console clichés, through a dramatization of the social nature of Wii video game play against the backdrop of the twentieth century's most iconic setting for social, mass entertainment. Nintendo itself in fact exploited this symbolism in a viral marketing campaign in the United Kingdom.[2] Before showings of *Pirates of the Caribbean: At World's End* during its opening weekend, the advertising reel was interrupted by a woman in the back of the darkened theater calling for her son, sitting down front. She loudly challenged him to a rematch of Wii Tennis, and the two—both actors—played a round live in front of the moviegoers, with the game projected onto the big screen. This professional campaign actually involved five teams of performer pairs doing the act across Britain in nine different theaters over two weekends, taking over the quintessential mass-entertainment space to perform the Wii's family-friendly gameplay out in public, in a deliberately social setting.

The three friends in the YouTube video are also demonstrating the Wii's nature as a social platform, playing video games in the social setting of the public movie theater—though in their case, with the theater closed. Their little group of three is still a social group, however. At one point, a player excitedly plans a party in the same space once *Metroid Prime 3* is released. We assume they didn't necessarily intend the media-landscape symbolism. But they're nonetheless part of larger trends, including the use of the newer, far-flung social space of YouTube (which, remember, was only about a year and a half old when their video was made), the ultimate social-media platform (and "theater") for this kind of performance. At any point during the video one of the three friends is presumably behind the camera, filming the other two at play. They're not just playing a video game; they're making a movie in the movie theater about playing video games. And it's expressly intended for YouTube, performed for an imagined audience—a mostly anonymous social group—of hundreds or thousands out there on the Internet. As you watch them play, you can almost hear the user comments they're anticipating.

What the uploaders more immediately intended was to respond to an earlier YouTube video in which someone else played *Wii Sports* with his friends using a data projector in his home, with the image projected onto a wall. As the second video maker says, "We figured we could one-up it with the equivalent of a 344" television screen." Yet then he goes on: "We wanted to use my friend's Nintendo Wii in the theater, but we didn't want to have to deal with yards of cabling. Inspired by doctabu's design, I built my own wireless sensor bar for less than $20."[3] And suddenly it's clear—both stunts are really hacks. That is, the social symbolism of the public theater's becoming a space for video game play is also social in another sense: it's about users appropriating a platform, and modding or hacking it in order to make it do something it wasn't designed to do. The point of competing with doctabu was not just to increase the screen real estate on which to play; it was to do this with the video maker's own idea—repurposing the simple and cheap wireless infrared LED sensor bar. In other words, Radio Shack was the initial social arena of this competition.

Watched with this context in mind, the theater video reveals its director's intentions: it opens with a quick tour of the back of the digital-projector setup, showing the Wii attached with a video cable and the significantly empty port for the sensor bar cable (making it clear, incidentally, that its only purpose is to deliver power to the LEDs). Then, at the conclusion, we see the new homemade sensor bar, which the friends set up on the backs of two velvet chairs down front. A link from YouTube to the maker's blog even points to a schematic drawing, with a detailed parts list and directions:

> I built the wireless sensor bar, brought it over to the theater and tested it on a regular television. Fortunately, it worked! After the patrons left, we hooked the Wii up to the data projector and house sound, put in *Wii Sports*, and brought the controllers and the wireless sensor bar downstairs. We set the emitters on the backs of two chairs and stood a few rows back. The wireless range of the controllers was great enough to work! We suffered no technical glitches from the distance; we could even play up on stage, craning our necks up at the gigantic image, immersing ourselves in the game.[4]

It's interesting that he views the results in terms of immersive game-play, since as far as we can see everything about the stunt works in the other direction—it turns the center of the gaming experience outward into the theater, and from there, further out, on to the Internet (not to mention Radio Shack, where supplies were purchased, and the home workshops where the sensor bars were built). The theater stunt illustrates an important connection between this kind of appropriation of a platform and the normal ways in which a platform is made the occasion, prompt, or catalyst for social interactions—whether a party or bout of online play or a friendly competitive hardware hack. Both are examples, in their different ways, of how people find their own uses for platforms. Both remind us therefore that platform is ultimately a social phenomenon.

In common parlance, a platform is something you build on. Rather than a completed structure in its own right, it provides a base or foundation on which other people can build. But the openness of platforms to being built on varies widely. An active, commercially viable video game console system in a competitive environment is not designed to be an open platform. Quite the contrary: it's the very definition of a proprietary platform, a dedicated entertainment system. In the terms used by Jonathan Zittrain, a video game console is a consumer "information appliance"—like a mobile phone, MP3 player, or DVR—designed to offer a controlled, consistent experience, as opposed to a traditional PC, which is a platform "open to a set of offerings from anyone who want[s] to code for it." Zittrain's argument is that the latter kind of platform is a "generative" one, since people build unanticipated edifices on it. It invites audience contributions, as opposed to a more closed, "appliance"-like platform such as Apple's iPhone or iPad—or any video game console. His point is that the "nongenerative" kind of platform is these days in the ascendancy and threatens to dominate people's uses of the Internet, and that the whole sphere of networked electronic devices is becoming increasingly "appliancized."[5]

When Apple released the iPad in 2010, activist and author Cory Doctorow posted a blog entry in opposition to the tablet device and general model of closed consumer devices. In it, he quotes the *Maker's Manifesto*: "If you can't open it, you don't own it. Screws not glue." He contrasts the new touchscreen device with the Apple II, which "came with schematics for the circuit boards, and birthed a generation of hardware and software hackers who upended the world for the better." The ideal user of an iPad, Doctorow says, is just a "consumer," and you don't tinker with or improve your iPad; you improve it only by buying apps.[6]

In response to similar criticisms and sparked especially by the controversial decision not to include Abode's Flash in the iPad support, Steve Jobs said that the increasing majority of users do not want or need a programmer's or hacker's kind of access to the system, particularly at the expense of security and a reliable online experience. He compared PCs to trucks—utility vehicles for mostly professional drivers—and devices like the iPad to cars—more attractive and comfortable to drive, with features such as the automatic transmission aimed at consumers.[7] What he didn't add is that like the iPad, today's cars tend to be "attractively styled," but have "their innards hermetically sealed," relying on onboard and external computers for diagnosis and repair as well as functions such as assisted braking and fuel system maintenance (especially in the case of hybrid vehicles)—so that how they work is essentially mysterious to the owner.[8]

The question of designing hardware and software platforms to be closed or open, to be left sealed or tinkered with, is only part of the issue. Doctorow's "screws not glue" language is in the end complicated by the multiple kinds of devices as well as interactions that people have or wish to have with their devices. It makes sense as an argument against a general trend in computing, and in favor of a hacker or maker ethos. It's most compelling when you imagine a future in which the old-school open-platform PC is no longer available—in other words, in Zittrain's unwelcome "future of the Internet."[9] But for now, a somewhat-different aspect of that future seems to be unfolding—one in which specially purposed, often smaller and more efficient, dedicated computing devices are proliferating, as we first suggested in chapter 2, in conjunction with a dispersal of the kinds of computing tasks that people expect these devices to enable. We believe that the design of the Wii as a platform can best be understood in the context of this new environment. What kind of openness is possible or desirable, on what level, in such an environment?

First, a little background about what it means for a system to be open. The whole idea of free/open-source software (FOSS) is focused on the low-level source code of a product or system along with its availability for study, use, and repurposing. But there are different degrees of free and open. For example, in the case of the GNU general public license (GPL), the software and any derivative works must by definition always remain completely open under the GPL. That is, anyone who modifies it under the license agrees that it will remain available under the original terms. Opinion differs, though, over which applications or devices should actually be open source—on the question of how far down and out into the world the openness of code should extend. A recent topic of discussion in the FOSS community, for instance, has been whether firmware code that has open-source drivers to "talk to it" needs to be open source as well.

In particular, the popular NVIDIA controller has its own proprietary firmware (and even proprietary drivers) that can be used to provide the "complete experience" even on open-source platforms like Ubuntu. There has been considerable FOSS community debate surrounding these kinds of hybrid platforms. In the end, users are afforded the option on systems like Ubuntu to install the proprietary drivers, but only after they have installed the OS on their computer. So if a user wants to run a high-resolution monitor by way of NVIDIA chips, say, they will have to install the proprietary drivers on top of the OS and—as the FOSS community views it—live slightly outside the "virtuous" limits of FOSS-compliant software. The debates can become fairly theological.

In everyday life, in the increasingly multiscaled environment of distributed computing with embedded dedicated processors everywhere, the pragmatic meaning of openness can be found not just in a particular instance of code but also in the bigger picture of networking protocols and services. Video game consoles—especially the Wii, with its deliberate shift to lower-powered and unobtrusive design—can be seen as fitting into this distributed environment and the accompanying trend toward more service-oriented design. In effect, setting up the Wii creates a PAN in the user's living room. This PAN enables communication among various components in the system.

Consider the Wii Remote for a moment. What exactly is exchanged across the boundaries of controller and sensor bar/television set, or controller and console? A good deal of data, as it turns out, and despite the closed nature of the game platform, much of these data remain open in some important ways. The Wii Remote transmits its accelerometer data (and data from other attached devices, such as the Nunchuk), and because this data feed is not encrypted, it can be accessed via other OSs besides the Wii—such as Linux and Windows. It's just a matter of creating a Bluetooth pointing device profile (much like what's created for a standard mouse) and adapting the software profile to handle additional data (multiple-axis acceleration).[10]

So what really makes a system open—and perhaps even generative, to use Zittrain's term—may be a matter of how it fits into the larger emerging distributed-systems environment. From a broader computer science perspective, the key question in most practical instances is whether the system can be integrated into a larger world that is increasingly networked, whether wired or wireless, point-to-point serial connection (USB, serial port, or parallel port), and so on. Consider just one example of a user hack, a simple demonstration that the Wii MotionPlus device, on its own, can be attached to a computer via a serial/parallel port, giving the user access to the data generated by the tuning-fork gyroscope. Does this mean that the MotionPlus device is an open one? In technical or legal terms, it does not. The device is about as proprietary as it gets when it comes to commercial computing. And yet this hack pretty eloquently shows that given the device's black-box nature, its boundaries for integration with wider systems are in practice open, and in this way the device is potentially generative in Zittrain's terms. You can get the data out of it with a simple modification, so that's a kind of openness, whatever its original design.

Consider the history of Sun, the company that effectively ushered in the open-systems era. Although Sun never positioned itself as an open-source company, it nevertheless was at the forefront of open standards and interfaces. Even when Java was in its infancy, the slogan associated with it was "the network is the computer."[11] Sun understood then what is widely recognized now: true openness requires designers and programmers to keep most of the networking protocols and standards open, because these form the boundaries of larger distributed *systems*. Clearly there are recent trends that challenge this view, particularly Apple's tightening control over its platform on various devices by setting up iTunes and the App Store, which though it runs on the Internet using its protocols (HTTP and TCP/IP), is mostly a closed architecture. In institutional terms, Apple's control over what gets published via the App Store is a serious issue. But this is not reducible, in the end, to whether the iPad's design and source code, for example, does or does not allow for easy hacking.

The overall trend, we think, is toward many smaller *linked* devices—however closed or open—in a relatively open distributed network that itself employs mostly open standards. To recognize this is to shift attention from source code per se to those standards; in other words, to the social and economic factors that might affect communication among the distributed parts of the network or any given platform. Such a shift makes it clear that hardware and software design—including the design of any platform—is always shaped by social contexts.

Even Zittrain acknowledges that "how much the system facilitates audience contribution is a function of *both* technological design *and social behavior*."[12] There is always a social layer at the highest level that's an essential part of how any computing platform works—and how open it is in practice. And this is especially true for a gaming system, the purpose of which is creative expression and interactive entertainment. Any platform with users is a function of this social layer. The reason that video game consoles still exist—at least for now—is that gamers continue to respond positively to the affordances of these dedicated systems, with their specialized controls, interfaces, and data-management systems, which are closely bound up with existing institutions for software development and distribution channels as well as communities that identify with particular franchises and producers of intellectual property, especially social "universes" surrounding the competing platforms. There is no reason, given a regularly updated library of software titles, that a PC or portable platform—such as Nintendo's 3DS, or any smartphone—could not serve just as well as a home game console. For many gamers, it already does.[13]

What the console offers are nonessential features, from a strictly computing point of view (but absolutely crucial from a social point of view): its special interface and control system, the tethered content of exclusive games, and the radiating sense of a cultural brand or creative hub provided by two social forces in (sometimes-tense) cooperation, the producers and the users. On the one side, there's a producing and publishing company like Nintendo, with its institutions, talent, and economic motives. On the other side, there are the users and their social networks, fandoms, attachments, and desires. Together these two forces give meaning to a platform. Meaning is never something constructed by the producing company alone. This is perhaps most obvious when certain users take over a platform and reshape it against the grain of how it was designed, by hacking the hardware or software, or both, for their own purposes. But in a less obvious or tangible way, it's also true for almost any video game played on any platform, because the whole idea of gameplay is to push back against the system (including the software running on it) to try to find loopholes, exploits, and clever ways to overcome obstacles and beat the game. A social platform is always defined in the space between the system and its users.

Some Wii Mods and Hacks

It will come as no surprise to anyone familiar with computing and gaming culture that there have been a wide array of creative hacks and mods performed on the Wii. These can be divided into two categories: the creative repurposing of the system itself or its components; and mods of the system in order to circumvent or break security measures, or DRM software or hardware controls. In the first category, there are actually two kinds of repurposing: game related, and nongame related.

The gadget-based Wii seems to invite nongame-related hacks that employ its motion-sensitive controllers as controllers for other devices and other systems. For example, one enterprising team at an Australian mining equipment company coded a control system in Python to allow them to use the Wii Remote to operate two fifteen-ton steel robot arms with grappling claws. Technically this hack is amusing because it takes the controller outside the game universe, into the world of heavy equipment, but the video of the robot arms in action recall video arcade claw machines, which are especially popular in Japan.[14] In another instance from Australia, University of Melbourne medical researchers disassembled a Wii Balance Board and discovered that the strain gauge system was surprisingly sophisticated for the price, and that the board was sensitive enough to serve as a cheaper substitute for similar "force platforms" used to measure patients' balance in physiology clinics, some of which cost nearly eighteen thousand dollars. The game controller was chosen because it's an inexpensive off-the-shelf product that's easy to adapt.[15] Even the US government's Department of Homeland Security has explored a security screening system combining an eye tracker with heart, respiration, and skin-temperature gauges, all working while a subject stands on a Wii Balance Board.[16]

But by far the best-known producer of Wii hacks is Johnny Chung Lee, a Microsoft researcher—and interestingly enough, one who has said he worked on Project Natal (which became Kinect). Lee's own Web site includes a number of articles and videos showing how to reverse engineer and repurpose the platform's technology in a spirit of experimentation.[17] In one hack, Lee literally turns the system the other way around, using the Wii Remote infrared sensor CMOS camera on the television set facing the user in order to track finger motions. (He points an LED array at the user to make his fingers reflect light for the Wii Remote to pick up.) Extending that idea, he constructs a head-tracking virtual reality program, with the components of the controller system reversed again, the Wii Remote on the television pointing out, and the sensor bar attached to a cap on his head. A 3D grid on the screen is then navigable with only his head motion. Lee's most famous Wii hack, however, may be the electronic whiteboard, using LED-equipped pens and, again, with the infrared camera in the Wii Remote serving as a sensor rather than as a controller, pointing at the screen on which he's projected the image from his laptop.

Lee is likely under a nondisclosure agreement at Microsoft, but it's not difficult to imagine that this kind of simple workbench experiment involving reverse engineering and literally reversing the Wii controller system might have been inspired by (or might have inspired) some of his work on the Kinect interface, which conceptually not unlike Lee's Wii hack, uses 3D sensor depth-of-field cameras to construct a "point cloud" map of the room, within which the software recognizes the human body in motion and translates that into the interface.[18]

As we suggested at the conclusion of the previous chapter, the gaming community has traditionally included a contingent of players interested in discovering clever exploits. The lines between sharing cheat codes, finding loopholes in a game's programming, modding a console's hardware, and installing the Homebrew Channel may be legally defined, but in practice, to many users, they seem somewhat blurry. When it comes to the Wii, the infamous "Twilight Hack" stands as an instructive example. Members of the Homebrew community discovered that *The Legend of*

Zelda: Twilight Princess afforded an exploit of a buffer-overflow error in the game by which Homebrew software could be loaded via an SD card. The hack involved loading a kind of Trojan horse save file containing a supposed new name for Link's horse, Epona, but that actually contained a small program. When the game loaded the "name" file into memory, it was tricked into loading and running the code from the SD card's root directory.[19] Nintendo's updates closed the loophole as quickly as possible. And hackers quickly replaced it with a new exploit, called Bannerbomb, which reportedly used a malformed banner to load from the SD card the code that allows a user to install the Homebrew Channel, for example. Such exploits and hacks are quite common when it comes to all video game consoles, though of course they are easier to pull off with older and no longer commercial systems.

While Nintendo software updates answer such widespread and organized hacks, there is little to stop individual hackers from modifying their own hardware or software for experimental purposes (aside from the voided warranty and good chance they will render the hardware useless). One of the more common mods is to replace an in-game music sound track with one's own choice of MP3 files. With the Wii, however, using the Wii Remote for musical purposes has occurred to a number of hackers. One modder used a *Guitar Hero* guitar controller with embedded Wii Remote, exploiting the controller's Bluetooth capability to send signals to their laptop so that they could play notes with the buttons rather than just play the in-game music.[20]

A little more sophisticated hack was involved in the creation of the Wii Loop Machine software by Yann Seznec, a sound designer and former graduate student at the University of Edinburgh, that turns the Wii Remote into a controller for a four-channel music-loop synthesizing program.[21] It runs on Mac OSX via the Bluetooth connection. Flicking or waving the Wii Remote while holding the B button works to digitally "scratch" the sampled tracks as if you were manually handling a turntable (or sliding fader switch) as well as using the D-pad button to reverse tracks or change their speed, and the A button (while waggling the controller) to produce other special audio effects. Conceptually, the Loop Machine takes advantage of the Wii's motion-control affordances in much the same way that Nintendo's own *Wii Music* does—to make a simple music-altering "instrument" out of the Wii Remote.

It's easy enough to advocate for the rights of users to alter the hardware and software they've purchased, as opposed to the rights of manufacturers and publishers (or content producers) to continue to control the devices as well as the software *after* purchase. This is what Doctorow really means by championing screws not glue, for instance, and debates surrounding copyright, patents, DRM, and sharing are especially urgent in the digital era. It's not our intention to take up those debates here. Our point is simply that mods and hacks are possible, and that they are reminders that platforms go out into the world (if the producing company is successful) and then users do things with them—some of which goes against the grain of the designers' and producers' intentions for those platforms. Notwithstanding the profit motive, there is a real sense that video game platforms in particular are *designed to be appropriated* to one degree or another, whether through choosing peripherals (some from third-party manufacturers), personalizing settings, making and sharing system content such as Miis, building a collection of software titles (again, some from third-party developers), and then playing them in individualized ways such that saved game data—levels completed and features unlocked, avatars customized, or characters named—will vary from user to user. These are all sanctioned, encouraged forms of appropriation. Unsanctioned ones, however, are also part of the continuum of possible uses, or the social meanings given to game platforms as well as the software played on them.

Wii Social Games

But games are certainly social media in other senses, too. One can play *New Super Mario Bros. Wii* in multiplayer co-op mode, but it's relatively difficult to learn to do it properly. The idea of fun social play is in this case somewhat in conflict with the demands of the gameplay based on this beloved core franchise. It's hard to avoid getting in each other's way and impeding rather than advancing game progress.[22] The more accessible and more casual social games for the Wii developed by Nintendo have tended to be minigame- or microgame-based, like *WarioWare: Smooth Moves*, in which an unlocked multiplayer mode allows up to twelve players to hand off and share the Wii Remote. The game's official Web site makes it explicit: "It's Party Time! Spice up any party with some smooth moves." Nintendo's Web site emphasizes in familiar terms the game's ability to make an "Off-Screen Party" (a resonant term)—"with games that are as much fun to play as they are to watch people play, *WarioWare: Smooth Moves* brings the party to its feet. It's hilarious for players and audiences alike."[23]

In *Wii Party*, the social purpose is explicit, especially in its use of feedback features to turn the Wii Remote into a physical game token in various guises. The same basic idea, of creating an "off-screen party" atmosphere by stimulating social interactions out in player space, lay behind some of the gameplay in *Wii Sports* and *Wii Fit* packs. Miyamoto's original sketch for the Wii's launch software included *Wii Play*, a miscellaneous collection of family or party games, including rec room games such as billiards and a pre-*Wii Sports Resort* Table Tennis game. The sports games allow for "versus" modes, of course, and the iconic Wii Bowling allows for multiple players to take turns. Though it's possible to Wii Bowl alone, it's not any more fun than is real bowling alone. Viewed one way, all of the mimetic-interface games for the Wii are multiplayer, in the sense that they are designed to be played in social settings, where others in the room can at least watch and interact with the player, if not take turns playing. The on-screen game is the occasion and pretext for an off-screen party, to use Nintendo's phrase. Even the NPC Miis that cheer in the stands or from the sidelines are meant to be tokens or surrogates for your friends and family or party guests, creating a cartoon version of a social setting within the game space that implies at least the desirability of a corresponding social group in the living room's physical space.

One game designed to encourage social interaction more than any other in Nintendo's own initial software offerings is *Wii Music* (2008). A pet project of Miyamoto's, this title was not as successful as *Wii Sports*, for example, perhaps because it affords social interaction in ways that some players don't find sufficiently gamelike when compared to the competition from other music games, or perhaps because it appeared near the end of the wave of popularity of music games in general. *Wii Music* simulates the playing of instruments, either in groups or alone, but always playing along with NPC Mii ensembles or orchestras. Part of the problem, when you compare it to other music games, is that its initial list of fifty unlockable songs—the music you can play along with and on which you can improvise—is so broad in its intended international and multigenerational reach that it may seem watered down to any given user. Tunes to which no one can object make for a bland playlist that includes "Twinkle, Twinkle, Little Star," "Do-Re-Mi," and "Happy Birthday to You." During actual gameplay, on the other hand, these generic songs often become merely the raw material for the simulation's effects, excuses to play around with the tune, and that seems to be the point of what the game offers in the way of entertainment. What you do alters the music in sometimes-surprising ways—as you play faster during jams, say, the game responds with fills and multiplied notes. Although you're not coming up with the actual improvisations, it feels as though you've prompted them by speeding up, so the feedback is fun.

You hold the Wii Remote like a horn, and push one and two buttons, or use the Wii Remote and Nunchuk in combination to play piano, guitar, violin, and many other instruments. A metronome track clicks through your Wii Remote speaker in your hand to keep time. Instrument design can show real ingenuity, as when you raise the volume of a horn part by tilting the Wii Remote up in front of you like a horn. But it's difficult to feel cool, even if you're a young player, while making air-guitar (or air-marimba, etc.) gestures with the Wii Remote and Nunchuk to control "Twinkle, Twinkle, Little Star," or "Chariots of Fire." More likely to appeal to Nintendo fans are the handful of tunes from video games, such as the *Super Mario Bros.* theme, and especially when one unlockable instrument turns out to be a melodica made from an NES (Famicom) controller (the "NES Horn"). Miyamoto is a banjo player of many years and a folk music fan himself, and clearly the idea was to choose songs that would appeal to the widest swath of potential players (presumably in Asia, the United States, and Europe, and adults as well as children; song descriptions include a little national flag for the country of origin), or tunes that the greatest number of people would be familiar enough with to play along to. The karaoke-style gameplay means that in most modes, basic tracks continue playing underneath whatever you play, so there's little chance of actual failure, and no chance that the music will come screeching to an embarrassing halt.

In the games, though, such as Handbell Harmony, you have to play color-coded notes on time as they scroll past, somewhat like in *Rock Band*, and you are scored after each performance. Though there's no booing crowd of Miis, as we might expect if this were *Rock Band* or *Guitar Hero*, your Mii hangs their head in shame as manga-style sweat drops fly—and if you're really bad, it clouds up and rains on you. The game is cute—arguably sometimes a little too cute. For instance, musical Miis may show up in cat costumes meowing their notes. And there's a whole different group of musical characters, the Tutes, who look and sound like a family of tiny Mii Muppets, and offer instruction and guidance. The relative easiness of the game as a whole along with the cartoony Mii (and Tute) cuteness led one snarky reviewer to call it "toddler friendly" and "overly casual."[24] Reviewers have not uniformly panned *Wii Music*, and sales are only relatively low (given expectations), but by Nintendo's standards the game has not been a real success.[25]

Miyamoto demonstrated the game in public for the first time himself, wearing a tuxedo onstage and conducting a Mii orchestra in Mii Maestro mode (called Open Orchestra in Japan). The staging, with cartoons and Miyamoto as the live actor, playing together in an orchestra, brought to mind Leopold Stokowski conducting in Disney's *Fantasia*. Miyamoto has answered the critics by stressing the game's positive opportunities for open-ended play and its room for improvisation of sorts. In-game prompts say things like, "There's no one way to play a song, there are millions of ways!" and "The most important thing is that you have fun, feel the music, and express yourself." It's true that the interface is actually well calibrated to make the music respond to different player gestures without crashing altogether: if you move the controllers in a faster rhythm, you can play grace notes or fill out solos; if you waggle the Wii Remote, it can cause tracks to speed up; and in Mii Maestro mode, you control the basic rhythms and pauses of the orchestra. This relative freedom to play with the controllers as if they were instruments contrasts with the constraints of the game's obvious primary competition, the *Guitar Hero* and *Rock Band* franchises (at least until later releases, which approach the difficulty of playing actual music). *Wii Music* is at its best as a social or party game, with multiple players waving their controllers around. But it's clearly a game at the far casual end of the scale.

Of course you can play third-party rhythm games on the Wii as well, such as Harmonix's *Rock Band 2* or *The Beatles: Rock Band*, just as you can on other platforms. The plastic instrument controllers in which the Wii Remote is inserted can be replaced with *Rock Band* or the custom Beatles instruments, which communicate with the console and game via Bluetooth, just as the Wii Remote does, by plugging USB dongles into the back of the console. What sets these games apart—and what has made them (along with their progenitor, *Guitar Hero*) the best-known and most popular rhythm games of the past decade—is the fundamental device of their gameplay. When you fail, you hear squawky notes, and eventually, if you miss enough of them, the music grinds to a halt, leaving you in awkward silence. Instead of cartoon Miis or Tutes, you see "rock-star" avatars, or in the most effective artwork of all these music games, animated images of the Beatles at various points in their history. Instead of the abstract game spaces of *Wii Music*, in *The Beatles: Rock Band*, for example, you perform in settings based on the band's storied career.

In every case, however, these settings and the avatars serve mostly as a kind of cinematic backdrop (though an often-stunning one) for the real interface layer superimposed in the foreground, which contains the gameplay graphics proper—the widely familiar color-coded notes streaming toward you and meters to mark your progress. The most fundamental affordances of *Wii Music*—being able to simulate playing music, and playing it together in a social group—are more or less provided by *Rock Band 2*. And *Rock Band* can even be rendered more "casual" by turning on the "no-fail" mode. But there are also online leaderboards where high achievements are listed and a real sense of failure when you lose. *Rock Band*'s affordances are arguably made more meaningful in the context of the game's more clearly defined constraints. In this case, Nintendo by contrast may have gone so far in the direction of "accessibility" that it limited the game's appeal in the context of existing music games.

An illustrative contrast can be found in a perhaps-unexpected corner of Nintendo's own software history—the bongo-drum controller introduced with *Donkey Konga* for the GameCube (2003–2004).[26] The DK Bongos use two touch sensors to measure hits and even have a built-in microphone for capturing hand claps up in the air above the drumheads. You have to match the beats in the sound track, visualized with horizontally streaming color-coded dots and lines much as in *Guitar Hero* or *Rock Band*, which includes thirty songs from eclectic mix of genres, much like *Wii Music*. But the game keeps score based on your level of accuracy, and it's possible to win coins and unlock different drum sounds. It allows for a multiplayer Jam Session mode, creating a kind of drum circle or beach bonfire party. One skilled player and game reviewer produced a video in which he single-handedly plays four bongo controllers at once in a Jam Session mode performance of the *Pokémon* theme song—not so much a game exploit or mod as a way to bend the game slightly in order to enhance the difficulty and show off, just for the challenge of it.[27]

Donkey Konga, like *Dance Dance Revolution* before it, and *Guitar Hero* and *Rock Band* immediately after it, is a true rhythm game. All of these make accurately timed control their object. This is obvious from the fact that another game for GameCube—and now revived for the Wii—*Donkey Kong Jungle Beat*, allows you to use the DK Bongos to control a conventional platformer fighting game.[28] The Wii's nature when it comes to software publishing, distribution, and compatibility means that you could theoretically play the original *Donkey Konga* on the Wii, given a set of DK Bongos to plug into one of the GameCube ports, just as you could play *Rock Band* with the right peripherals.

Or you could go to WiiWare on the Wii Shop Channel, purchase points, and download the independent third-party games in the *Bit.Trip* series, developed by Gaijin Games. *Bit.Trip Beat*, *Bit.Trip Core*, and *Bit.Trip Void*, released in 2009, and the follow-ups in 2010, *Bit.Trip Runner* and *Bit.Trip Fate*, are art games as well, homages to a 1980s' Atari-style eight-bit aesthetic. They're also a self-consciously pared-down take on the essential elements of the rhythm game. They could be seen as differently designed and themed levels in one large game, and the playable hero-character in all of them is Commander Video, a spritelike abstraction in the eight-bit tradition of Mario himself (who was after all once named "Mr. Video"), but including graphic references to *Pitfall!*, for example. Commander Video is a tall figure with a television screen or computer monitor where his face should be. He looks a little like a Keith Haring graffiti character from the 1980s—but then everything in *Bit.Trip* invokes *something*, from dance-club videos to the psychedelic on-rail shooter, *Rez*. Commander Video runs from left to right with a rainbow trailing behind him, facing challenges on escalating levels that conclude with boss battles according to classic game structure.

In all the games, gameplay consists of rhythmically matching controller actions to a continuous sound track of beat-heavy music and abstract animated visualizations in the game. The original sound tracks in a techno-chiptune style are carefully structured to build and then release tension. *Bit.Trip* games can be hypnotic and engrossing, with their sometimes-relentless sound tracks, but they do allow for co-op mode and emphasize something crucial about music-based rhythm games: even if only one person in a room is playing them, the music can itself contribute to a social atmosphere, like having the stereo on during a party. Watching people play, taking turns, or playing in co-op mode, playing games like these remind us that what makes video games social is not necessarily the obvious things (say, multiplayer modes, online play, and the constant opportunities for communication in massively multiplayer online games). The social layer of video gaming is often invoked by more basic features such as rhythm and music, or by somatic or mimetic controllers that make players more fun to watch as they play.

The Wii as a Social Platform

Trip Hawkins, the founder of Electronic Arts and an early video game industry pioneer, has seen the Wii as the initial wake-up call to the video game business, an early warning sign in 2006 of the huge wave of online social games—exemplified by the popularity of *Mafia Wars* and *FarmVille* on Facebook—that was just about to sweep across the culture.[29] Though *FarmVille* uses Facebook for its platform of asynchronous click-based play, and the Wii encourages interactions in the shared space of the living room, both kinds of casual gaming work by tracking what the player does in different kinds of social spaces, and creating a feedback loop between those player actions and the digital games. The larger climate change to which Hawkins refers is a shift toward making gameplay more and more about that kind of loop, about forging links between game space and social space. Such links have always been part of video gameplay, across platforms. But the Wii places those links, those feedback loops with social space, at the center of attention for developers, publishers, other console makers, and players.

Jesper Juul, who, as we have said, sees the Wii and its mimetic interface as being at the center of the casual revolution, has conducted interesting Internet experiments along these lines. He shows that if you search Flickr, for example, for "*Gears of War 2*," you get pictures of in-game battles, among other things. Whereas if you search "Wii Tennis," you get a much higher percentage of pictures of people playing *Wii Sports*, moving around in their living rooms and waving their arms around.[30] The focus is on the player rather than on the screen.

We'll come back to Juul's Flickr-mining experiment later, but for now we want to look a little more closely at the idea, shared by Juul and other critics, that the Wii by design shifts the center of attention to the player's body in physical space, the living room in front of the television. Recall that Will Wright has said essentially the same, and that the Wii is all about nonimmersive gaming, in which most of "the entertainment is not happening on the screen," it's happening out in the room with your friends. And Wright compares this to other mimetic interface games (as Juul calls them), like *Guitar Hero* or *Rock* Band, in which "most of the entertainment is off the screen, it's in the social group around you."[31] Similarly, what Bart Simon has referred to as the "material imaginary" when playing the Wii foregrounds the importance of the "physical context of play," even to the point of "gestural excess," where—"*especially in social settings*"—players act out more than is necessary to actuate the controls.[32] The fact that mimetic interface games like those played on the Wii "allow players to play from the perspective of their physical presence in the real world," as Juul says, marks a shift from 3D game space to "concrete player space."[33] We would add that the related shifts in game mechanics, the setting of gameplay, and the ascendancy of certain genres and styles of play over others (namely, the rise of casual gaming) can all be seen at work in Nintendo's strategy in building as well as marketing the Wii as a platform.

When the product name was changed from Revolution to Wii in spring 2006, Nintendo issued the following statement:

> While the code-name "Revolution" expressed our direction, Wii represents the answer. . . . Wii will break down that wall that separates game players from everybody else. Wii will put people more in touch with their games . . . and each other.[34]

By now, readers of this book will be familiar with this formulation of Nintendo's blue-ocean strategy. It's about breaking down the marketing "wall" on the other side of which is "everybody else" with their money—people waiting to buy a Wii, people who don't own a PlayStation or an

Xbox, or people who have until now have only played *Tetris*, *Solitaire*, or *Bejeweled* on their PCs. Nintendo's solution is straightforward: fewer buttons/motion-sensitive controllers equals "accessibility" equals more product sold. That's certainly a driving motive of Nintendo's plan: breaking down the wall between gamers and everyone else in order to reach new, untapped markets. But it's not *only* a matter of simplifying the controls or even of rendering them more intuitive through motion-sensitive technology. It's about leveraging that technology to promote (and then exploit) kinds of gameplay that will appeal to everyone else.

The initial television campaign for the Wii, produced by Leo Burnett Company for the US market (which won an advertising industry Effie Award in 2008), opened with two Japanese men in suits, presumably Nintendo employees.[35] They show up in various locations, hold up a Wii Remote in a ceremonious gesture in two hands, like a samurai weapon, and say together, "We ['Wii'] would like to play," then bow.[36] Then, over a sound track of Japanese-flavored world music with a techno beat, we see montages of gameplay. The spots conclude with the Nintendo team putting on their dark sunglasses and driving off, literally into the sunset—which frames the Wii logo with two animated letter **i**'s that bow. In one spot the suited team arrives at a big-city high-rise, where they play *The Legend of Zelda: Twilight Princess* and *Metroid Prime 3: Corruption* with a mixed-race and mixed-gender group of three twentysomethings. (A woman stands and watches, and cheers, but never takes a turn with the controller. In other ads, however, girls and women do play.) A longer compilation ad with clips from all the other ads ends with the two suited men onstage in front of a cheering crowd, repeating the slogan loudly: "Wii would like to play!"[37]

These ads, which aired starting in November 2006, were for many US consumers their first encounter with the Wii. They depict and enact Nintendo's strategy of reaching out to a wide swath of potential players in their own living rooms. In fact, the blatant strategy of capturing the nonstereotypical market share goes a long way back at Nintendo. Peter Main, vice president of sales and marketing, was quoted in David Sheff's book *Game Over* in 1993 as saying that the company "wanted to break out from the historic video game user . . . because the thirteen-year-old boy will soon be fourteen years old and pass from our grip. Our objective from day one was to move beyond that narrow base."[38]

Yet to take Miyamoto at his word for a moment, breaking down the wall between gamers and everyone else does have other, less blatantly commercial meanings. From an artist's or a developer's point of view, the Wii's strategy for reaching new markets contains other dimensions—aesthetic, engineering, and cultural dimensions. Miyamoto himself later commented on Sheff's book (which had clearly become an issue at Nintendo), saying that the cover image of a hypnotized-looking little boy sitting in front of the screen, and what it signified about the public perception of Nintendo and gaming in general, bothered him personally, and that it ultimately lay behind the direction taken by the company that resulted in the Wii. Whereas Main worried about the zombie boy slipping from Nintendo's grip as he grew up, Miyamoto said that the picture made him want to "break out of that image" itself, to "break free of the stereotypical definition of what a gamer is, because until we do, we'll never be part of the national or worldwide culture."[39] When asked by the interviewer what he'd like the new image of the gamer to be, Miyamoto pointed to the photos being used in the company's campaign for the Wii—pictures of older people and children, a large number of them female, all standing and moving around, having active fun.

So the cover image on Sheff's book (representing what was at the heart of the 1990s' cultural panic) of the lone player, male, young, hypnotized—shot from the perspective of the television out—found its antithesis in all those Nintendo ads showing ethnically and gender-diverse groups of happy people—also shot from the television out—playing and laughing together, moving around in player space. The design strategy for the platform aimed to break down the wall between gamer culture and "worldwide culture," as Miyamoto put it, beginning with the wall between the isolated gamer and other people, including other people in the house or the room with them. The shift to player space that Juul rightly identifies is not to *the* player in isolation. It's ultimately a shift to the wider *culture*, the space of collectively constructed meanings, a social space.

This starts with a heightened self-consciousness on the player's part about what they're doing when they play, about the movements that they are making in physical space, and a recognition that the player can be observed by others in the same space while they play, that it's fun to watch one another play. Just to be clear: to some degree this is always the case on any platform and playing any kind of game. Gamers socialize by watching one another play, even when they're not playing in co-op or multiplayer modes, or in LANs. But before the Wii, this was rarely made the focus of attention, or the whole purpose of the platform as it was designed and marketed. Wii gameplay, as Nintendo imagines it, is social gameplay, *not* in the sense that *FarmVille*, for instance, is a "social game," or in the sense that multiplayer modes in traditional gaming allow for social interactions, but in a more fundamental sense. The Wii is designed to be enjoyed in a room with other people, or at least with the expectation of being observed by others, whether or not they engage with you in competitive or cooperative play. Though of course in real life people play alone or in any number of different social arrangements, it seems clear that from the point of view of Nintendo's designers, a party in the living room is the ideal setting for playing Wii games.

Remember that Nintendo began by making playing cards, those historical tokens for quintessential party games. And this aspect of the entertainment company, which includes the Laser Clay Ranges in bowling alleys, was rooted in the carnival midway or the pub. The earliest video game by the company that became a commercial venture was installed in a tavern, in a horizontal tabletop cabinet that could also hold drinks. In the later 1970s and early 1980s, playing video games was almost always something done out in public, in a social setting, showing off for other people. The arcade was a social space, and it was with this space in mind that Miyamoto designed the hit *Donkey Kong*. The Wii is just the latest attempt by Nintendo to bring a version of this kind of social gaming into the living room, closer to arcade parties and karaoke than to, say, bouts of online multiplayer military simulations.

This is the background for the Wii no Ma Channel (including its incorporation of the marketing Miis) and the wider effort to create a playful social space in the family living room. Its design as a party console is reflected even in the simplified casual online play of games like *Mario Kart Wii*, or the design of *WarioWare: Smooth Moves*, with its fast-moving microgames, or *Wii Party*, an explicit manifestation of the Wii's social aims that builds on the example of the *Mario Party* franchise, but in the new context provided by the Wii. *Wii Party* contains eighty minigames, some of which—especially the group called House Party games—make use of the Wii Remote's built-in speaker and rumble effect for the "time bomb" passing game, one that matches animals on-screen with sounds emitted from different Wii Remotes in people's hands, and a hide-and-seek game in which you rely on its sound to find a hidden controller. These minigames turn the Wii Remote into a physical game token reminiscent of the mechanical game tokens of 1960s' and 1970s' games, such as the windup ticking plastic objects of Milton Bradley's *Time Bomb* and *Spudsie* the hot potato. (The time bomb depicted on-screen in the Wii game even looks like the old plastic *Time Bomb* object.) In this way we see that the Wii Remote is not only a game controller, it's a game *object* that mediates between players and shapes what happens in the physical space in which they interact socially, around the game, at its prompting. As the copy accompanying the House Party games says, "These use your living room as part of the fun!" *Wii Party* exaggerates this aspect of the system, its role as an excuse for social interaction out in physical space, which is also evident in different ways across all sorts of Wii games.

The Wii's most characteristic games have been social games in that precise and delimited sense. In terms of design, they are living room games closer to *Twister* than to *Call of Duty*. In both *Twister* and *Wii Sports* you use a pointer device of sorts, people take turns moving, and the rules and simplified mediating objects or tokens are designed to help players lose their inhibitions as their bodies contort in a fun social setting—and so become less self-conscious.[40] A big part of the fun in either game is watching each other play and even having chance physical encounters. The game running on the console provides a pretext for such interactions. Remember Juul's Flickr experiment, in which searching Flickr images for "Wii Tennis"—rather than, say, "*Gears of War 2*"—produces pictures of people playing Wii Tennis, not their Mii avatars in the game space. Partly this is not surprising; it's usually less interesting to photograph somebody on the couch holding a control pad and executing a difficult button combination.

But look again at the specific results of our own attempt to replicate his Flickr search.[41] They point to some areas in common between hardcore and Wii games, and allow us to see what the Wii does to emphasize its precise differences within that range of general similarities. The search results for "*Gears of War 2*" don't include as many images of the immersive 3D game world, as many in-game screenshots, as you might expect. They reveal other kinds of images: box art, for example; packaging and Zune tie-in promotions; an odd marketing campaign out in the streets of Hong Kong with bikini-clad women wearing game-art body paint; Lego figures posed in scenes from the game (of course); collectible action figures and other game-related objects; people posing with their collectible objects, including plastic replicas of Lancer assault rifles with chainsaw attachments. All of these are instances of the stuff, the paraphernalia, that everyone knows goes with a good deal of even hard-core gaming.

If the pictures of people playing Wii Tennis are pictures of player space, and in-game screenshots are images of game space, then what can we say about a picture of a hard-core fan holding up a replica weapon, with the *Gears of War* box at their feet? We would suggest that they occupy what we might think of as fan space, and fan space is a kind of *social* space. All of these activities, packages, art, and collectibles in fan space, the universe of objects radiating out from a game, are analogous to what textual theorist Gerard Genette has called the paratext. In the case of book-based texts, the paratext consists of the prefaces, acknowledgments, notes, and even (under the subcategory of "peritext") the book's binding, paper, cover, and—extending out to what Genette labels the "epitext"—the advertisements, posters, author interviews, and publisher's marketing, all of which frame the text for the reader and shape its reception.[42]

The theory of the paratext is a way to describe the "wrappers" or layers of media and prompted social interactions by which texts are conveyed to the world as well as experienced. *Context* is what's given in the culture, but *paratext* is the outer edge of the text that interfaces with the given context, forming a "threshold" to the text, or a transitional space between the text and the world that shapes the reception of the text along with how readers approach and judge it. A book appears, is published, in a particular time and place (which provides part of its context). But *how* it's published—including how it's embodied and presented, announced and marketed—determines the parts of the context that will actually come into play as readers encounter the book. Paratext is the threshold or border between the book and its aura—all the paraphernalia of publishing that surrounds it—and the wider culture that forms the context for the book's reception and interpretation.

According to this analogy, we can quickly identify some basic paratextual features of video games: the box art and included operation manual, say, or even the Entertainment Software Rating Board's rating printed on the box—a giant E, T, or M—all features that bridge from the game to the player or critic, shaping expectations of everything from which players are likely to buy the game, to players' reactions to the purchase, their responses (which might be captured on video) during the initial unpacking of the optical disc that conveys the creative work (by way of the software burned on it), to how the game is displayed on a retail store's shelf (or how it appears as a thumbnail graphic online). Closer to the "inside" of the game, some paratexts are even built in to the game's code—for example, in the boot and log-in screens, opening music, or even the layered animated logos that signify studio, developer, and publisher, as you make your way into the actual start screen.

But the distinctions get a little more complicated as we imagine moving in the other direction, outward in concentric circles from the game itself to its outer paratextual "wrappers." Some of these features are part of marketing, and some are part of the game's cultural reception. And many are both. The "outer" paratext or epitext clearly consists of the online review sites, help pages, boards and forums, collectibles, and fan art Web sites. Yet what about third-party shells for controllers, a plastic inflatable go-kart, say, or what about machinima movies made using the game engine and assets, or user-generated levels, or game mods? How do these paratextual (epitextual) objects count in relation to the primary object, the "game itself"? Where does that game itself begin and end, anyway? With what's on the screen? Or in the code that users don't see? What about updates received online after purchase or expansion packs? Paratext is a shifting and uncertain threshold, a dynamic and often-concealed border. We believe, though, that it's where things get interesting, because it's where the meanings of games are made.

The point is not to force the term paratext to fit the case of video games in any precise or rigorous way. Still, we contend that Genette's concept offers a way to think about how the value and meaning of video games can't be restricted to just one layer of signification, analogous to the "text itself," whether that's the ROM, the code, what can be seen on the screen, or some other rigid idea of the game itself. The meaning of video games is *made*, constructed socially, at the places where the game crosses boundaries of hardware, software, and unpredictable player interactions, but most of all by repeated acts of play—which means that other, epitextual activities (those outside the game itself) always figure in, activities *out in social space*. Fans know this, whether or not they think about it in these theoretical terms. They inhabit a social space built from and around the cultural expressions they love, an ever-expanding series of thresholds, ripples spreading out from a cultural object or its franchise, its "universe."

A successful game or platform spawns its own "wider culture," extrudes its own paratext as it makes its way through the world. Paratext is an inherently cultural and social phenomenon. It's a series of transactions between creative works and the people who receive it, among multiple such people, across groups and institutions. All games and game platforms are social in this sense: they're designed to provoke those social transactions—starting with somebody actually playing the game, in the living room (or wherever), but including, potentially, other people watching and commenting on the gameplay as well as paratextual objects that prepare and extend those transactions—collectibles, coffee-table art books, blog reviews, and discussion boards, and also hacks, mods, machinima, and gameplay videos. That's what we're watching in the video with which this chapter began of the group of friends playing *Wii Sports* in an empty movie theater: paratext at work, the ongoing reception of the Wii as a social platform.

In his now-famous talk at the Design, Innovate, Communicate, Entertain summit in 2010, designer and former Disney imagineer Jesse Schell described a trend: that games and other media were everywhere "busting through to reality." For him, this is a phenomenon that includes the Wii but culminates in online social games like *FarmVille*, which are played with "real friends—the friends that you have already established as a part of your social network." This is part of a larger trend in which games are leaking out into the real world and inserting themselves into people's everyday experience. In the talk, Schell extrapolates this into a pretty dystopian vision of the future that's only just beginning, where pervasive computing and pervasive marketing blend with games in ways that sound frankly Orwellian (or Huxleian).[43]

In a later interview he labeled this the "gamepocalypse," and it was much discussed online under the label of "gamification." But this is to some degree because the marketers are starting to exploit those features of gaming and distributed systems that have been emerging for a decade or more, and that grew out of video game culture: live-action role-playing, costume role-playing, alternate reality games, locative art, augmented reality and geocaching, and Foursquare and Gowalla. Fictive worlds from game-based models have been overlaid onto the physical and social worlds in all sorts of playful, serious, and sometimes-ominous ways. Much of this emerges out of game culture, because games have always been about drawing magic circles—then playing at the edge of them, more like throwing marbles than putting on a play. Schell acknowledges that "the idea of the single-player video game is a weird anomaly."

> If you look at the history of games going back thousands of years, those games are multiplayer 99 percent of the time. You might have Solitaire, but most of the time games are about connecting with other people. Computer technology of 20 or 30 years ago didn't really permit that, so there was no choice but to have single-player games. I think the single-player thing is a bit of a blip on the history of games.[44]

The history of video games, even including single-player video games, is more social than the clichés would allow.

Understanding the social nature of games and game platforms requires that we understand the permeable boundary between what's inside and what's outside the game. Like other critics, Alexander R. Galloway has applied the notions of *diegetic* versus *nondiegetic* elements to video games. These terms come from film theory and narrative theory, where diegetic space is the space of narrative or story (from the Greek word *diegesis*, "to narrate"), and nondiegetic space includes the formal devices that are part of a film, say, but not directly part of its story—such as the musical score, or the titles and credits. Fair enough. But Galloway also usefully makes room in his theory for "gamic elements that are inside the total gamic apparatus yet outside the portion of the apparatus that constitutes a pretend world of character or story"—which is to say, the nondiegetic elements, such as the player or "operator" setting up or configuring the game.[45]

In the end, Galloway realizes that despite the schematic relationships that his terms imply, diegetic and nondiegetic elements actually coexist along a complicated continuum, and it's not always easy to define the difference between them. He acknowledges, for example, that "nondiegetic elements are often centrally connected to the act of gameplay," that in fact "the nondiegetic is much more common in gameplay than in film or literature," and admits that ultimately "in some instances it will be difficult to demarcate the difference between diegetic and nondiegetic acts in a video game, for the process of good game continuity is to fuse these acts together as seamlessly as possible."[46]

Precisely so; and in fact, we would go further and say that video games are normally played *at the border between* diegetic and nondiegetic spaces. This is never clearer than when you are playing a multiplayer game or a game with a mimetic interface like the Wii's. But almost all video games have an important social dimension in this sense, because almost all video games are played at the paratextual threshold between the fictive game world and player operations, the border between diegetic and nondiegetic spaces, the boundary of text and paratext. Skilled gamers have always been adept at moving from Hyrule to the health meter to the Z button and back again. They have also frequently negotiated the border between actual social space (in the living room) and the make-believe worlds (game spaces) in which they're engaged, whether ghost-filled mazes, space stations, or WuHu Island. A network of displays, haptics, controllers, and channels of communication has always linked game space to the physical and social worlds. That's what a console-based platform is, in the end—that series of links or transactional objects that mediate between player and game. What the Wii has done so impressively is to make that threshold space, that transactional space, the main focus of its system and the focus of the best games for its system. This means actively embracing the idea that when it comes to gameplay, the center of the action is paratextual, and the paratextual is inherently social.

Platform is an abstraction, in part a dynamic function of the circumstances of the company that builds and markets it, the environment constructed and inhabited by competing systems, available software developers, existing fan culture, and game history—the whole complex of determining factors that give the Nintendo Wii, for example, a special kind of social or cultural aura, makes it more than the sum of its parts. Ultimately, this constructed cultural aura, which is a function of so many external factors, cannot be separated from the more tangible components of the platform. Any successful platform has a social or cultural layer, starting with the behaviors and expectations of its user base. This social layer of a video game platform is an essential part of what the system means, because it's the environment in which the platform gets used. It determines the way that users perceive the platform and what it means to them. Thus, in many subtle as well as some obvious ways, the social layer helps determine the meanings of the expressive works—the games and other software—that get created for and run on the platform. That's what we mean when we say that platform is a social phenomenon.

At the Los Angeles, E3 2010 conference, June 13, 2010, in what seemed at first like a deliberate postmodern parody of a "media circus," Microsoft deployed acrobats from the Cirque du Soleil troupe to help introduce its new controller-free motion-sensitive device, Kinect (formerly code-named Project Natal) at a theatrical kick-off event, the Project Natal Experience. The voice-over was over the top: "History is about to be rewritten. . . . Human beings will be at the center, and the machine will be the one that adapts. Might the next step be an absence of an object? Is the future of humanity . . . humanity itself?"[1] High above the giant room, suspended from the ceiling, actors played a family sitting on a living room couch, watching the event as if it were on their television. One child actor climbed a rocky slope to stand on a huge Xbox logo ball and interact with a giant screen, where a cartoon avatar imitated their gestures. Then the screen slid open to reveal a living room with a family waiting on the couch. The whole set rotated until it was upside down. Brief demos of games followed on the screen, as players' avatars responded to their movements. They played through a list of noticeably Wii-like games: sports, racing, adventure sports, and a hip-hop dance game by Harmonix (the answer to *Just Dance*), a brief preview of a LucasArts *Star Wars* game involving light-saber battles.

The Kinect was released in November 2010, sold separately for Xbox 360 or bundled with a new smaller, more elegant Xbox Slim. The symbolism of the E3 event was clearly based on Nintendo's own previous four years of marketing for the Wii—an impression only reinforced the next day at Microsoft's press conference. The press conference included descriptions of the Kinect interface as "controller-free, simpler," and "what happens when technology gets out of your way," but also significantly, "more social than ever before," and its accessibility was stressed: "entertainment that everyone can enjoy."[2] Later, the Microsoft Kinect Web site contained catchphrases such as "No controllers, just you," and "you are the controller."[3] At E3, some attendees arrived in their hotel rooms to find Kinect ads stuck to the bathroom mirrors, reading: "14 buttons replaced by your body."[4] The emphasis was on the player—"the people playing, they're the stars of our games"—and just as it had been at the glitzy show, the press conference and advertising stressed the social space of the living room: "Kinect brings your living room to life," and "This is your living room, more social than ever."[5] The lessons of the Wii had clearly been communicated: new casual consoles should shift attention to player space, the social space of the physical living room.

The central symbol of the circus performance was the couch, hanging from the ceiling and framed by the square proscenium of the main stage. The most symbolic moment at the event may have been the hall's entryway, which apparently forced developers and journalists attending to pass through optical-illusion portals into sets designed to represent a family living room, where actors were playing parents and kids playing with Kinect:

> Through a window, we were face-to-face with a Latino family—mom, dad, big brother, and little sister—who were sitting in a small mock living room staring at us. They started pointing excitedly and greeting us, beckoning us to step through the window. Entering the window into their living room, we wheeled around and noticed that we'd just popped out of their TV set. They ushered us onto the theater floor.[6]

The same day, an initial trailer was released on the Internet, set in what looks like a spacious upper-middle-class living room (it would later be made clear that a very large, cleared-out space in front of the television was necessary to play Kinect). A family sits or stands in front of a symbolic blazing hearth beside, in turn, the electronic hearth: a large screen television. Two at a time, they take turns competing in racing and dancing games, while other family members on the couch or floor cheer them on ("Good job, Mom!").[7] Obviously derived from the "Wii Would Like to Play" ads, this campaign for the Kinect also fits into a longer-term campaign by Microsoft. Bill Gates had declared years before, speaking of the Xbox, that it was a "general purpose computer" and that "it was about strategically being in the living room."[8]

Turning the Blue Ocean Red

The Kinect debut at E3 opened a three-way competition with Nintendo and Sony for market share in the motion-control arena. With the radical decision to forego controllers altogether, Microsoft moved aggressively into Nintendo's blue-ocean market space, aiming to capture a segment of the new casual demographic. It's as if one of the larger dinosaurs (to use Miyamoto's metaphor) decided to turn the tables, and compete in the wider niche that the small and nimble dinosaur had been dominating. In the process, Microsoft (along with Sony, perhaps to a less significant degree, in terms of its differences from the Wii) has joined Nintendo in redefining game platforms for this generation (or, in the case of Xbox and PlayStation, half-generation) of consoles. In reaction to the "controller-free" rhetoric, for example, both Sony and Nintendo stressed in their presentations at E3 that their controllers still had buttons. And when Miyamoto himself came out on the stage later in the week to demo *The Legend of Zelda: Skyward Sword*, his two-handed use of the Wii Remote and Nunchuk, to wield both shield and sword or a bow and arrow, for the first time looked oddly normal, quaintly like a standard video game control system. The context of the mimetic interface revolution had shifted.

While Microsoft took the spotlight at E3 for its new console technology and extravagant show, Nintendo shifted its focus to the portable hand-held successor to the DSi, the 3DS, and a range of new software titles for it and the Wii. Everything about Kinect was big, so Nintendo concentrated on the small, while at the same time aligning itself to compete with Sony for the claim that it offered a 3D experience, except in this case it was without special glasses. Nintendo's 3DS was in one sense an answer to the critics of the Wii's graphics capability. On the 3.5-inch screen, using 3D technology based on a parallax barrier stereoscopic image LCD and with a *proportionately* powerful processor, the 3DS can claim to be a kind of mini HD system—HD in your hand. It has two screens, and the lower one is a touch-sensitive controller for the upper display. A slider switch allows the user to adjust or turn off the 3D view. It contains the same kind of accelerometer and gyroscope combination as the Wii, allowing for motion-sensitive games. It has two cameras, facing out and back, with which users can take their own 3D pictures or capture the surrounding environment so that it can be combined with characters and objects in augmented reality games. (In this way, the 3DS extends the design ethos of the Wii to shift attention to the living room and player space as the site of game play.) It includes a WiFi connection for downloading content from the eShop (like the Wii's Virtual Console) and Web browsing, and to allow for the sharing of some content with other 3DS users when in Street Pass mode. It has a new and improved Mii creator, and can show downloaded 3D videos as well as play games from game cards. In general, Nintendo has positioned the device as the logical follow-on to the Wii. One reviewer noted that "Nintendo's success in making 3D work without glasses in an easy-to-use, immediately accessible fashion is a triumph akin to how the Wii reshaped home gaming by rethinking what a game controller is, how it functions and who might be able to use it."[9]

Presenting the handheld at the E3 press conference with his characteristic gesture (holding it aloft in one hand), Iwata emphasized its purpose as a "mass-market device." Compared to the Wii, which must be hooked up to whatever television set the user owns, the 3DS comes with its own screen and thus offers programmers guaranteed control of the display, so, as Miyamoto pointed out at a developers' roundtable at E3 2010, "everyone has the same setup, the same 3D screen. Developers can work around that set 3D spec."[10] Another crucial factor is the burgeoning market for tablets and smartphones as mobile gaming platforms. In an interview on October 21, 2010, with a reporter blogging for *Forbes*, Nintendo of America's President Fils-Aime admitted that "in the near term," Apple could "hurt" Nintendo more than Microsoft, clearly thinking of the competition provided by the iPhone, the iPad, and perhaps more significantly, the App Store.[11] As if in response to that latter threat, Fils-Aime claimed that Nintendo's competitive edge in the mobile gaming market will come from its deep catalog of software. As with any Nintendo platform, the company's own software is the primary given in the case of the 3DS, providing major goals and determining constraints of the system's design, as well as a selling point well beyond the system's initial release—since promised titles are in effect virtual or potential benefits of the platform even before they are actually made available. Consumers are likely to buy the 3DS on the basis of the promise of Mario and Zelda titles, for example, which may take months or years to appear.

Any game platform develops in stepwise fashion, with software and hardware emerging in relation to one another. The software announced for the 3DS at E3 2010 included a new version of the hit virtual-pet game *Nintendogs*, now with cats—which looked especially diminutive after Microsoft's large-screen demo of *Kinectimals*, but also looked, in a way, reassuringly tested, both in terms of technology and market. The 3DS actually benefited in general by seeming compact and manageable, less a revolutionary replacement and more a logical successor to a successful handheld line, more likely to provide recognizable forms of entertainment. The 3DS was repeatedly presented in the initial publicity as literally *tangible*—it has a touchscreen, and you hold it in your hands to view it— something Kinect was specifically designed *not* to be. When you wanted to pet your *Nintendog* cat, you touched its image right there on the screen, rather than, as with *Kinectimals*, gesturing at a distance in thin air. The list of 3DS software also included *Animal Crossing*; versions of *Star Fox 64*, *Mario Kart*, and *Paper Mario*; numerous third-party games including hard-core titles such as *Resident Evil: Revelations*, a *Final Fantasy* game, and *Assassin's Creed: Lost Legacy*.

The most enthusiastic reaction by the crowd, though, may have been to the trailer for Nintendo's own *Kid Icarus: Uprising*. This is a new version, with newly impressive 3D graphics, of a 1986 platformer for the NES about an angel named Pit. The eight-bit original is already available in emulation on the Virtual Console, and a portable game, *Of Myths and Monsters*, was published for the Game Boy in 1991. The new game for the 3DS was clearly an appeal to nostalgia among the Nintendo fan base. After a few years of promoting the idea of revolution, Nintendo turned to the 3DS— which is actually a solid and tested *kind* of platform, despite the publicity touting its use of a new display technology—and fell back on the depth of its catalog and the cultural resonance provided by its storied franchises.

A Software Phase

This retrenchment was even more apparent in the Wii's case. For whatever reason, the Vitality Sensor, which had been recognized by the American Heart Association earlier in the year in a carefully planned public relations announcement, was nowhere to be seen at E3 2010. After the conference, Nintendo of America's Cammie Dunaway responded to questions about it in this way:

> We're continuing to work on the Vitality Sensor. As we thought about what we wanted to bring to E3, we realized we had a really packed agenda. We also thought about the atmosphere at E3 which is noisy and adrenaline-filled, and loud and stressful, and it just didn't seem like the best environment to introduce a product that's really about relaxing, so we decided we'd think about other venues that would be more appropriate.[12]

In the same interview, she articulated Nintendo's post-Revolution strategy, saying that "you have to have great and innovative technology, but it has to be paired with best-in-class game design. I think Zelda is the absolute definitive proof point," and stressed the "very large install base in the U.S. . . . close to 29 million units of Wii sold."[13] With the speculative console that became the Wii U at that point still a year in the future, and its place in effect having been temporarily held by the 3DS, Nintendo focused on a software list for the Wii calculated to play to a sense of history. At the E3 press conference, Fils-Aime remarked that the conference had seen plenty of talk about "button control, motion control, and"—smiling— "no controller at all." But, he said, "technology is only a tool. . . . [T]he thing that matters is an experience." After several years of emphasizing the role of revolutionary technology in creating that experience, the company shifted gears in 2010 to concentrate on software's role.

For Nintendo fans, one big announcement was for the adventure-action title, *The Legend of Zelda: Skyward Sword*. Long anticipated, the game was shown in a playable state, but its release date was pushed off to 2011 (our own descriptions here are therefore based on the demos, trailers, and reports by journalists). This is the first new Zelda game fully designed for the Wii, since *Twilight Princess* had been originally started for the Game-Cube and ported to the Wii late in its development.

Second only to Mario in iconic status in Nintendo's catalog, the Zelda franchise is Miyamoto's other great contribution to video game history. The Kingdom of Hyrule is the original game world as "miniature garden," to again cite Miyamoto's favorite metaphor. Writer Tom Bissell has compared the "impressively open-ended gameworld" of *The Legend of Zelda: Ocarina of Time* in particular (1998, for the Nintendo 64) to later open-world or sandbox games like those in the *Grand Theft Auto* series; Hyrule offered the player a similar sense of extensive freedom, and was "ingenious, fun, and beautiful." Bissell's book *Extra Lives* is an interesting case study actually—a strange kind of confessional autobiography about his obsession with gaming. In it he also contrasts Zelda's appeal to the "hairlessly innocent parts of [his] imagination" with his later cocaine-enhanced experiences with *Grand Theft Auto: Vice City*, for example, evincing the kind of deep-seated nostalgia that many older core gamers still feel for Nintendo classics.[14]

This is the kind of loaded context into which any new game in the Zelda series is introduced—a complex emotional identification with multiple generations of a franchise across several different platforms, which adds up over time to a sense of the Zelda universe. It was deliberately triggered by the trailer introducing the game, in which ghostlike Links from previous games ride (on horseback) sail (in a ship) and leap forward (as a wolf) into the image of the new game's version of the hero, who stands calmly and unsheathes his sword. Ensuring the proper succession of games in a long-loved franchise is always important to dedicated fans.

Imagery like this is a kind of ritual pageant, meant to reassure and establish the lineage of the new installment. In the same spirit, Miyamoto himself came onstage (after appearing first on the large video screen) to demonstrate *Skyward Sword*.

In terms of story, it's a deep prequel that recounts the origin of the famous Master Sword, just as fans had speculated when preview artwork of a personified sword-figure made its way on to the Web a year earlier. The Skyward Sword of the title guides Link in the new game and is eventually transformed into the Master Sword. The artwork is subtly different from previous games in the series, based more on the look of impressionist paintings, according to Miyamoto and confirmed by those who played the demo. Earlier titles in the franchise had a cel-shaded cartoon look, and some had speculated that this new game might go in that direction again, given the graphics limitations of the Wii. The softer-focus painterly graphics, especially for the many scenes of the sky, may be an alternative design solution toward addressing the same limitations.

Several key design decisions have been made based on the Wii's specific affordances and constraints. Link is right-handed, of course, as he has been since *Twilight Princess*, when the use of the Wii Remote instead of only button controls made the statistically more common choice of right hand for sword hand necessary for the first time, altering the famously left-handed hero. You play with two hands, the shield controlled by the Nunchuk and the sword by the Wii Remote, and you can use the shield to volley shots back to enemies, not only for protection during melee battles. The swordplay takes advantage of the MotionPlus attachment, just as *Red Steel 2* does, for instance. The Deku Babas, the giant Venus-Flytrap monsters that you encounter in the game, have been designed to open their mouths either vertically or horizontally, and since MotionPlus affords the possibility of measuring the difference, you have to match the direction of the open mouth as you swing your sword in order to kill them. When you hold the sword (by holding the Wii Remote) pointed straight up, it charges with the power of heaven and can shoot lightning bolts. You can shake either controller to produce a weapon: sword, shield, slingshot, whip, or bow and arrow. With some refinements, the bow and arrow works more or less the way it does in *Wii Sports Resort*. Bombs can now be dropped or "bowled" using the same arm motion as in Wii Bowling. The weapons are accessible using the Wii Remote to call up a radial menu of items that appears in a heads-up display, superimposed on the gameplay screen. In his demo, Miyamoto characterized this feature as a way to imagine that you're reaching in your pocket for the next implement.

During the press conference, when it came time to demonstrate the bow and arrow, Miyamoto found his controllers lagging and breaking contact with the game. He blamed the glitch on wireless interference, probably accurately, since this was a problem faced earlier the same year during high-profile tech demos by Steve Jobs at Apple and at a Google demonstration of its Internet television, due to the recent increase in the use of "MiFi" personal wireless devices among those attending the presentations. Yet the glitch serves as an interesting reminder of how dependent new game platforms are becoming on networking communications protocols, and how much any modern computing platform is likely to depend on a distributed model to one degree or another outside any given device. The network—whatever technical form it takes—is becoming a vital component in game platforms. As the wireless failures at these demos remind us, this goes beyond any specific design for user interactions or online modes of play to the matter of basic infrastructure.

Another important demo at the same press conference reinforced the appeal to nostalgia, taking the cultural associations to levels rarely seen even in the highly allusive world of video games. *Disney Epic Mickey* is an exclusive title for the Wii developed by respected game designer Warren Spector and Junction Studios (now part of Disney Interactive Studios), in collaboration with Disney and Pixar. Spector is a designer with "core" credibility, best known for the dark cyberpunk hybrid FPS-RPG series, *Deus Ex* (2000, 2003).[15] But he has an interesting background, which includes a graduate degree in film and communications, and before his earliest work on games, he did a brief stint as an archivist in the David O. Selznick Collection of the Harry Ransom research library at the University of Texas. One of the earliest games he worked on was *Toon: The Cartoon RPG* (Steve Jackson Games, 1984), in which you play as a cartoon character who's a close parody of an actual classic cartoon. Spector's sense of film history, cartoon art as well as the role of imitation, parody, and reconstruction in dealing with cartoon-based intellectual properties all read like qualifications for the job of developing a modern action-adventure game based on the world's most famous eighty-year-old cartoon-mouse movie star.

The issues of Disney aesthetics and values, the squeaky-clean image promoted for later incarnations of the mouse, the company's history when it comes to intellectual property battles, and the social politics surrounding Walt Disney and the company he founded make the context for this project especially complicated. Early public expectations were that Spector would bring a steampunk aesthetic to the character, "darkening" Mickey Mouse in keeping with the kind of FPS and RPG games he had produced before. Early concept art encouraged this notion. Though this has been borne out to some degree in the released game, the result was bound to look disappointingly conventional to some.

The game's overall plan is based on deepening the context for the mouse as action-adventure hero. The story takes place in Wasteland, which basically is a world of discarded, forgotten Disney intellectual properties—characters, sets, films, and old theme park rides—all held under a spell and threatened by a Phantom Blot, by way of Oswald the Lucky Rabbit, who was in real life Walt Disney's first creation before Mickey Mouse, but for whom he lost intellectual property rights. Oswald is jealous of Mickey's fame and lives a twisted shadow existence in Wasteland, accompanied by a series of uncanny copies of Disney characters that were Mickey's friends, Donald Duck and Goofy, as well as the Beetleworx, dark cyborg versions of Mickey's fellow cartoons. Mickey meddles with the Sorcerer's created world (as in *Fantasia*), then enters Wasteland, climbing through a mirror like Alice through the looking glass, and has to stop the Phantom Blot in order to save the world, in part by regaining the trust of Oswald, his lost half brother.

It's all heavily metanarrative, a dark version of Disney lore, with precedent in various actual cartoons, including in the famous short from a competing studio, Warner Brothers, *Duck Amuck*, the feature film *Who Framed Roger Rabbit?*, and more directly the previous video game series, Square Enix's *Kingdom Hearts*, a critically successful mashup combining Disney worlds and characters with the characters of the Japanese *Final Fantasy* series. Spector has said that the core mechanic of the game is about the essence of cartoon being: ink or paint. You play as Mickey, and use a paintbrush and paint thinner to either bring objects into being or dissolve them, so the 3D platformer action involves literally shaping the game world—both positively and negatively—as you play. These actions have consequences in the story as well, so that "play style matters," as Spector likes to put it.[16] This kind of divergence or split is manifest in the game world, too, where there are varying "states of matter," colorful painted objects that you can affect with your brush and thinner along with dark and sharp inert objects that you cannot affect. In a corresponding way, you can choose to play Mickey (also after all an object in the game world) in varying states of character, from "hero" (more like the late Mickey that Spector calls "mom-friendly") to "scrapper" (more like the mischievous Mickey of the early black-and-white cartoons), or a hybrid of the two, and his appearance will vary slightly based on the choice.[17] The range of styles in this one game in some ways mirrors the different styles of play implicit in the spectrum of hardcore to casual gaming, one end of which the Wii has helped to define. It's as if the game were designed to grapple with the perceived contradictions inherent in the whole situation of Warren Spector's making a Disney game exclusively for the Wii.

Play style, states of matter of objects in the game, and character style become interrelated variables affecting diegetic events as well as the form and appearance of the game world itself. Mixtures of genre are part of the overall experience, since the game is basically an action-adventure game with RPG elements and 3D platformer architecture. Old-fashioned movie screens serve as portals that take you between levels, by way of playable transitions, 2D platformers based directly on early black-and-white Disney cartoons such as *Steamboat Willy*.

There are some clear resemblances between the platformer gameplay and, say, *Super Mario Galaxy*, since in both games diminutive, plucky, cartoon heroes with squeaky voices run and jump across vast landscapes. Of course, this is no accident, since Mickey Mouse was surely among Miyamoto's inspirations for Mario in the first place, especially the later 3D Mario, with his rounded torso and limbs along with white gloves. This character kinship serves as an index to the larger connections between Nintendo and Miyamoto, and Nintendo and Disney Corporation—the first major licensing agreement that Nintendo signed was to make Japanese playing cards with Mickey Mouse and other Disney characters printed on them—all of which would seem to make the game a natural for the Wii.[18] Still, development began first for other platforms, including the PC, but when faced with porting it to the Wii, Spector demurred, worried about not giving the system its due in a mere port, and this led eventually to simply making the game a Wii exclusive. Spector's own comments have stressed the connections on various levels—cultural, marketing, and technology—that he believes make the Wii the right platform for the game.

> Nintendo, like Disney, is all about reaching a broad audience of gamers, nongamers, kids, adults: the Wii is popular with all of those. I also like the idea of Mickey and Mario and Link together on the same platform—at least virtually. And if I was going to take a break from realistic stealthy shooter RPGs, why not go someplace where color and cartooniness are the norm rather than the exception? Finally, once you start talking about a game that involves painting and erasing and such, the Wii Remote and Nunchuk just seemed like a good fit.[19]

These remarks touch on all the basic premises of platform studies, including how much cultural factors and other intangibles matter in accounting for the relationship of platform to creative work. This particular creative

work, *Disney Epic Mickey*, was in the end developed for the Wii as a platform because:

- The technology of the mimetic interface, the Wii Remote, afforded
the intuitive gestures of painting and erasing that matched the core
game mechanic
- The general style of art associated with the platform—in part for
reasons of the affordances and constraints of its processors and
other technology—is compatible with the game's own "color and
cartooniness"
- The other games and franchises associated with and playable on the
platform are compatible in terms of the diegetic elements of character, story, and genre (Mario and Link belong together with Mickey
Mouse)
- The perceived audience for the platform, both its installed base and
potential demographic reach, seems "right" for the new game:
"Nintendo, like Disney, is all about reaching a broad audience of
gamers, nongamers, kids, adults."

Undoubtedly, platform studies must attend to direct connections
between hardware, software, and creative work. But we believe, as we have
tried to illustrate throughout this book, that even the most obviously
material of these connections are ultimately matters of social, cultural,
and economic factors. Some of these factors affect platform via marketing,
or socially, by way of the reaction of players and fans. Attending to these
factors is part of the job of platform studies, just as book history or the
history of material texts must attend to matters of readership or audience
and genre, ideas of the "literary," or the social class of readers when it
comes to certain kinds of poems, plays, or novels. Ultimately, this is the
premise behind our claim throughout this book that platform is a social
phenomenon.

It might seem as if attention to these social factors would risk dema-
terializing the idea of platform, dissolving it in the stew of cultural theory
the way that an object is dissolved by paint thinner in *Disney Epic Mickey*.
On the contrary, we think it's a necessary way to acknowledge that platform spans *multiple* materialities—from microchips to social institutions.
They're all material, and they all matter. As a platform, a video game
console is a computing-based foundation for running games, but it's also
an example of industrial design, a consumer product, a generator of
expectations as well as a media system that mediates between the various

layers of hardware, code, interface, game, the screen, the player's body, the peripherals, the living room, the invisible networks of communication technologies and the larger network, and the world.

Platforms emerge, evolve, and sometimes disappear from common use over time. Any understanding of the life cycle of a platform must take into account its development after release, and the significance of the development of software for the platform, from launch to the transition to a new platform (which may entail ports, or even more radical forms of redesign and recoding) later in the life cycle. As we write, the Wii's successor, the Wii U, has just been unveiled and the original Wii is fast approaching the traditional five-year limit of a game system's life cycle. The 3DS, released in 2010, has served as a bridge to the new console, as well as a shift by Nintendo into the mobile market. At this interesting moment in the life cycle of the three platforms—Wii, 3DS, and Wii U—under the pressure brought by the new motion-control competition, Nintendo has paid increased public attention to its software, including the appeal of that software to the nostalgia of its core fans.

Another example of this software phase is the James Bond game, *GoldenEye 007* for the Wii—a resuscitation of what many consider the most important FPS of its generation, *GoldenEye 007* for the Nintendo 64. Yet another is *Metroid: Other M*, the new installment of the science-fiction shooter franchise with a solid place in video game history, in part because of its female hero, Samus Aran (whose alien DNA and cybernetic Power Suit worked to conceal her sex for most of the first game). Or the colorful *Kirby's Epic Yarn*, which exhibits the kind of artwork and central conceit associated with independent games on WiiWare (the game world of this mostly 2D scroller looks entirely made of fabric, and threading, sewing, scrunching up, and unraveling become core mechanics), and combines that artwork with the cultural capital of yet another well-loved Nintendo franchise.

Viewed in a wider context, this shift to software is part of the normal staged development of game platforms, which emerge not with hardware and software all at once together (except for some strategic launch titles) but rather in a kind of spiraling double helix. No matter how early the SDKs ship, the greatest production of software titles has to wait for some testing and familiarity with a new console in the actual market—and this is bound to be exaggerated in the case of any truly new developments in hardware or controller system, like the motion control introduced by Nintendo in 2006. The case of the two *Red Steel* games illustrates this. The distance traveled between the first and second games is the story of an upgrade to the platform's technology (Wii MotionPlus) as well as the developer's learning over time to work within the constraints and with the affordances of the new system. Complicated schedules of various kinds affect all the agents involved, which are sometimes large institutions, corporations, and teams involved in producing and publishing games, and producing and marketing the platforms on which they run. The overall impact of a platform on the wider culture is dependent on all these complexly interrelated schedules of invention, development, emergence, and then convergence with software.

Emerging and Converging Technologies

It might be a good idea at this point to remember that the history of computing in general can be understood as the interrelation of emerging and converging technologies. *Emerging technologies* are those that represent new and significant developments in the field. *Converging technologies* represent sets of previously distinct ideas that in some way are moving to stronger interconnection and similar goals. Both are moments, as it were, in the longer process of technological innovation and change. The most basic technology bears this out.

Consider the wheel. It may have been invented in multiple places simultaneously and is an ancient device. Wherever it first appeared, it could be considered an emerging technology, and played a significant role in agriculture and military applications, transporting implements and weapons. (A novel by Emily Barton, *The Testament of Yves Gundron*, imagines the emergence of the wheel and horse-drawn plow in an accidentally isolated community in the twentieth century—and the radical social consequences of this emergence.) Many centuries later, the wheel converged in various innovative ways with other emerging ideas, such as the steam engine, or the combustion engine to create pulleys, sewing machines, railroad trains, and automobiles. Each of these new inventions can itself be considered a kind of revolution, a significant shift from previous technological paradigms, but in many ways the overall story is one of technological convergence, which takes place not in one smooth trajectory but instead as stuttered responses to feedback. While the wheel remained a crucial enabling component of these inventions, the whole of each was greater—or at least different—than the sum of the parts. Something else emerged as a result of the convergence process.

Video game consoles are for economic reasons (among others) especially likely to develop according to the mode of technological convergence. The Wii is a vivid case in point. Again, the idea of using accelerometers—or infrared sensors or Bluetooth—is in itself anything but revolutionary. These are tested technologies with many existing applications. What makes the Wii innovative is its combination of available technologies in particular contexts and design decisions such as separating the two hands of even two-handed gameplay with two cable-connected components. Its design combines mostly commodity components in new combinations, given its particular uses in the specific market of video game consoles. In contrast with the other systems in its generation, the Wii offered a system comparable in computational power merely to a late-generation Pentium processor, packaged in the smallest "die" possible. Yet the Wii can still be considered innovative. In 2006 it offered the smallest form factor of any gaming console, aimed at a casual audience that was only then beginning to emerge, using Nintendo's signature style of abstract or manga-based games. It did this while reducing power use, mostly for economic and marketing reasons (what "mom" would buy), but in a way that ended up responding, even if by accident, to some environmental and sustainability concerns in the general arena of computing systems.

Moreover, even though it's tethered to the television set, the Wii can fit into a trend of the convergence of mobile technologies (a connection that's even stronger in the case of the Wii U, with its wireless, tablet-like touchscreen controller). The Wii Remote uses the same technology found in various mobile devices, including smartphones and tablets. As we have seen, Nintendo recently suggested that Apple was its new chief competitor, and the emphasis on the 3DS is part of exploiting the long-term success of the DS (and before that, the Game Boy). The 3DS can be thought of as in the general orbit of the Wii. Power-sipping processors are part of its success, too, and they connect it to mobile computing and trends in pervasive computing, and will likely play an increasing role in gaming and game platforms, while also contributing to a modestly hopeful trend toward at least relatively greener computing (a field of technology that in general is anything but ecologically friendly).

We are not referring here to the popular media's idea of convergence: the notion that every application will merge into one set-top box, for example. As Jesse Schell said in his Design, Innovate, Communicate, Entertain talk in 2010, this kind of technological convergence is "total bullshit. . . . Technologies *diverge* . . . like species in the Galapagos Islands."[20] Yet like the evolutionary processes that Schell invokes, the convergence and divergence of specific technologies within devices—rather than of devices into each other—take place over time, all the time, more like shifting phases in an uneven process of development, innovation, and retrenchment.

On the other hand, when it comes to the old idea of device convergence, we do see forces that are driving the industry as it attempts to respond to that overall divergence and the rise of casual gaming—forces in the somewhat-unexpected recent dominance of the living room metaphor, especially evident in the Wii's marketing (and most literally in the Wii no Ma Channel), and now in its competitors' attempts to enter the casual gaming market. The attempt to return to the centrality of the television as the hub of all household entertainment, probably doomed in the long term, nevertheless says something important about the console companies' (and some consumers') *desire* for this kind of convergence and perhaps stability in home entertainment, and that desire alone has consequences for the further development of creative software and the forms of user experiences afforded by future platforms.

New and not-so-new technologies are always opportunistically combined in game platforms, the development of which then feeds back into the next phase of development. Until recently, this led to a new generation of consoles about every five years. Assuming they remain viable platforms for a while, dedicated game consoles are likely to continue to overlap with PCs for some time, and they are almost certain to increasingly have to compete with mobile devices, phones, and tablets as well as dedicated handheld platforms in an environment of always-on pervasive computing. To remain economically viable, any new gaming system would be well advised to avoid inventing anything too "revolutionary." This is just the logic of the market. Instead it should focus strategically on technologies with the highest (social) impact. Under this definition, the Wii is indeed a leading-edge product—one that has helped redefine the console market and the social platform of gaming for its generation.

The Absence of an Object?

Although it began by imitating the Wii's approach to the gaming market, in the end Microsoft's Kinect went in a different direction from the Wii, attempting to define itself as an even more extreme revolution in console design. In contrast to Nintendo's Wii design, as we've been describing it throughout this book, Kinect aims to use its gestural interface to produce an experience of total immersion. "With Kinect," as the slogan goes, "there are no gadgets, no gizmos, just you."[21] What might it mean, in terms of platform, to develop a system without gadgets? What might be gained, and what might be lost?

At E3 2010, the theatrical circus performance we described at the beginning of this chapter played with the line between the living room and game space, with various "screens" serving as mere "windows" (surely an intended allusion by Microsoft) opening onto virtual worlds and the real world virtualized (literally turned upside down at one point, so that a little girl walked on the ceiling and a couch hung suspended). The family of players were repeatedly absorbed into staged representations of what looked like an indistinctly bounded and transcendent space, often represented through sublime images of infinite regress: the square proscenium stage looked like a television screen, but it contained the living room in which the performers played a family playing Kinect on another screen, and so on. This performance was being watched by crouching circus acrobats in elaborate costumes that suggested they were "primitive" jungle dwellers. A little like the apes before the obelisk in *2001: A Space Odyssey*, they gesticulated and murmured as they watched the controller-free game demos, the family of players like strange gods with their new technology (that was billed as magic). Out beyond the lights, the audience became part of the spectacle, as their LED-enabled ponchos were activated from the control room in a giant light show of patterned colors across the hall.

Rhetorically, the show seemed to be saying that Kinect would turn your living room into a sublime, transcendent game space, realizing the fantasy of cyberspace or the holodeck, which some had predicted that the Wii would fulfill (wrongly, it turned out). As sociologist Bart Simon has cogently argued, the Wii is more likely to make your television seem like a kind of pragmatic heads-up display than it is a magic window onto a transcendent realm. "The traditional VR fantasy," he says, "is transcendental; it is about layering or superimposing another world over and beyond our living room," and it's represented with terms like "immersion" and "escape." But, he concludes, "the Wii is different, almost in spite of itself."[22]

We would disagree only with Simon's final clause, since it's clear that Nintendo's intended strategy all along has been to "capture" the living room in a pragmatic way that avoids having to pursue the transcendent, immersive fantasy of game space as cyberspace. It has done so in part by domesticating the virtual, bringing it into mundane contact with the living room (and in an explicitly nonrealistic, cartoon form), aiming for augmented not virtual reality, and in part by embracing the continued use of an array of stubbornly material—physical and mechanical—controllers and peripheral objects in a self-conscious way.

Author William Gibson famously invented the term cyberspace, inspired by watching arcade gamers play video games.[23] Gibson was not a gamer. His idea of cyberspace was based on imposing his interpretation of gameplay on what he saw in the arcades. As the gamers leaned into their machines, bumping the cabinets and staring at the screens for hours, Gibson fantasized about the world behind the screen. Since Gibson did not have much experience with it himself, he took the player's application of body English for a desire to meld with the game world, or a kind of longing for total immersion.

Historically, total immersion in this sense has never had all that much to do with actual, thriving gameplay, not even, most of the time, in most persistent-world MMOs. Yes, the decade before 2006 for the big-budget game industry was consumed with developing highly immersive and realistic graphics for more detailed and lavishly rendered game worlds. But even in triple-A titles for the major consoles before 2006, in most cases conventions and features like the heads-up display, not to mention back-chat over headsets or Byzantine LAN party configurations, all the often highly social activities of fans surrounding game play, gave away the truth: gaming has never been entirely about total immersion. Actual gameplay is an impure, mixed, borderline activity. Its pleasures include talking to friends in the room while you play—snacking and also thrashing button combinations from the couch.[24] It's not in the end about suspending disbelief and fantasizing about being, say, a cybernetic supersolider on a distant artificial ring world. It is not at all clear that gamers, as a group, have ever been motivated primarily by the desire to be totally immersed in a kind of realistic out-of-body experience—as opposed to being meaningfully engaged *at the interface*, which has historically been constituted by peripherals and controllers.

Nonetheless, the desire for total immersion seems to have been assumed in the marketing of Kinect. Its sensors and cameras work by capturing and mapping the living room the way that certain security systems do, rendering it as a field, the disturbances of which can be detected as bodies in motion. In this sense, it turns your living room into the game space in a much more literal way than the Wii's motion-control system does. Kinect interprets the goal of the gestural interface as pointing to increasing dematerialization, as allowing for pure gestures with the unencumbered body, so, somewhat counter-intuitively, it has to incorporate the player's body in its interface. When the *Wii Fit* robotic voice says "measuring," and a wire-frame Mii figure gets "scanned," it's just a visual fiction, a metaphor. You're actually standing on a Balance Board being weighed (and your center of balance is being determined) while your *data* are being scanned and matched up to those measurements. But when Kinect sets up a new account, or produces an avatar for its sports or fitness games, it really does perform a full body scan with its cameras, graphing the key forty-eight joints of your body—in many ways a much more thorough scan than what the Transportation Security Administration uses for airport security, including using sensors to measure how far from the screen you're standing in the mapped 3D space of your living room. It then tracks your movements at thirty frames per second.[25]

Given the rhetoric at the launch event, and given the stated need for a large, well-lit play space, it was surprising to us in our early experiences with the system that when playing most of the initial titles released for Kinect, you effectively have to remain in an imaginary box about six to eight feet from the screen. If an additional player wants to join in a game, they step into this box, and the sensor quickly sees them and adds an avatar. If you move too far to one side while playing, however, a warning prompts you to move back into the device's field of vision.

For example, in *Kinect Adventures!* you may see a rendering of an expansive game world—a large gym, a glass undersea observatory, a winding riverbed, or a series of tracks in a vast mountainous landscape— but most of it is not playable. Your actual gameplay, the part of that environment you can control with your gestures, is bounded in a much smaller box. Visual cues in the game for the space in which you actually move are provided by a conduit-pipe cage extending about as far as you can reach, the glass walls of a small underwater room, a raft on which you stand and walk from side to side to steer, or the rolling cart on which you traverse the tracks. These can be seen as a kind of virtual counterpart to the Wii's physical Balance Board.

As a result, at least in our initial experiences of gameplay, *Kinect Adventures!* games at least—which are obviously early applications of what the system might do in the future—can feel a bit claustrophobic, like a theme park ride in which you have to keep your hands inside the car or an on-rails game where the contextual animations move past you.

Conceptually, Kinect is a much more technically sophisticated version of Sony's earlier EyeToy camera peripheral. Taking into account its combination of sensors and camera, it's clear, of course, that Kinect doesn't really offer gadget-free gaming; it just takes the gadgets out of the player's hands and moves them into the sensor bar, which sits like a vaguely anthropomorphic robot head near the television screen, where it can see the room and any players.

Structurally, it works like something of an inverted Wii setup. Instead of having a CMOS camera sensor in your hand and the LED signals beamed to it from the area of the television, as the Wii does, Kinect puts the cameras in the area of the television and trains them on the player's body. The lack of a light-emitting piece of hardware for calibration is one reason early reviews have noted that the lighting in the game space has to be just right for the Kinect. Too much sunlight, for instance, or even a player's skin tone being too dark for easy reflection in low light can confuse the cameras.[26]

In making the decision to remove the gadgets, the controllers, from the player, the Kinect developers had to sacrifice certain affordances, not only the data provided by the accelerometers—which are replaced (with a slight lag, in our experience with the release titles) by image-captured data—but also the immediate responsiveness of digital input—such as the on/off/shoot/release signals provided by buttons. Like the Kinect, the Wii also makes use of a gestural interface. You just gesture with a controller in your hand, and this offers certain advantages. As Chris Kohler observes, "When you press a button on a standard controller, it sends a very clear signal. A switch is flipped; a zero becomes a one. Kinect doesn't possess this ability. All it has is fuzzy analog input."[27]

> Bowling in *Kinect Sports* presents the same problem. The Wii version of bowling is markedly superior for one reason—you hold down a button when you're holding the ball, and release it to let it go. The accelerometer does the fuzzy stuff, tracking the swing of your arm, but the button reports when, exactly, you release the ball.[28]

Every system has its unique constraints as well as affordances. Our point is simply that the rhetoric of total immersion through "controller-free" gaming in the case of Kinect masks certain practical trade-offs. Despite the marketing, the Kinect and the Wii have much in common. (They are in some ways structurally inverted versions of one another, as we have shown.) Yet Kinect's move to jettison the gadgets not only comes at a certain cost, it also sheds light on the importance of gadgets in the Wii's case—that is, on the significance of the network of interrelated control devices. A gadget is something you handle, something you with which you engage.[29] These devices are objects in their own right, or components in the larger system, that shape and mediate the player's experience of the system as a whole.

By contrast, the symbolism at the E3 Kinect pageant was focused on erasing those mediating devices, dismissed as mere gadgets and gizmos, as if to play to an imagined nontechnical consumer. As the voice-over announcer said, "History is about to be rewritten. . . . Human beings will be at the center, and the machine will be the one that adapts. Might the next step be an absence of an object?" The *absence of an object* literally meant the absence of a controller, pad, or joystick or remote, but because of the dramatic way it was worded, it had a more sweeping, philosophical ring to it: the absence of an object implies a total, sublime domination by the *subject* ("it's all about you"), or the dominance of subjectivity itself, which is one version of the old dream of total immersion.[30]

Kinect's version of the mimetic interface, rather than merely shifting attention to physical player space (the living room), as the Wii can be said to do, imagines the subsuming of player space into a kind of immaterial game space—a game space as cyberspace—through erasing the object and making the player, as subject, one with the game's representations. Instead of the game leaking out into your living room, you're sucked into the virtual space behind the screen. But when it comes to the notion of cyberspace, even Gibson has in more recent work had his characters observe that nowadays, cyberspace seems to be "everting"—meaning that it's turning inside out and spreading into the world.[31] As it does so, its "innards" are inevitably exposed; the scaffolding of its infrastructure are bared.

The Wii, it seems to us, has participated in this trend by in effect opting out of the drive for total immersion.[32] It assumes that gaming is less about *cyberspace* than it is about *cybernetics*—in Norbert Wiener's sense, based on mechanisms and devices providing control and feedback—which has a long history in relation to video games.[33] Steven Poole, for example, makes the connection to cybernetics and explains that "the perfect video game 'feel' requires the ever-increasing imaginative and physical involvement of the player to stop somewhere short of full bodily immersion. After all, a sense of pleasurable control implies some modicum of *separation*: you are apart from what you are controlling."[34]

Poole's point implies that to design a platform for "pleasurable control" requires a focused attention on the separation—the space between the player and the game—a space of possibilities for interesting mediations. This is basically the same assertion that we have made throughout the book about the importance of "adequate space" for Wii game play, as seen for example in chapter 4's discussion of the Balance Board's exploiting the active periphery of gameplay, and is in keeping with the larger argument that Katie Salen and Eric Zimmerman make against the dominance of the "immersive fallacy" in game design—the idea that the whole purpose of video games is to "transport a player into an illusory reality" or an "imaginary world." Salen and Zimmerman challenge game designers to give up "pining for immersion," for that total transcendence that "will only evolve . . . when the technology arrives." Instead, they say, designers of games should take seriously the more common gamer's experience of a "hybrid consciousness"—a fluid moving from states of immersion, to "deep engagement" with game mechanics, to full awareness of "the space outside the magic circle."[35] Gaming, we think, is indeed all about that movement, in and out of the game and the physical room, the magic circle and its outer perimeter, the action at the periphery of game space.

Writing a couple of years before the Wii appeared, Salen and Zimmerman suggest that such a shift in attention by designers—a shift from "pining for immersion," to encouraging multilayered and (therefore) *deep engagement*—might help games reach a more "diverse mass audience," or all those potential gamers and more casual gamers who have little or no interest in the romantic dream of total immersion in a cyberspatial game world, but who would just like to play, and for whom play involves playing with the platform, not expecting it to disappear.[36] As we have been arguing thought this book, platform is a social phenomenon. Its meaning is determined by ideas along with social and cultural contexts as much as by abstract principles of engineering and design. Watching the Kinect E3 2010 show, it was hard not to think of that boxy, rotatable main stage as a giant television set turned into a single magic portal to cyberspace, an instance of what the romantic poet John Keats called "magic casements, opening on . . . faery lands, forlorn," the subjective end point of an interface about which no one has to be self-conscious because it is an extension of consciousness itself ("Might the next step be an absence of an object?").[37] The marketing of Kinect highlights, by contrast, how "object oriented" Nintendo's version of the mimetic interface is—how the experience of playing Wii games involves increased attention to the mediating role played by the various controllers that are all parts of the system.[38]

The design ethos behind the Wii is not focused so much on the unique properties of the Wii Remote, Nunchuk, Balance Board, or other component objects. Nor is it all about an idealized and unencumbered player as the controlling subject. Instead, it's focused more on making possible engaging events in the space *between* the user and the game, via the mediating material objects with which the player is directly engaged. As a system, the Wii is designed not to elide or conceal but rather to call attention to the player's interactions with objects of various kinds—hardware and software, in the hand and on the screen, Mii avatars as well as weapons, balls, and vehicles, stored in the console or beamed to the living room as services. As a platform, the Wii more often than not focuses attention on the charged relationship between subject and object, the repeated material transactions between player and game—transactions that are mediated by technology (gadgets—that is, peripherals and components), but that always take place in the context of the social spaces of the living room and the wider culture. In that sense, the Wii makes player space itself an important object of (and in) the system.

As the emergence of the Wii and its recent competition has demonstrated, there are multiple possible vectors for the evolution of game platforms going forward. Different permutations of components offer varying affordances and constraints that shape the possibilities, and the possibilities include greater or lesser emphasis on the social contexts for gameplay. In all gaming systems, regardless of the components, and how they are arranged or connected, in the end the most important thing is the kind of (social) interaction they afford, as we have contended. Almost every new technology these days is described as revolutionary. But in bringing the social nature of game platforms to the center of the discussion, the Wii has lived up to its codename.

Notes

Chapter 1

1. Satoru Iwata, "Iwata Asks: *New Super Mario Bros*. Wii," Nintendo, http://us.wii.
   com/iwata_asks/nsmb/vol1_page2.jsp. Given the lack of information about the
   internal history and development at Nintendo, we depend on these Nintendo-
   published columns throughout the book, though we realize (and want our readers
   to realize) that the company produces them for many purposes—chiefly, for marketing and public relations. In addition, in several instances throughout the book
   we cite Wikipedia, since its socially constructed articles on video games, by
   numerous knowledgeable contributors, are often among the most reliable on the
   site. Something of the same goes for game blogs and reviews, which we cite as
   appropriate, which frequently have the most detailed and up-to-date information on current games and platforms.
2. Robert D. Putnam, *Bowing Alone: The Collapse and Revival of American Community*,
   Kindle ed. (New York: Simon and Schuster, 2000), 1827–1833, 1670–1676. We
   make use of some Kindle editions e-books throughout this book, as indicated,
   citing them by location number or range of numbers.
3. The Wii U, unveiled at the E3 2011 conference (June 7, 2011), is at the time of
   writing scheduled for release during 2012. It should be noted that the new console
   is said to be backward compatible with the Wii and to make use of the iconic Wii
   Remote in addition to its own newly designed touchscreen controller.
4. Jesper Juul, *A Casual Revolution: Reinventing Video Games and Their Players* (Cambridge, MA: MIT Press, 2010), 2, 18.
5. See Sebastian Deterding, with contributions by Staffan Björk, Stephan Dreyer,
   Aki Järvinen, Ben Kirman, Julian Kücklich, Janne Paavilainen, Valentina Rao,
   and Jan Schmidt, "Social Game Studies: A Workshop Report" (Hamburg: Hans
   Bredow Institute for Media Research, 2010), http://socialgamestudies.org/
   report.
6. Juul, *A Casual Revolution*, 5.

7. Ibid., 16–17.
8. Ibid.
9. As pointed out by Jonathan Zittrain, *The Future of the Internet: And How to Stop It*, Kindle ed. (New Haven, CT: Yale University Press, 2008), 1384–1397.
10. Steven E. Jones, *The Meaning of Video Games: Gaming and Textual Strategies* (New York: Routledge, 2008).
11. On the practical significance of play space in earlier exercise games, including economic inequalities, see Ian Bogost, *Persuasive* Games: *The Expressive Power of Videogames*, Kindle ed. (Cambridge, MA: MIT Press, 2007), 3778–3786.
12. Ian Bogost and Nick Montfort, "New Media as Material Constraint: An Introduction to Platform Studies," http://www.bogost.com/downloads/Bogost%20Montfort%20HASTAC.pdf.
13. Ian Bogost and Nick Montfort, *Racing the Beam: The Atari Computer System* (Cambridge, MA: MIT Press, 2009); see http://platformstudies.com/levels.html.
14. In the field of book history, see especially the debates between Elizabeth Eisenstein (*The Printing Press as Agent of Change* [Cambridge: Cambridge University Press, 1980]) and Adrian Johns (*The Nature of the Book: Print and Knowledge in the Making* [Chicago: University of Chicago Press, 1998]).
15. Dan Frommer and Leah Goldman, "iPad Survey Results," *Business Insider*, http://www.businessinsider.com/ipad-survey-results-2010-11.
16. "Mario," Wikipedia, http://en.wikipedia.org/wiki/Mario.
17. Chris Kohler, *Power Up: How Japanese Video Games Gave the World an Extra Life* (Indianapolis: Brady Games, 2004), 61, 57, 58.
18. Iwata, "Iwata Asks: *New Super Mario Bros.* Wii."
19. Tom Bissell, *Extra Lives: Why Video Games Matter*, Kindle ed. (New York: Pantheon Books, 2010), 261, 751.
20. On the role of abstraction in manga especially, and its ability to draw the viewer into the work, see Scott McCloud, *Understanding Comics: The Invisible Art* (New York: Harper Perennial, 1993), 26–36, 43–44.
21. Quoted in Osamu Inoue, *Nintendo Magic: Winning the Videogame Wars*, trans. Paul Tuttle Starr (New York: Vertical, 2010), 142.
22. Seth Schiesel, "Back-Seat Jumpers Now Have Their Day," review of *Super Mario Galaxy 2*, *New York Times*, May 24, 2010, http://www.nytimes.com/2010/05/25/arts/television/25mario.html.
23. This playing with multiple perspectives or multiple views of the game world carried forward to the design of the Wii U (as revealed in June 2011), which affords two "windows"—the handheld controller screen and the TV—onto the same game world.

Chapter 2

1. *Oxford English Dictionary*, citing *U.S. News and World Report*, November 29, 1976, 73.
2. On Nintendo's history, see Stephen L. Kent, *The Ultimate History of Video Games: From Pong to Pokemon—The Story behind the Craze That Touched Our Lives and Changed the World* (New York: Three Rivers, 2001); David Sheff, *Game Over: How Nintendo Zapped an American Industry, Captured Your Dollars, and Enslaved Your Children* (New York: Random House, 1993); Chris Kohler, *Power Up: How Japanese Video Games Gave the World an Extra Life* (Indianapolis: Brady Games, 2004).

3. Donald A. Norman, *Emotional Design: Why We Love (or Hate) Everyday Things*, Kindle ed. (New York: Basic Books, 2005), 26. More recently, Norman has critiqued gestural interfaces like those on the iPad, iPhone, and Android for violating basic HCI principles. He also cites the original strapless Wii Remote as among the problematic applications of gesture and foreshadows some of the contradictions we discuss in chapter 7 when it comes to Microsoft's "controller-free" Kinect. See Donald A. Norman, "Natural User Interfaces Are Not Natural," *Interactions* 17:3 (May–June 2010): 6-10, DOI: 10.1145/1744161.1744163l; http://portal.acm.org/citation.cfm?doid=1744161.1744163.

4. Satoru Iwata, E3 2005 press conference (May 17, 2005), http://www.youtube.com/watch?v=2361Ei14Kak.

5. As pointed out by Osamu Inoue, *Nintendo Magic: Winning the Videogame Wars*, trans. Paul Tuttle Starr (New York: Vertical, 2010), 39.

6. Quoted in Kenji Hall, "The Big Ideas behind Nintendo's Wii," interview with Shigeru Miyamoto and Ken'ichiro Ashida, *Business Week Online*, November 16, 2006, http://www.businessweek.com/technology/content/nov2006/tc20061116_750580.htm?chan=search.

7. Jesper Juul, *A Casual Revolution: Reinventing Video Games and Their Players* (Cambridge, MA: MIT Press, 2010).

8. Norman, *Emotional Design*, 411–414.

9. Hall, "The Big Ideas behind Nintendo's Wii."

10. See Adrienne L. Massanari, "Designing for Imaginary Friends: Information Architecture, Personas, and the Politics of User-Centered Design," *New Media and Society* 12, no. 3 (2010): 401–416, DOI: 10.1177/1461444809346722, http://nms.sagepub.com/content/12/3/401.abstract.

11. See Justine Cassell and Henry Jenkins, ed., *From Barbie to Mortal Kombat* (Cambridge, MA: MIT Press, 1998).

12. Both examples are discussed in Steven E. Jones, *The Meaning of Video Games: Gaming and Textual Strategies* (New York: Routledge, 2008), 143–145.

13. Announced at the corporate strategy meeting held on October 26, 2007, as reported in Satoru Iwata, "Iwata Asks: Wii Fit," Nintendo, http://us.wii.com/wii-fit/iwata_asks/vol4_page1.jsp.

14. Iwata, "Iwata Asks: WarioWare: Smooth Moves," Nintendo, http://us.wii.com/iwata_asks/warioware_smooth_moves/part_4.

15. Scott McCloud, *Understanding Comics: Invisible Art* (New York: Harper Perennial, 1993), 43.

16. Cited in Kohler, *Power Up*, 6.

17. James Brightman, "Nintendo's Reggie on Wii Core Games, Wii HD, Shortages & More," *Industry Gamers*, March 16, 2010, http://www.industrygamers.com/news/nintendos-reggie-on-wii-core-games-wii-hd-shortages--more.

18. Greg Kasavin, "*Red Steel* Review," Gamespot, November 17, 2006, http://www.gamespot.com/Wii/action/redsteel/review.html.

19. Matt Casamassina, "Why You'll Love *Rabbids Go Home*," IGN, November 3, 2009, http://wii.ign.com/articles/979/979811p3.html.

20. Neon Kelly, interview with Jason Vandenberghe, February 22, 2010, http://www.videogamer.com/wii/red_steel_2/preview-2225.html.

21. Quoted in Hamza CTZ Aziz, "*Red Steel 2* May Have Defeated the Waggle," July 7, 2009, http://www.destructoid.com/red-steel-2-may-have-defeated-the -waggle-138687.phtml.

22. "MEMS Gyroscopes for Gaming," InvenSense, http://invenSense.com/mems/ gaming.html.

23. Chris Kohler, "Stand, Shoot, and Slash in *Red Steel 2* Wii," *Wired*, March 23, 2010, http://www.wired.com/gamelife/tag/red-steel-2.

24. Quoted in Totilo, "No Graphical Complaints from This Wii Developer," Kotaku, 2009, http://kotaku.com/5372026/no-graphical-complaints-from-this-wii- developer.

25. Seth Schiesel, "Way Down Deep in the Wild Wild West," review of *Red Dead Redemption*, *New York Times*, May 16, 2010, http://www.nytimes.com/2010/05/17/ arts/television/17dead.html.

26. The exception that proved the rule was the release in 2010 of *GoldenEye 007* for the Wii, which Nintendo touted as proof that core games can succeed on the Wii. See James Newton, "*GoldenEye*'s Success 'Proves Core Games Sell on Wii,'" NintendoLife, November 17, 2010, http://wii.nintendolife.com/news/2010/11/ goldeneyes_success_proves_core_games_sell_on_wii.

27. Noah Horowitz et al., "Lowering the Cost of Play: Improving Energy Efficiency of Video Game Consoles," National Resources Defense Council, November 2008, http://www.nrdc.org/energy/consoles/contents.asp. Our own real-time measurements of the Xbox 360 running the Kinect extension versus the Wii running *Wii Sports* (June 2011) suggest that the Xbox consumes 3.5 to 5 times as much electricity as the Wii during this kind of comparably casual gameplay.

28. Ibid.

29. On some of the problems associated with multicore architectures, see http:// view.eecs.berkeley.edu/blog.

30. Quoted in Iwata, "Iwata Asks: Wii Fit."

31. Ibid.

Chapter 3

1. Video of the keynote, posted on Gamespot, September 16, 2005, http://www. gamespot.com/wii/action/metroidprime3/video/6133401. Iwata had presented the prototype system earlier in the year, in much the same preliminary way, at the E3 conference in Los Angeles in May 2005, but his talk in Tokyo involved a more complete presentation.

2. Ibid.

3. Matt Casamassina, live blogging for IGN Cube News, http://cube.ign.com/ articles/651/651320p1.html.

4. Donald A. Norman, *Emotional Design: Why We Love (or Hate) Everyday Things*, Kindle ed. (New York: Basic Books, 2005).

5. Satoru Iwata, "Iwata Asks: Wii Remote," Nintendo, http://us.wii.com/iwata_asks/ wii_remote/part_2.

6. Quoted in ibid.

7. Video of the keynote, posted on Gamespot, September 16, 2005.

8. Quoted in Iwata, "Iwata Asks: Wii MotionPlus," Nintendo, http://us.wii.com/ iwata_asks/wiimotionplus/vol1_page1.jsp.

9. Alan S. Brown, "Tearing Down the Nearly Invisible," *Mechanical Engineering*, August 2006, http://memagazine.asme.org/articles/2006/August/Tearing_Down_Nearly_Invisible.cfm.

10. W. Chan Kim and Renée Mauborgne, *Blue Ocean Strategy: How to Create Uncontested Market Space and Make the Competition Irrelevant*, Kindle ed. (Boston: Harvard Business School Press, 2005).

11 Genyo Takeda, quoted in Stephen L. Kent, *The Ultimate History of Video Games: From Pong to Pokemon—The Story behind the Craze That Touched Our Lives and Changed the World* (New York: Three Rivers, 2001), 523.

12. On the Power Pad, Roll 'n' Rocker, Joyboard, Power Glove, and so forth, especially in the context of "exergames," see Ian Bogost, *Persuasive Games: The Expressive Power of Videogames*, Kindle ed. (Cambridge, MA: MIT Press, 2007), 3529–3622.

13. Kent, *The Ultimate History of Video Games*, 287–288.

14. Norbert Wiener, "Men, Machines, and the World About" (1954), in *The New Media Reader*, ed. Noah Wardrip-Fruin and Nick Montfort (Cambridge, MA: MIT Press, 2003), 65–72.

15. The recent exception might be Microsoft's Kinect, where all the mechanical "gadgets" are taken away from the players, and their functions are replaced by technology hidden inside the sensor-and-camera device near the television (see chapter 7).

16. Cited in Satoru Iwata, "Iwata Asks: Wii MotionPlus," Nintendo, http://us.wii.com/iwata_asks/wiimotionplus/vol1_page2.jsp.

17. "MEMS Gyroscopes for Gaming," InvenSense, http://invensense.com/mems/gaming.html. Takamoto cited in Iwata, "Iwata Asks: Wii MotionPlus," Nintendo, http://us.wii.com/iwata_asks/wiimotionplus/vol1_page1.jsp.

18. Iwata, "Iwata Asks: Wii MotionPlus," http://us.wii.com/iwata_asks/wiimotion plus/vol1_page2.jsp.

19. Ibid., http://us.wii.com/iwata_asks/wiimotionplus/vol1_page4.jsp.

20. InvenSense, http://invensense.com/mems/gaming.html.

21. David Sheff, *Game Over: How Nintendo Zapped an American Industry, Captured Your Dollars, and Enslaved Your Children* (New York: Random House, 1993), 200.

22. Alexander R. Galloway, *Gaming: Essays on Algorithmic Culture* (Minneapolis: University of Minnesota Press, 2006), 12–13.

23. Osamu Inoue, *Nintendo Magic: Winning the Videogame Wars*, trans. Paul Tuttle Starr (New York: Vertical, 2010), 72–73.

24. "Link's Crossbow Training," Nintendo, http://www.nintendo.com/games/detail/9xKcFNixgDWMPXxoDGuo_77F_6Hwbk2s.

25. Quoted in Satoru Iwata, "Iwata Asks: *WarioWare: Smooth Moves*," Nintendo, http://us.wii.com/iwata_asks/warioware_smooth_moves.

26. Quoted in Satoru Iwata, "Iwata Asks: WarioWare: Smooth Moves," Nintendo, http://us.wii.com/iwata_asks/warioware_smooth_moves/part_2.

27. For a discussion of the mimetic interface, see Jesper Juul, *The Casual Revolution: Reinventing Video Games and Their Players* (Cambridge, MA: MIT Press, 2010), 103.

28. "The Legend of Zelda: Wind Waker," Nintendo, http://www.zelda.com/gcn.

29. And now the series has come full circle with *WarioWare D.I.Y.* for the DS and the companion game, *WarioWare D.I.Y. Showcase*, for the Wii (see chapter 5 below).

30. Quoted in Satoru Iwata, "Iwata Asks: WarioWare: Smooth Moves," Nintendo, http://us.wii.com/iwata_asks/warioware_smooth_moves.

31. Chaim Gingold, "Miniature Gardens and Magic Crayons" (master's thesis, Georgia Institute of Technology, 2003), iii, http://levitylab.com/cog/writing/thesis.

32. Douglas Engelbart and William K. English, "A Research Center for Augmenting Human Intellect," in *The New Media Reader*, ed. Noah Wardrip-Fruin and Nick Montfort (Cambridge, MA: MIT Press, 2003), 233–246.

33. Ibid., 235.

34. Quoted in Iwata, "Iwata Asks: Wii Remote," Nintendo, http://us.wii.com/iwata_asks/wii_remote.

Chapter 4

1. Our description is based on various videos of the event at E3 2007 on YouTube. See, for example, http://www.youtube.com/watch?v=pJGJEt9hwD8&feature=fvsr.

2. Miyamoto, quoted in "E3 2007 Nintendo E3 Media Briefing Live Blog," IGN, http://wii.ign.com/articles/803/803335p1.html.

3. Osamu Inoue, *Nintendo Magic: Winning the Videogame Wars*, trans. Paul Tuttle Starr (New York: Vertical, 2010), 69.

4. Quoted in Satoru Iwata, "Iwata Asks: Wii Balance Board," Nintendo, http://us.wii.com/wii-fit/iwata_asks/vol3_page1.jsp.

5. Okamoto et al., "Storage Medium Storing a Load Detecting Program and Load Detecting Apparatus," United States Patent Application Publication (Pub. No. US 2009/0093305 A1). April 9, 2009, http://www.freepatentsonline.com/20090093305.pdf, cited in Jeremy Jacquot, "How the Wii Balance Board Works," How Stuff Works, http://electronics.howstuffworks.com/wii-balance-board5.htm; ; Matt Casamassina, "GDC 2008: Sawano on Wii Fit," IGN, February 20, 2008, http://wii.ign.com/articles/853/853708p1.html.

6. A fossil trace of the early stage in the Balance Board's evolution as a tethered extension controller has been identified in its circuitry, where the Balance Board's button is mapped to the A button on the Wii Remote and the strain gauge sensors are mapped to an extension controller. See http://Wiibrew.org/wiki/Wii_Balance_Board.

7. Quoted in Inoue, *Nintendo Magic*, 193.

8. On exergames as a genre, see Ian Bogost, *Persuasive Games: The Expressive Power of Videogames*, Kindle ed. (Cambridge, MA: MIT Press, 2007), 3513–3801.

9. Quoted in Iwata, "Iwata Asks: Wii Fit," Nintendo, http://us.wii.com/wii-fit/iwata_asks/vol4_page1.jsp.

10. *Wii Fit* parody, http://www.youtube.com/watch?v=_iYBmAVuBns.

11. Ibid.

12. Our thanks to Ian Bogost for reminding us of this precursor to the Balance Board.

13. Inoue, *Nintendo Magic*, 125.

14. Quoted in ibid., 142.

15. Press conference at E3 2009, YouTube, http://www.youtube.com/watch?v=dZlte_4xkUI.

16. Inoue, *Nintendo Magic*, 130–131.

17. Nick Jones, "Miyamoto: 'Vitality Sensor for New Zelda Possible,'" *Now Gamer*, March 22, 2010, http://www.nowgamer.com/news/91639/miyamoto_vitality_sensor_for_new_zelda_possible.html.

18. Ian Bogost, Guru Meditation, http://www.bogost.com/games/guru_meditation.shtml.

19. Bogost also points to a meditation game that uses fingertip controllers strikingly like the Vitality Sensor to measure the player's heart rate and skin galvanic response, *Journey to Wild Divine*, http://www.wilddivine.com.

20. Iwata, "Iwata Asks: Wii Fit:" http://us.wii.com/wii-fit/iwata_asks/vol2_page4.jsp.

21. Scott Sharkey, for 1up.com, http://www.1up.com/features/top-5-wtf-moments-e3. Sharkey sardonically dubbed the future game for the sensor "You're Still Not Dead: The Game."

22. Tor Thorsen, "Wii Sales Near 71 Million, DS Almost 129 Million," Gamespot, May 6, 2010, http://www.gamespot.com/news/6261400.html?tag=recent_news;title;1.

23. Yoshiyuki Oyama, quoted in Iwata, "Iwata Asks: Wii Balance Board," Nintendo, http://us.wii.com/wii-fit/iwata_asks/vol4_page3.jsp.

24. Yohei Miyagawa, quoted in Iwata, "Iwata Asks: Wii Balance Board," http://us.wii.com/wii-fit/iwata_asks/vol4_page5.jsp.

25. Iwata, "Iwata Asks: *Wii Fit*," Nintendo, http://us.wii.com/wii-fit/iwata_asks/vol4_page1.jsp. These figures on gender were reportedly announced at the corporate strategy meeting held on October 26, 2007.

26. Quoted in Iwata, "Iwata Asks: *Wii Fit*," http://us.wii.com/wii-fit/iwata_asks/vol4_page1.jsp and http://us.wii.com/wii-fit/iwata_asks/vol4_page4.jsp.

27. In the context of the Wii's focus on the space between the player and the game, or between the peripheral and the screen, we find suggestive a recent industrial design manifesto by Branko Lukić and Barry M. Kātz, *Nonobject*: iPad App Version (Cambridge, MA: MIT Press, 2010), which focuses through imaginative "design fictions" on "the charged space between the user and the object" (Introduction). See as well footnote 38, chapter 7 below.

28. Jesper Juul, *A Casual Revolution: Reinventing Video Games and Their Players* (Cambridge, MA: MIT Press, 2010), 17, 107.

29. "Why 3D Projection Makes Sense," http://nintendo-revolution.blogspot.com/2006/02/why-3d-projection-makes-sense.html.

30. Juul, *A Casual Revolution*, 18.

31. Johan Huizinga, *Homo Ludens: A Study of the Play Element in Culture* (1938; repr., Boston: Beacon Press, 1950), 10.

32. Chaim Gingold, "Miniature Gardens and Magic Crayons" (master's thesis, Georgia Institute of Technology, 2003), http://levitylab.com/cog/writing/thesis.

33. Ibid.

34. Will Wright interview, Web 2.0 Expo, 2009, *Wired* video, http://link.brightcove.com/services/player/bcpid1813626064?bctid=21523091001.

35. Ibid.

36. Gingold, "Miniature Gardens and Magic Crayons."

37. Bart Simon, "Wii Are Out of Control: Bodies, Game Screens, and the Production of Gestural Excess," *Loading* 3.4 (2009), http://journals.sfu.ca/loading/index.php/loading/article/viewArticle/65.

38. Inoue, *Nintendo Magic*, 190.

39. The Wii no Ma Web site (in Japanese) is available at http://www.Wiinoma.co.jp; accessed May 30, 2011. We have also consulted several user-made video tours of the channel on YouTube, as well as reports with translations such as that found at Eurogamer (April 30, 2009) at http://www.eurogamer.net/articles/nintendo-unveils-wii-video-service.

Chapter 5

1. Wii Channels, Nintendo, http://www.nintendo.com/wii/channels.
2. Hisashi Nogami, quoted in Iwata, "Iwata Asks: Wii Channels," Nintendo, http://us.wii.com/iwata_asks/wii_channels/part_6.
3. See David Morley, *Home Territories: Media, Mobility, and Identity* (London: Routledge, 2000), 88.
4. Chris Kohler, "Coverage Wrapup: Why WiiWare Needs Work," *Wired*, March 25, 2008, http://www.wired.com/gamelife/2008/03/coverage-wrapup/#ixzzopFtoSuBo.
5. E3 2005 Nintendo press conference reported on 1Up.com, May 22, 2005, http://www.1up.com/do/blogEntry?bId=4980481.
6. Iwata presentation, E3 2005 Nintendo Press Conference, http://video.google.com/videoplay?docid=5740279523739566758#.
7. Wikipedia, "Virtual Console," http://en.wikipedia.org/wiki/Virtual_Console.
8. James Newton, "Reggie: We're Not Interested in 'Garage Developers,'" *Nintendo Life*, March 18, 2011, http://www.nintendolife.com/news/2011/03/reggie_were_not_interested_in_garage_developers.
9. Matt Casamassina, interview with Tom Prata, "Nintendo: 100 WiiWare Games in Queue," IGN, May 30, 2008, http://uk.Wii.ign.com/articles/877/877761p1.html.
10. John Linderman, "Pearl Harbor Interview with Dan Muir," *Nintendo World Report*, January 20, 2010, http://www.nintendoworldreport.com/interview/20807.
11. Quoted in *Edge* magazine staff, "WiiWare: Developer Impressions," *Edge*, May 13, 2008; http://www.next-gen.biz/features/wiiware-developer-impressions.
12. *Edge* magazine staff, "Industry Focus: The Economics of Motion Control," *Edge*, May 2010, 24–25.
13. James Brightman, "Nintendo's Reggie on Wii Core Games, Wii HD, Shortages & More," *Industry Gamers,* March 16, 2010, http://www.industrygamers.com/news/nintendos-reggie-on-wii-core-games-wii-hd-shortages--more.
14. *Cave Story* Web site, http://www.cavestory.org.
15. Quoted in *GoNintendo* staff, "The *Cave Story* Interview," *GoNintendo*, October 6, 2008, http://gonintendo.com/viewstory.php?id=58250.
16. See, for example, "What Is Cave Story?," http://www.cavestory.org/info_1.php.
17. Quoted in *GoNintendo* staff, "The *Cave Story* Interview."
18. "Who Are You, 2D Boy?," 2D Boy, http://2dboy.com/about.php.
19. Corbie Dillard, "2D Boy's Ron Carmel Talks about Indie Game Development," *NintendoLife*, March 23, 2009, http://wiiware.nintendolife.com/news/2009/03/2d_boys_ron_carmel_talks_about_indie_game_development.
20. VGChartz, http://www.vgchartz.com.
21. Brad Gallaway, "Interview with *World of Goo* developer, 2D Boy," *GameCritics*, November 4, 2008, http://www.gamecritics.com/brad-gallaway/interview-with-2d-boy.

22. "The World (of Goo) Wasn't Built in a Day," part 2, 2D Boy blog, http://2dboy.com/2009/03/09/the-world-of-goo-wasnt-built-in-a-day-part-2-of-7.

23. Bubbles prototype, http://2dboy.com/2007/06/23/new-prototype-word-association-network-game.

24. Jon Erik Ariza, "We Are the World of Goo," *GameObserver*, January 2, 2010, http://www.gameobserver.com/features/inside/all-platforms/we-are-world-of-goo-part-1-the-goo-filled-hills-211.

25. Ibid.

26. Quoted in Gallaway, "Interview with *World of Goo* Developer, 2D Boy."

27. Ibid.

28. "*WarioWare D.I.Y.*: Ron Carmel Made It Too," http://www.youtube.com/watch?v=oFMOaU4wHlw&feature=related; *WarioWare D.I.Y.*: Gaijin Games feature, http://www.youtube.com/watch?v=cdXMp4sfZTQ&feature=player_embedded.

29. "*WarioWare D.I.Y.*: Ron Carmel Made It Too."

30. *WarioWare D.I.Y.*: Gaijin Games feature.

31. Wikipedia, "Doom WAD," http://en.wikipedia.org/wiki/WAD_file.

32. Wii Homebrew Web site, http://wiihomebrew.com.

33. William Gibson, *Burning Chrome* (New York: Ace Books, 1986), 186.

Chapter 6

1. "Wii-diculous," video of movie-theater hack, http://www.youtube.com/watch?v=lzfJUHVrWhs&feature=player_embedded.

2. Steven E. Jones, *The Meaning of Video Games: Gaming and Textual Strategies* (New York: Routledge, 2008), 148–149.

3. Jon Peck, blog, http://jonpeck.blogspot.com/2006/12/wii-diculous.html.

4. Ibid.

5. Jonathan Zittrain, *The Future of the Internet: And How to Stop It*, Kindle ed. (New Haven, CT: Yale University Press, 2008), 573.

6. Cory Doctorow, "Why I Won't Buy an iPad (and Think You Shouldn't, Either)," BoingBoing, April 2, 2010, http://boingboing.net/2010/04/02/why-i-wont-buy-an-ipad-and-think-yo.html.

7. Steve Jobs, "Thoughts on Flash," April 2010, http://www.apple.com/hotnews/thoughts-on-flash.

8. For an earlier analogy between competing OSs and vehicles, see Neal Stephenson, "In the Beginning Was the Command Line" (1999), http://www.cryptonomicon.com/beginning.html.

9. Zittrain, *The Future of the Internet*.

10. This is based on the results of our own test of what the device can do under Linux.

11. John Gage is credited with the slogan. http://en.wikipedia.org/wiki/John_Gage.

12. Zittrain, *The Future of the Internet*; emphasis added.

13. Indeed, one trend is toward cloud-based gaming, where consoles give way to what are in effect terminals for virtual consoles on the server. See David Kushner, "Cloud-Based Gaming Still Up in the Air," *Wired*, February 22, 2010, http://www.wired.com/magazine/2010/02/pl_games_cloud.

14. Interestingly, we've seen Wii consoles serving as the prizes in such claw machines. On the claw, see http://gizmodo.com/5309536/ultimate-Wiimote-control-hack-15+tonne-giant-robot-claws.

15. Paul Marks, "Wii Board Helps Physios Strike a Balance after Strokes," *New Scientist* 2743 (January 16, 2010), http://www.newscientist.com/article/mg20527435.300-wii-board-helps-physios-strike-a-balance-after-strokes.html.

16. Jordy Yager, "New Security System Uses Wii Technology and Worries GOP," *Hill*, November 15, 2009, http://thehill.com/homenews/house/67839-new-security-system-uses-wii-technology-and-worries-gop.

17. Johnny Chung Lee projects, http://johnnylee.net/projects/Wii. Lee's blog reports on his work on Project Natal (which became Kinect), http://procrastineering.blogspot.com.

18. According to Lee's explanation on his project blog, http://procrastineering.blogspot.com.

19. WiiBrew wiki, http://Wiibrew.org/w/index.php?title=Twilight_Hack.

20. *Wii Guitar Hero* hack video, http://www.youtube.com/watch?v=JDd4E6bgLfs.

21. Loop Machine, http://www.theamazingrolo.net/2009/05/the-wii-beatlooper.

22. Seth Schiesel, "Mario and Luigi, Back to the Wii: The More Players, the Deadlier," *New York Times*, November 15, 2009, http://www.nytimes.com/2009/11/16/arts/television/16mario.html.

23. See http://www.nintendo.com/sites/software_warioware.jsp; http://www.nintendo.com/games/detail/7vgUzwrkjswZ6wiUXTtZQB8ji6_uPB3v.

24. Alexander Sliwinski, "Nintendo: Wii Music Not Competing against *Rock Band*, *Guitar Hero*," *Joystiq*, August 8, 2008, http://www.joystiq.com/2008/08/08/nintendo-wii-music-not-competing-against-rock-band-guitar-hero.

25. Chris Kohler, notably, defended the game to some degree in "*Wii Music* Puts Improv before Gameplay," *Wired*, October 23, 2008, http://www.wired.com/gamelife/2008/10/wii-music-revie.

26. On the particular procedural rhetorics of such rhythm games, see Ian Bogost, *Persuasive Games: The Expressive Power of Videogames*, Kindle ed. (Cambridge, MA: MIT Press, 2007), 3749–3755.

27. *Donkey Konga* hack video, http://www.youtube.com/watch?v=osHK65IOn5M.

28. See Bogost, *Persuasive Games*, 3755.

29. J. P. Mangalindan, "Is Casual Gaming Destroying the Traditional Gaming Market?" *CNN.Money*, March 18, 2010, http://tech.fortune.cnn.com/2010/03/18/is-casual-gaming-destroying-the-traditional-gaming-market.

30. Jesper Juul, *A Casual Revolution: Reinventing Video Games and Their Players* (Cambridge, MA: MIT Press, 2010), 117.

31. Will Wright interview, Web 2.0 Expo, 2009, *Wired* video, http://link.brightcove.com/services/player/bcpid1813626064?bctid=21523091001.

32. Bart Simon, "The Material Imaginary of the Wii: Bodies, Spaces, and the Not-at-All Virtually Real," Interfaces, Concordia University, Montreal, March 10, 2009, http://www.interfacesmontreal.org/en/videos/the-material-imaginary-wii-bodies-spaces-the-not-at-all-virtually-real; and "Wii Are Out of Control: Bodies, Game Screens, and the Production of Gestural Excess," *Loading* 3.4 (2009), http://journals.sfu.ca/loading/index.php/loading/article/viewArticle/65.

33. Juul, *A Casual Revolution*, 107, 117.

34. Nintendo Press Release quoted in "Nintendo Revolution Renamed to Nintendo Wii," Console Watcher, May 2, 2006, http://www.consolewatcher.com/2006/05/nintedo-revolution-renamed-to-nintendo-wii.

35. Press release, June 5, 2008, http://Wii.ign.com/articles/879/879595p1.html.
36. The television commercials are available in multiple copies in YouTube, for example: http://www.youtube.com/watch?v=UP-THj032k4.
37. The long-form compilation ad is available at GameTrailers.com: http://www.gametrailers.com/video/wii-would-nintendo-wii/15154.
38. Quoted in David Sheff, *Game Over: How Nintendo Zapped an American Industry, Captured Your Dollars, and Enslaved Your Children* (New York: Random House, 1993), 292.
39. Stephen Totilo, "Nintendo's Design Guru, Shigeru Miyamoto, Says Wii Can Destroy Gamer Stereotype," *MTV News*, May 26, 2006, http://www.mtv.com/news/articles/1532607/20060526/index.jhtml.
40. Steven Poole observes that *Dance Dance Revolution* is really a "speedy techno version of *Twister*" (*Trigger Happy: Videogames and the Entertainment Revolution* [New York: Arcade Publishing, 2004], 61).
41. These were results from Flickr image searches, April–June 2010. In a couple of cases, we have conflated searches made on one occasion with those made on another. Of course, as is the ephemeral nature of this kind of evidence, the results will change over time.
42. Gerard Genette, "Introduction to the Paratext," *New Literary History* 22, no. 2 (Spring 1991): 261–279; Gerard Genette, *Paratexts: Thresholds of Interpretation*, trans. Jane E. Lewis (Cambridge: Cambridge University Press, 1997).
43. Jesse Schell, "Design outside the Box" (presentation at Design, Innovate, Communicate, Entertain, February 18, 2010), http://www.g4tv.com/videos/44277/DICE-2010-Design-Outside-the-Box-Presentation.
44. Jesse Schell, "Matt Helgeson Interview, 'Contemplating the Gamepocalypse,'" *Gameinformer* 205 (May 2010): 37.
45. Alexander R. Galloway, *Gaming: Essays on Algorithmic Culture* (Minneapolis: University of Minnesota Press, 2006), 6–8, 12–13.
46. Ibid., 8.

Chapter 7

1. Our descriptions of this event, the Project Natal Experience, are based on video shown first on the Internet and then played on MTV the following day, June 15, 2010, as well as on multiple live blogging accounts by participating developers and journalists. Later in 2010, after the product release, we were able to actually play Kinect games ourselves as we completed this chapter, as our comments indicate.
2. Microsoft Press Conference, E3 2010, June 14, 2010, G4TV, http://www.g4tv.com/videos/46342/E3-2010-Microsoft-Press-Conference. And cf. liveblog on Cnet Reviews, June 14, 2010, http://reviews.cnet.com/8301-21539_7-20007501-10391702.html.
3. Microsoft Kinect: http://www.xbox.com/en-US/kinect.
4. "Microsoft Kinect Team Kicking Advertising up a Notch," Eight08 Gaming, June 14 2010, http://hyperkind808.wordpress.com/2010/06/14.
5. Microsoft Press Conference, E3 2010; and liveblog on Cnet Reviews. See note 2.
6. Chris Kohler, "Microsoft Throws Glitzy Coming-out Bash for Kinect at E3," *Wired*, June 14, 2010, http://www.wired.com/gamelife/2010/06/kinect-e3/all/1.

7. Kinect Sports trailer, June 14, 2010, http://www.youtube.com/watch?v=am2 RdxbakiE.

8. Quoted in Jonathan Zittrain, *The Future of the Internet: And How to Stop It*, Kindle ed. (New Haven, CT: Yale University Press, 2008), 101–114.

9. Seth Schiesel, "New in Gadgetry: 3-D Escapades without Glasses," *New York Times*, June 20, 2010, http://www.nytimes.com/2010/06/21/arts/television/21videogame .html?hpw. After this chapter was completed, we were able to spend time with the 3DS and found the AR (augmented reality) games in particular to be an extension of the design ethos of the Wii as we've described it throughout this book. That highly symbolic coffee or tea table in our Wii configuration is replaced in 3DS play with an actual table (or any other surface) on which you place an AR card with an image printed on it. When viewed through the 3DS, the paper card and the wooden table *become* the game world, as a dragon emerges from the card as if from a hole in the table, for example, and you shoot at it from multiple angles, circling around the table, holding the console in front of you as a viewer. A similar focus on the possibilities of augmented reality has apparently informed the design of the Wii U, which makes use of the touchscreen controller as a second, alternative window, to "take the game world off the TV and spread it all around you" in the living room so that "you can peer into it from any angle." Iwata, Nintendo E3 2011 press conference, June 7, 2011, http://e3.nintendo.com.

10. Jeremy Parish, "Notes from Nintendo's E3 2010 Developer Roundtable," 1Up. com, June 15, 2010, http://www.1up.com/news/notes-nintendo-e3-2010 -developer.

11. Brian Caulfield, "Apple Bigger Near-Term Threat Than Microsoft, Nintendo of America President Says," Shiny Objects blog for *Forbes*, http://blogs.forbes.com/ briancaulfield/2010/10/21/apple-bigger-near-term-threat-than-microsoft -nintendo-of-america-president-says.

12. *GameSetWatch* staff, "E3: Nintendo's Dunaway on 3DS, Kinect/Move, and Wii Momentum," *GameSetWatch*, June 18, 2010, http://www.gamesetwatch. com/2010/06/e3_nintendos_dunaway_on_3ds_ki.php.

13. Ibid.

14. Tom Bissell, *Extra Lives: Why Video Games Matter*, Kindle ed. (New York: Pantheon Books, 2010), 2222–2235.

15. Wikipedia, "Warren Spector," http://en.wikipedia.org/wiki/Warren_Spector.

16. M. H. Williams, "Playstyle Matters: Warren Spector on Disney's Epic Mickey," *Industry Gamers*, October 11. 2010, http://www.industrygamers.com/news/ playstyle-matters-warren-spector-on-disneys-epic-mickey---part-1.

17. Warren Spector, voice-over for demonstration video for Disney Epic Mickey, http://www.youtube.com/watch?v=AvNcQhdBVGM.

18. See Nintendo Wiki, "Disney Playing Cards," http://nintendo.wikia.com/wiki/ Disney_playing_cards.

19. Warren Spector, voice-over for demonstration video for *Disney Epic Mickey*, http://www.youtube.com/watch?v=AvNcQhdBVGM.

20. Jesse Schell, "Design outside the Box" (presentation at Design, Innovate, Communicate, Entertain, February 18, 2010), http://g4tv.com/videos/44277/DICE -2010-Design-Outside-the-Box-Presentation.

21. Xbox Kinect Web site, Microsoft, http://www.xbox.com:80/en-US/kinect.

22. Bart Simon, "Wii Are Out of Control: Bodies, Game Screens, and the Production of Gestural Excess," *Loading* 3.4 (2009), http://journals.sfu.ca/loading/index.php/loading/article/viewArticle/65.

23. William Gibson first used the term in a short story, but it became widely known in his cyberpunk novel *Neuromancer* (New York: Ace Books, 1984). On the inspiration for the word cyberspace, see William Gibson, interviewed in documentary film, *No Maps for These Territories*, directed Mark Neale (Chris Paine/907 Productions, 2001).

24. For different perspectives on the borderline and impure nature of actual gameplay, see, for example, Jesper Juul, *Half-Real: Video Games between Real Rules and Fictional Worlds* (Cambridge, MA: MIT Press, 2005); Rune Klevjer, "In Defense of Cutscenes," in *Computer Games and Digital Cultures Conference Proceedings*, ed. Mäyra Frans (Tampere, Finland: Tampere University Press, 2002), 191–202. Available at http://www.digra.org/dl/db/05164.50328.

25. Ellie Gibson, interview with Alex Kipman, *Eurogamer*, June 5, 2010, http://www.eurogamer.net/articles/e3-post-natal-discussion-interview.

26. See Chris Kohler, "Flawed Kinect Offers Tantalizing Glimpse of Gaming's Future," *Wired*, November 4, 2010, http://www.wired.com/gamelife/2010/11/review-kinect/?intcid=postnav. On the issue of skin tone, see Larry Frum, "Lighting Affects Kinect's Face Recognition, Report Says," CNN, November 4, 2010, http://premium.edition.cnn.com/2010/TECH/gaming.gadgets/11/04/kinect.dark.skin/index.html.

27. Kohler, "Flawed Kinect Offers Tantalizing Glimpse of Gaming's Future."

28. Ibid.

29. One possible etymology for gadget is from the French word *engager*, to engage (*Oxford English Dictionary*).

30. In a blog entry, Mitu Khandaker ("On existenz and Immersion," October 1, 2009, http://mitu.nu/2009/10/01/on-existenz-and-immersion-from-the-immersive-fallacy-to-the-immersive-apogee) speculates about a number of the same issues we are considering here, including the danger of solipsism when it comes to immersive gaming. And Steven Poole (*Trigger Happy: Videogames and the Entertainment Revolution* [New York: Arcade Publishing, 2004], 63) poses general questions that are now being raised again by the release of Kinect: "What about total immersion? . . . Will this, then, become the dominant means of videogame control? . . . [I]f so, the spirit of [Martin] Heidegger will rise again to warn that such cybernetic hegemony will necessarily *narrow* the field of possibilities."

31. William Gibson, *Spook Country* (New York: Putnam, 2007), 20, 64.

32. In some ways, the Wii U, with its presumably more powerful system and HD capability, marks a pendulum swing back in the direction of immersive experiences—at least as one affordance of the same system that in other ways continues the trend toward casual gaming. See Miyamoto's comments on immersion quoted in Iwata, "Iwata Asks: Wii U," Nintendo, http://iwataasks.nintendo.com/interviews/#/e32011/newhw/0/0.

33. Norbert Wiener, "Men, Machines, and the World About" (1954), in *The New Media Reader*, ed. Noah Wardrip-Fruin and Nick Montfort (Cambridge, MA: MIT Press, 2003), 65–72.

34. Poole, *Trigger Happy*, 61, 63.

35. Katie Salen and Eric Zimmerman, *Rules of Play: Game Design Fundamentals* (Cambridge, MA: MIT Press, 2004), 458, 451, 455.

36. Ibid., 455.

37. John Keats, "Ode to a Nightingale," in *John Keats: Complete Poems*, ed. Jack Stillinger (Cambridge, MA: Belknap Press of Harvard University Press, 1982), 279.

38. We use the term object oriented only as a reminder of the questions that surround the relationship of the user to hardware and software components. In this light, see Ian Bogost's recent philosophical work on object-oriented ontology, a succinct public statement of which is available at http://www.bogost.com/blog/what_is_objectoriented_ontolog.shtml. Bogost has said that he views platform studies as a kind of "applied" instance of this philosophical project (see http://www.bogost.com/blog/i_prefer_not_to.shtml). As should be clear from our discussions in this book, our view is generally consonant with this perspective, except perhaps that our focus remains more relational, more about the roles of players and objects in the inter-relational space they co-define, where players meet platforms (as objects and constellations of objects) and engage with them. Interestingly, this way of viewing game systems finds an echo in theories of (social) network analysis (see David Easley and Jon Kleinberg, *Networks, Crowds, and Markets: Reasoning about a Highly Connected World* [Cambridge: Cambridge University Press, 2010]), where the usefulness of the network at least in part is about the formation of ties—in this case, ties between players, nonplayers, and the system components themselves, which can all be viewed as a network or graph in computer science terms.

Bibliography

Ariza, Jon Erik. "We Are the World of Goo." *GameObserver*, January 2, 2010. http://www.
gameobserver.com/features/inside/all-platforms/we-are-world-of-goo
-part-1-the-goo-filled-hills-211.

Aziz, Hamza. "*Red Steel 2* May Have Defeated the Waggle." July 7, 2009. http://www.
destructoid.com/red-steel-2-may-have-defeated-the-waggle-138687.phtml.

Barton, Emily. *The Testament of Yves Gundron*. New York: Washington Square Press,
2001.

Bissell, Tom. *Extra Lives: Why Video Games Matter*. Kindle ed. New York: Pantheon
Books, 2010.

Bogost, Ian. *Persuasive Games: The Expressive Power of Videogames*. Kindle ed. Cambridge, MA: MIT Press, 2007.

Bogost, Ian, and Nick Montfort. "New Media as Material Constraint: An Introduction
to Platform Studies." http://www.bogost.com/downloads/Bogost%20
Montfort%20HASTAC.pdf.

Bogost, Ian, and Nick Montfort. *Racing the Beam: The Atari Computer System*. Cambridge, MA: MIT Press, 2009.

Brightman, James. "Nintendo's Reggie on Wii Core Games, Wii HD, Shortages &
More." *Industry Gamers*, March 16, 2010. http://www.industrygamers.com/news/
nintendos-reggie-on-wii-core-games-wii-hd-shortages--more.

Brown, Alan S. "Tearing Down the Nearly Invisible." *Mechanical Engineering*, August
2006. http://memagazine.asme.org/articles/2006/August/Tearing_Down_Nearly
_Invisible.cfm.

Casamassina, Matt. "GDC 2008: Sawano on *Wii Fit*." IGN, February 20, 2008. http://
wii.ign.com/articles/853/853708p1.html.

Casamassina, Matt. Interview with Tom Prata. "Nintendo: 100 WiiWare Games in
Queue." IGN, May 30, 2008. http://uk.Wii.ign.com/articles/877/877761p1.html.

Casamassina, Matt. "Why You'll Love *Rabbids Go Home*." IGN, November 3, 2009.
http://wii.ign.com/articles/979/979811p3.html.

Cassell, Justine, and Henry Jenkins, ed. *From Barbie to Mortal Kombat*. Cambridge, MA:
MIT Press, 1998.

Caufield, Brian. "Apple Bigger Near-Term Threat Than Microsoft, Nintendo of America President Says." Shiny Objects blog for *Forbes*. http://blogs.forbes.com/briancaulfield/2010/10/21/apple-bigger-near-term-threat-than-microsoft-nintendo-of-america-president-says (accessed November 14, 2010).

Deterding, Sebastian, with contributions by Staffan Björk, Stephan Dreyer, Aki Järvinen, Ben Kirman, Julian Kücklich, Janne Paavilainen, Valentina Rao, and Jan Schmidt. "Social Game Studies: A Workshop Report." Hamburg: Hans Bredow Institute for Media Research, 2010. http://socialgamestudies.org/report.

Dillard, Corbie. "2D Boy's Ron Carmel Talks about Indie Game Development." *NintendoLife*, March 23, 2009. http://wiiware.nintendolife.com/news/2009/03/2d_boys_ron_carmel_talks_about_indie_game_development.

Doctorow, Cory. "Why I Won't Buy an iPad (and Think You Shouldn't, Either)." Boing-Boing, April 2, 2010. http://boingboing.net/2010/04/02/why-i-wont-buy-an-ipad-and-think-yo.html.

Easley, David, and Jon Kleinberg. *Networks, Crowds, and Markets: Reasoning about a Highly Connected World*. Cambridge: Cambridge University Press, 2010.

Edge magazine staff. "WiiWare: Developer Impressions." *Edge*, May 2008.

Edge magazine staff. "Industry Focus: The Economics of Motion Control." *Edge*, May 2010, 24–25.

Eisenstein, Elizabeth. *The Printing Press as Agent of Change*. Cambridge: Cambridge University Press, 1980.

Engelbart, Douglas, and William K. English. "A Research Center for Augmenting Human Intellect." In *The New Media Reader*, edited by Noah Wardrip-Fruin and Nick Montford, 233–246. Cambridge, MA: MIT Press, 2003.

Frommer, Dan, and Leah Goldman. "iPad Survey Results." *Business Insider*. http://www.businessinsider.com/ipad-survey-results-2010-11.

Frum, Larry. "Lighting Affects Kinect's Face Recognition, Report Says." CNN, November 4, 2010. http://premium.edition.cnn.com/2010/TECH/gaming.gadgets/11/04/kinect.dark.skin/index.html.

Gallaway, Brad. "Interview with Ron Carmel." *GameCritics*, November 4, 2008, http://www.gamecritics.com/brad-gallaway/interview-with-2d-boy.

Galloway, Alexander R. *Gaming: Essays on Algorithmic Culture*. Minneapolis: University of Minnesota Press, 2006.

GameSetWatch staff. "E3: Nintendo's Dunaway on 3DS, Kinect/Move, and Wii Momentum." *GameSetWatch*, June 18, 2010. http://www.gamesetwatch.com/2010/06/e3_nintendos_dunaway_on_3ds_ki.php.

Genette, Gerard. "Introduction to the Paratext." *New Literary History* 22, no. 2 (Spring 1991): 261–279.

Genette, Gerard. *Paratexts: Thresholds of Interpretation*. Translated by Jane E. Lewis. Cambridge: Cambridge University Press, 1997.

Gibson, Ellie. Interview with Alex Kipman. *Eurogamer*, June 5, 2010. http://www.eurogamer.net/articles/e3-post-natal-discussion-interview.

Gibson, William. *Neuromancer*. New York: Ace Books, 1984.

Gibson, William. *Burning Chrome*. New York: Ace Books, 1986.

Gibson, William. Interviewed in documentary film, *No Maps for These Territories*. Directed Mark Neale. Chris Paine/907 Productions, 2001.

Gibson, William. *Spook Country*. New York: Putnam, 2007.

Gingold, Chaim. "Miniature Gardens and Magic Crayons." Master's thesis, Georgia Institute of Technology, 2003. http://levitylab.com/cog/writing/thesis.

GoNintendo staff, "The *Cave Story* Interview," *GoNintendo*, October 6, 2008, http://gonintendo.com/viewstory.php?id=58250.

Hall, Kenji. "The Big Ideas behind Nintendo's Wii." Interview with Shigeru Miyamoto and Ken'ichiro Ashida. *Business Week Online*, November 16, 2006. http://www.businessweek.com/technology/content/nov2006/tc20061116_750580.htm?chan=search.

Huizinga, Johan. *Homo Ludens: A Study of the Play Element in Culture*. 1938. Reprint, Boston: Beacon Press, 1950.

Horowitz, Noah, Riley Neugebauer, Brooke Frazer, Peter May-Ostendorp, and Chris Calwell. November 2008. "Lowering the Cost of Play: Improving Energy Efficiency of Video Game Consoles." National Resources Defense Council with Ecos Consulting. http://www.nrdc.org/energy/consoles/contents.asp.

Inoue, Osamu. *Nintendo Magic: Winning the Videogame Wars*. Translated by Paul Tuttle Starr. New York: Vertical, 2010.

Iwata, Satoru. "Iwata Asks" columns. Nintendo Web site (by topic). http://us.wii.com/iwata_asks/index.jsp.

Iwata, Satoru. "Iwata Asks: Wii U." Nintendo. http://iwataasks.nintendo.com/interviews/#/e32011/newhw/0/0.

Iwata, Satoru, and Associates. Nintendo E3 2011 press conference, June 7, 2011. http://e3.nintendo.com.

Johns, Adrian. *The Nature of the Book: Print and Knowledge in the Making*. Chicago: University of Chicago Press, 1998.

Jones, Nick. "Miyamoto: 'Vitality Sensor for New Zelda Possible.'" *Now Gamer*, March 22, 2010. http://http://www.nowgamer.com/news/91639/miyamoto_vitality_sensor_for_new_zelda_possible.html.

Jones, Steven E. *The Meaning of Video Games: Gaming and Textual Strategies*. New York: Routledge, 2008.

Juul, Jesper. *Half-Real: Video Games between Real Rules and Fictional Worlds*. Cambridge, MA: MIT Press, 2005.

Juul, Jesper. *A Casual Revolution: Reinventing Video Games and Their Players*. Cambridge, MA: MIT Press, 2010.

Kasavin, Greg. "*Red Steel* Review." Gamespot. November 17, 2006. http://www.gamespot.com/Wii/action/redsteel/review.html.

Keats, John. Ode to a Nightingale. In *John Keats: Complete Poems*, ed. Jack Stillinger, 279. Cambridge, MA: Belknap Press of Harvard University Press, 1982.

Kelly, Neon. Interview with Jason Vandenberghe, February 22, 2010. http://www.videogamer.com/wii/red_steel_2/preview-2225.html.

Kent, Stephen L. *The Ultimate History of Video Games: From Pong to Pokemon—The Story behind the Craze That Touched Our Lives and Changed the World*. New York: Three Rivers, 2001.

Khandaker, Mitu. "On existenz and Immersion." October 1, 2009. http://mitu.nu/2009/10/01/on-existenz-and-immersion-from-the-immersive-fallacy-to-the-immersive-apogee.

Kim, W. Chan, and Renée Mauborgne. *Blue Ocean Strategy: How to Create Uncontested Market Space and Make the Competition Irrelevant*. Kindle ed. Boston: Harvard Business School Press, 2005.

Klevjer, Rune. "In Defense of Cutscenes." In *Computer Games and Digital Cultures Conference Proceedings*, edited by Mäyra Frans. Tampere, Finland: Tampere University Press, 2002.

Kohler, Chris. *Power Up: How Japanese Video Games Gave the World an Extra Life*. Indianapolis: Brady Games, 2004.

Kohler, Chris. "Coverage Wrapup: Why WiiWare Needs Work." *Wired*, March 25, 2008. http://www.wired.com/gamelife/2008/03/coverage-wrapup/#ixzz0pFtoSuBo.

Kohler, Chris. "*Wii Music* Puts Improv before Gameplay." *Wired*, October 23, 2008. http://www.wired.com/gamelife/2008/10/wii-music-revie.

Kohler, Chris. "Stand, Shoot, and Slash in *Red Steel 2* Wii." *Wired*, March 23, 2010. http://www.wired.com/gamelife/tag/red-steel-2.

Kohler, Chris. "Microsoft Throws Glitzy Coming-out Bash for Kinect at E3." *Wired*, June 14, 2010. http://www.wired.com/gamelife/2010/06/kinect-e3/all/1.

Kohler, Chris. "Flawed Kinect Offers Tantalizing Glimpse of Gaming's Future." *Wired*, November 4, 2010. http://www.wired.com/gamelife/2010/11/review-kinect/?intcid=postnav.

Kushner, David. "Cloud-Based Gaming Still Up in the Air." *Wired*, February 22, 2010. http://www.wired.com/magazine/2010/02/pl_games_cloud.

Linderman, John. "Pearl Harbor Interview with Dan Muir." *Nintendo World Report*, January 20, 2010. http://www.nintendoworldreport.com/specialArt.cfm?artid=20807.

Lukić, Branko, and Barry M. Kātz. *Nonobject: iPad App Version*. Cambridge, MA: MIT Press, 2010.

Mangalindan, J. P. "Is Casual Gaming Destroying the Traditional Gaming Market?" *CNN.Money*, March 18, 2010. http://tech.fortune.cnn.com/2010/03/18/is-casual-gaming-destroying-the-traditional-gaming-market.

Marks, Paul. "Wii Board Helps Physios Strike a Balance after Strokes." *New Scientist* 2743 (January 16, 2010). http://www.newscientist.com/article/mg20527435.300-wii-board-helps-physios-strike-a-balance-after-strokes.html.

Massanari, Adrienne L. "Designing for Imaginary Friends: Information Architecture, Personas, and the Politics of User-Centered Design." *New Media and Society* 12 (2010): 401. DOI: 10.1177/1461444809346722. http://nms.sagepub.com/content/12/3/401.

McCloud, Scott. *Understanding Comics: The Invisible Art*. New York: Harper Perennial, 1993.

MiraiGamer. "What Is Cave Story?" http://www.miraigamer.net/cavestory/info_1.php.

Miyamoto, Satoru. Quoted in "E3 2007 Nintendo E3 Media Briefing Live Blog." IGN. http://wii.ign.com/articles/803/803335p1.html.

Morley, David. *Home Territories: Media, Mobility, and Identity*. London: Routledge, 2000.

Newton, James. "*GoldenEye*'s Success 'Proves Core Games Sell on Wii.'" *Nintendo Life*, November 17, 2010. http://wii.nintendolife.com/news/2010/11/goldeneyes_success_proves_core_games_sell_on_wii.

Newton, James. "Reggie: We're Not Interested in 'Garage Developers.'" *Nintendo Life*, March 18, 2011. http://www.nintendolife.com/news/2011/03/reggie_were_not_interested_in_garage_developers.

Nintendo. Press release quoted in "Nintendo Revolution Renamed to Nintendo Wii." *Console Watcher*. May 2, 2006. http://www.consolewatcher.com/2006/05/nintendo-revolution-renamed-to-nintendo-wii.

Norman, Donald A. *Emotional Design: Why We Love (or Hate) Everyday Things*. Kindle ed. New York: Basic Books, 2005.

Norman, Donald A. "Natural User Interfaces Are Not Natural." *Interaction* 17 (May–June 2010). http://interactions.acm.org/content/?p=1355.

Nutt, Christian. "The Sony Situation." *Gamasutra*, May 21, 2010. http://www.gamasutra.com/view/feature/4709/the_sony_situation_sceas_rob_.php?page=5.

Parish, Jeremy. "Notes from Nintendo's E3 2010 Developer Roundtable." 1Up.com, June 15, 2010. http://www.1up.com/do/newsStory?cId=3179908.

Poole, Steven. *Trigger Happy: Videogames and the Entertainment Revolution*. New York: Arcade Publishing, 2004.

Putnam, Robert D. *Bowling Alone: The Collapse and Revival of American Community*. Kindle ed. New York: Simon and Schuster, 2000.

Salen, Katie, and Eric Zimmerman. *Rules of Play: Game Design Fundamentals*. Cambridge, MA: MIT Press, 2004.

Schell, Jesse. "Design outside the Box." Presentation at Design, Innovate, Communicate, Entertain, February 18, 2010. http://g4tv.com/videos/44277/DICE-2010-Design-Outside-the-Box-Presentation/.

Schell, Jesse. "Matt Helgeson Inteview, 'Contemplating the Gamepocalypse.'" *Gameinformer* 205 (May 2010): 37.

Schiesel, Seth. "Mario and Luigi, Back to the Wii: The More Players, the Deadlier." *New York Times*, November 15, 2009. http://www.nytimes.com/2009/11/16/arts/television/16mario.html.

Schiesel, Seth. "Way Down Deep in the Wild Wild West." Review of *Red Dead Redemption*. *New York Times*, May 16, 2010. http://www.nytimes.com/2010/05/17/arts/television/17dead.html.

Schiesel, Seth. "Back-Seat Jumpers Now Have Their Day." Review of *Super Mario Galaxy 2*. *New York Times*, May 24, 2010. http://www.nytimes.com/2010/05/25/arts/television/25mario.html.

Schiesel, Seth. "New in Gadgetry: 3-D Escapades without Glasses." *New York Times*, June 20, 2010. http://www.nytimes.com/2010/06/21/arts/television/21videogame.html?hpw.

Sheff, David. *Game Over: How Nintendo Zapped an American Industry, Captured Your Dollars, and Enslaved Your Children*. New York: Random House, 1993.

Simon, Bart. "The Material Imaginary of the Wii: Bodies, Spaces, and the Not-at-All Virtually Real." Video of lecture/demo at Interfaces, Concordia University, Montreal, March 10, 2009. http://www.interfacesmontreal.org/en/videos/the-material-imaginary-wii-bodies-spaces-the-not-at-all-virtually-real.

Simon, Bart. "Wii Are Out of Control: Bodies, Game Screens, and the Production of Gestural Excess." *Loading* 3.4 (2009). http://journals.sfu.ca/loading/index.php/loading/article/viewArticle/65.

Sliwinski, Alexander. "Nintendo: Wii Music Not Competing against *Rock Band*, *Guitar Hero*." *Joystiq*, August 8, 2008. http://www.joystiq.com/2008/08/08/nintendo-wii-music-not-competing-against-rock-band-guitar-hero.

Stephenson, Neal. "In the Beginning Was the Command Line" (1999). http://www.cryptonomicon.com/beginning.html.

Thorsen, Tor. "Miyamoto Plays up Wii Music," *Gamespot*, October 25, 2008: http://uk.gamespot.com/news/6200061.html.

Thorsen, Tor. "Wii Sales Near 71 Million, DS Almost 129 Million." Gamespot, May 6, 2010. http://www.gamespot.com/news/6261400.html?tag=recent.news;title:1.

Totilo, Stephen. "Nintendo's Design Guru, Shigeru Miyamoto, Says Wii Can Destroy Gamer Stereotype." *MTV News*, May 26, 2006. http://www.mtv.com/news/articles/1532607/20060526/index.jhtml.

Totilo, Stephen. "No Graphical Complaints from This Wii Developer." Kotaku, 2009. http://kotaku.com/5372026/no-graphical-complaints-from-this-wii-developer.

Wardrip-Fruin, Noah, and Nick Montfort, eds. *The New Media Reader*. Cambridge, MA: MIT Press, 2003.

Wiener, Norbert. "Men, Machines, and the World About" (1954). In *The New Media Reader*, edited by Noah Wardrip-Fruin and Nick Montfort, 65–72. Cambridge, MA: MIT Press, 2003.

Williams, M. H. "Playstyle Matters: Warren Spector on Disney's Epic Mickey." *Industry Gamers*. October 11, 2010. http://www.industrygamers.com/news/playstyle-matters -warren-spector-on-disneys-epic-mickey---part-1.

Yager, Jordy. "New Security System Uses Wii Technology and Worries GOP." *Hill*, November 15, 2009. http://thehill.com/homenews/house/67839-new-security -system-uses-wii-technology-and-worries-gop.

Zittrain, Jonathan. *The Future of the Internet: And How to Stop It*. Kindle ed. New Haven, CT: Yale University Press, 2008.

Games Discussed

For the Wii

Active Life: Outdoor Challenge

The Beatles: Rock Band

BioShock 2

Brain Training

Cave Story

Disney Epic Mickey

Donkey Kong

Donkey Konga

Donkey Kong Jungle Beat

GoldenEye 007

Guitar Hero

Introduction to Wii Zapper (Link's Crossbow Training)

Journey to Wild Divine

Kirby's Epic Yarn

The Legend of Zelda: Ocarina of Time

The Legend of Zelda: Skyward Sword

The Legend of Zelda: Twilight Princess

The Legend of Zelda: Wind Waker

Link's Crossbow Training

LIT

LittleBigPlanet

LostWinds

Mario Kart Wii

Mario Paint

Mario Party 8

Metroid: Other M

Metroid Prime 3: Corruption

Metroid Prime TrilogyMonster Hunter Tri

New Super Mario Bros. Wii

Okami

Paper Mario

Pearl Harbor: Red Sun Rising

Rabbids Go Home

Radar Scope

Red Steel

Red Steel 2

Rock Band

Rock Band 2

Space Wars

Suck Goo

Super Mario All-Stars

Super Mario Bros.

Super Mario Galaxy

Super Mario Galaxy 2

Super Paper Mario Wii

Super Smash Bros.

Tiger Woods PGA Tour

WarioWare D.I.Y.

WarioWare D.I.Y. Showcase

WarioWare, Inc.: Mega Microgame$!

WarioWare: Smooth Moves

WarioWare: Twisted! 3

Wii Fit

Wii Fit Plus

Wii Music

Wii Party

Wii Play

Wii Sports

Wii Sports Resort

Via WiiWare

Bit.Trip Beat

Bit.Trip Core

Bit.Trip Fate

Bit.Trip Runner

Bit.Trip Void

Max and the Magic Marker

World of Goo

For Other Platforms

Brain Training

Dance Dance Revolution

Duck Hunt

Family Fun Fitness

Family Trainer

FarmVille

Gears of War 2

GoldenEye 007

Grand Theft Auto: San Andreas

Grand Theft Auto: Vice City

Guru Meditation

Gyromite

Innergy

Kid Icarus: Uprising

Kinect Adventures!

Kinectimals

Kirby Tilt 'n' Tumble

Mafia Wars

Mogul Maniac

Nintendogs

Pitfall!

Pocket Pikachu

Red Dead Redemption

The Sims

Spore

Stack-Up

Wild Gunman

World of Warcraft

Index